The International Labor Movement in Transition

EDITED BY
Adolf Sturmthal and James G. Scoville

The International Labor
Movement in Transition

ESSAYS ON
AFRICA, ASIA, EUROPE, and SOUTH AMERICA

UNIVERSITY OF ILLINOIS PRESS
Urbana, Chicago, London

PREFACE

FOR THE American observer the terms "trade union" and "labor movement" are synonymous. And unionism is about collective bargaining. For most foreign students of labor, trade unions are only one element in a variety of organizations which together form the labor movement. Collective bargaining is one device among many in labor's arsenal. Indeed, viewed on a world scale, collective bargaining is by no means the most important way of determining wages and working conditions, at least not in a statistical sense.

Apart from the obvious restrictions on collective bargaining,[1] such as legal prohibitions of the formation or functioning of unions, some forms or stages of economic development seem to be more conducive to the formation of a collective bargaining system than others. How else can we explain the almost universal failure of American attempts after World War II to spread the gospel of free collective bargaining throughout the world into countries that had never known it? Or—as a counter-example—what caused the tremendous advance of collective bargaining in France during the post–World War II era, and especially since 1968?

In principle, collective agreements are regarded in the traditional Anglo-Saxon view as private contracts between two and only two partners: employer and union. While the government was used in the U.S. experience to make bargaining in good faith a legal obligation, public authority was not to intervene in the substance of the

1 Are they really obvious? Is it not important to ask why and under which conditions they exist?

contract itself. This view of collective bargaining is hardly compatible with long-term full employment as it has existed in many industrial nations since the early 1950's. Collective bargaining, regardless of who is physically present at the bargaining table, increasingly involves public authority. Has the traditional system of private bargaining come to an end?

It is widely held in the United States and some other Western countries that collective bargaining is not only the basis of the industrial relations system in America—which is a more or less correct statement of fact—but also that it is a most desirable and, given good will on all sides, universally applicable system. The essays in this volume are designed to put this second proposition to a test. One of the main results of these investigations appears to be evidence that the political, social, and labor market milieu in which the labor movement arises has a powerful impact on its strategy which in turn influences its structure and ideology. Thus labor movements start out with a great variety of strategies. Moreover, as the political and social status of labor advances, modernization progresses and the average standard of living improves; changes in strategy also occur, even though often with a considerable lag. Political and social discrimination against manual labor diminishes, many of the original objectives of the movement are attained, and basic changes occur in the relationship of supply and demand on the labor market. New objectives and new strategies come to the fore. Some of these changes are concealed from the casual observer by the retention of symbols and language that properly belong to an earlier stage in the evolution of the movement. Yet more careful investigation makes the changes visible and often understandable.

It would be oversimplifying history if one were to describe one factor as the *causa causans* (or what A. O. Hirschman in his *Strategy of Economic Development* calls the *primum mobile*) of this evolution. However, that changes in the long-term labor market situation play a key role in it, seemed a hypothesis worth exploring. The theoretical foundations for this exploration are outlined in the first two essays of this volume. The third essay extends this analysis beyond strategies to consideration of the factors shaping the labor movement's concrete forms. The editors' concluding survey draws a tentative balance sheet of the explorations that form the bulk of this volume.

The scope of the investigations in this volume ranges from situations, on one end of the scale, in which collective bargaining is nonexistent, given the lack of appropriate institutions and a long-term excess supply on the labor market, to the other extreme—where overfull employment is profoundly changing the nature of the collective agreement.

Beyond this, these essays must stand on their own merit as contributions to comparative work in the areas of labor economics and industrial relations.

The editors express their thanks to the Center for International Comparative Studies at the University of Illinois and the Ford Foundation for financial assistance in producing this volume, to Dorothy Wetzel for editorial help, and to Anice Birge for having mastered the difficult art of deciphering manuscripts of the most diversified national origins.

ADOLF STURMTHAL
JAMES G. SCOVILLE

Champaign, Illinois
March, 1972

CONTENTS

Adolf Sturmthal

Industrial Relations Strategies

SEVERAL YEARS AGO I attempted to find answers to two questions that seemed important in formulating hypotheses for a theory of the evolution of labor movements.[1] First, what were the conditions which caused some labor movements in some periods to emphasize political rather than economic objectives and means of action? And second, what were the circumstances that led to the development and vast expansion of the collective bargaining system in the United States and Great Britain? The two questions hang together, and the terms in which I formulated these questions need definition and refinement. Before proceeding I shall review this essential preliminary work.

Of the two phenomena—objectives and methods—it is perhaps easier to apply the distinction to the first. Economic objectives deal with wages and working conditions, in other words, the employment relationship; political objectives concern the life of the worker outside his work place. Unfortunately, from the point of view of the classification, the two are closely related. Workers with full citizenship rights rarely tolerate inadequate wages and unbearable working conditions for long. They use their political power to remedy the situation. When labor is in short supply, it is difficult to deny

1 Adolf Sturmthal, "Economic Development and the Labour Movement," in Arthur M. Ross, ed., *Industrial Relations and Economic Development* (London: Macmillan, 1966), pp. 165–81; "Some Thoughts on Labor and Political Action," *Industrial Relations,* Laval University, Quebec, vol. 17, no. 3 (July, 1962): 244–58.

workers their rights as citizens for very long. Still, the classification is of some value, even if it is less neat than we may wish.

The nature of the group to whom workers' demands are addressed can be of some help in classifying unclear cases. Demands addressed to employers or their associations are most likely to be of an economic nature. Those aimed at political objectives usually have a public authority (national, state, or municipal government) or some legislative body or the general public as their addressee. However, the second proposition has less validity than the first: minimum wage legislation, maximum working hours, safety, vacations, and the processes of collective bargaining have been the object of labor's political activity. We are thus dealing with a distinction of "more" or "less," rather than a clear-cut division.

The same applies to the issue of economic versus political means. This tends to become less significant and more elusive, the closer one examines it. A strike can be classified as an economic weapon when problems of wages, hours, and working conditions are at stake. A strike may also serve as a weapon in a political conflict whose outcome may change a government, prevent a *coup d'état,* or change a social system—as the revolutionary syndicalists advocated. Collective bargaining, commonly considered the main economic instrument of labor action, has been used, at least in a secondary fashion, to put pressure on employers to induce them to support union demands addressed to the government.[2] The history of industrial relations in France and other countries in the last fifteen years provides a number of examples of collective agreements concluded between all-industry employers' federations and union confederations under governmental guidance and regulating essential aspects of the employment relationship. It would not be easy to classify such agreements neatly under the headings of "economic" or "political" methods of settling industrial relations problems.

The main concern here is with the conditions under which a reasonably permanent collective bargaining system can be established and is in fact likely to come into being. The purposes to which it is put, ranging from wage improvements to safeguarding jobs and preserving or establishing the dignity of the employees,

2   One example is the supplementary unemployment benefit bargained for by the United Automobile Workers in the United States. Since the level of the employer's contribution under the contract varied inversely with the government-sponsored benefits, an increase of the latter reduced to some extent the employer's contribution under the collective agreement. This tended to induce the employers to associate themselves with union demands for higher benefits under the public system.

vary from situation to situation. But whatever its purposes, genuine collective bargaining is possible only under certain conditions still to be explored. Similarly, we are interested in exploring the conditions under which political action is the main instrument of labor.

While the objectives chosen, the nature of the opponents, and the means utilized all help to some extent to identify economic versus political strategies, they tend to overlap in specific circumstances. Nevertheless, the major focus of industrial relations activities and the predominant allocation of the parties' resources to these focal activities do permit a rough but useful classification of industrial relations strategies.

In part, this usefulness is demonstrated by the high degree of correlation between the respective emphasis on the two kinds of weapons and the systems of organization devised by labor. Where collective bargaining dominates the scene, trade unionism is the main or only form of labor organization. When a political party is created by the unions, possibly with the collaboration of some ideologically pro-labor intellectuals, the party is primarily intended to supplement and support union action. In contrast, primary emphasis on political activity tends to call for the formation of political parties of the working class—often ahead of unions, which are then created for specific action in the industrial relations field. Such unions are then usually subordinated, at least in their early stages, to the political branch of the movement.

Another reason why such a classification is of considerable use, untidy as it may be, is the fact that the problem of the "appropriate" means of labor action has played such a large role in both the history of labor movements and the literature about them. By historic circumstance the issue became intimately tied up with the sharp ideological conflicts of labor during the nineteenth and twentieth centuries, and it continues to be the object of passionate debates. In the past, the main (but by no means only) protagonists were the syndicalists, who relied exclusively on revolutionary action by unions culminating in a series of general strikes, and the Marxists, for whom political action was the main instrument of working-class liberation. Such action was to range from the use of voting rights to massive violence and the struggle "on the barricades." Generally, but especially since the end of World War II, the advocates of the primacy of economic action have been concentrated in the Anglo-American nations. The Marxian position is more difficult to describe, as its philosophic range is still at least as wide as it was in earlier periods. Indeed, the dispersion has been accentuated by the victory of the Bolsheviks in Russia. From it resulted a sharp division of political strategies between Social Democrats, who rely almost exclusively on democratic voting procedures, and the various shades of Communism in whose arsenal violence remains a main item of faith, though not always of action.

As to the literary debates, it may be sufficient to recall the Webbs' prediction and Selig Perlman's view of the "mature" labor movement. While the Webbs expected a gradual shift from economic to political means as the labor movements were to grow in power and stature,[3] Perlman in his most noted work foresaw exactly the opposite evolution: a "mature" labor movement, freed from the ideological freight which intellectuals have imposed upon it, would abandon its political aims and methods and rely upon its economic power. Collective bargaining would become its main activity.[4]

On the whole, it must be admitted that the evolution in the advanced industrial nations has been far closer to Perlman's predictions than to those of the Webbs. Yet it is easy to overstate Perlman's victory. In the first place, one would be lacking in historic insight were he to regard most of continental European labor history in the nineteenth and even the first half of this century as simply an aberration or a prelude to what was to follow. The reasoning that what came later is of necessity better, more mature, or more appropriate in some sense, is tempting but likely to be misleading. In the second place, the trend toward increased emphasis on collective bargaining in Europe in the last two decades, though clearly observable, has nevertheless taken some forms that require special examination and qualification before they can be accepted as full evidence for the progress of collective bargaining. Third and most important, it would be foolhardy and totally unrealistic to infer from this evolution, to the extent to which it has taken place, that collective bargaining is the one and only proper method of labor action anywhere and at any time.

Merely setting down this last proposition may make it sound too absurd to have even been asserted. But this has been the case all too

3   The classic, widely quoted statement of this view is contained in Sidney and Beatrice Webb, *Industrial Democracy* (London, 1920), p. 538: "The Trade Unionists, having obtained the vote, now wish to make use of it to enforce by Legal Enactment, such of their Common Rules as they see a chance of getting opinion to support."
4   Selig Perlman, *A Theory of the Labor Movement* (New York, 1949).

frequently. A brief reflection upon recent history may be permitted at this point.

THE UNIVERSALITY OF COLLECTIVE BARGAINING

Post–World War II events produced, especially in the Anglo-American sphere, a naïve belief in the universal applicability of some form of collective bargaining as the fundamental method of settling industrial relations problems. The idea that those directly involved settle their own problems without outside (government) interference appeals to all those committed to the ideas of liberalism—in the European meaning of the term—and self-government. Moreover, collective bargaining appears likely to produce a "just" solution in an area in which it is well-nigh impossible to establish objectively where justice lies. If roughly equal forces confront each other at the bargaining table in an adversary relationship, yet within a framework of common interests, a reasonable and mutually acceptable outcome may be expected.[5]

Early practitioners of collective bargaining in the Anglo-American countries, while convinced of its virtues, were conscious of the stringent prerequisites that had to be met before bargaining could be a fair and effective method of determining wages and working conditions. Thus Samuel Gompers was deeply convinced that only skilled workers were capable of establishing solid and lasting organizations of their own and of engaging in collective bargaining. He pointed out that unskilled workers were not yet ready to set up effective unions and to engage in genuine collective bargaining. This was indeed the main issue separating the AFL from the Knights of Labor. This recognition that collective bargaining has prerequisites not readily achieved at all times and in all places seems to have been forgotten by many people and influential organizations.

The strongest support for the idea that free collective bargaining is universally applicable in time and space has come from the countries that come closest to the realization of this idea: the United States and Great Britain. However, the stamp of international approval was put on this view by the evolution of the policy statements of the International Labor Organization (ILO). A first step in this

5 It is of some interest to draw attention to the contrast between the basic optimism of this view and the pessimism with which Marxian theoreticians analyzed this kind of situation. Marxians, especially those of the Austrian school, regarded a "balance of hostile class forces" as a situation most likely to lead to a stalemate, ending in the establishment of a dictatorship which would subject both of the balancing class forces to its rule.

direction, still containing some reservations, was made before World War II. In its Minimum Wage Convention of 1928, the ILO followed British thinking in making minimum wage–setting by authority subsidiary to wage determination by collective agreement.[6] In setting such wages, "regard should primarily be had to the rates of wages being paid for similar work in trades where the workers are adequately organized and have concluded effective collective agreements. . . ." Other sections of the convention and of the recommendation attached to it made it clear that such wage setting was to be limited to situations where effective unionization was not yet possible. The process of minimum wage–setting was to approximate the process of collective bargaining as much as possible; employers and workers in the trade concerned should be represented in equal numbers on the wage-setting authority. In short, the process should be as similar to collective bargaining as possible and should provide a transitional mechanism.[7]

While the long-term ideal of universal collective bargaining was implied in these ILO pronouncements, it was clearly and explicitly stated after World War II. The Convention of 1949 on the Right to Organize and Collective Bargaining required the affiliates "to encourage and promote the full development and utilization of machinery for voluntary negotiation between employers or employers' organizations with a view to the regulation of terms and conditions of employment by means of collective agreements." The same principle had already been enunciated two years earlier in the Convention on Social Policy in Non-Metropolitan Territories. While in the earlier stages the British model seems to have predominated in ILO thinking (the United States not being a member of the organization during this period), American ideas came to have more and more influence after World War II. As might be expected, they operated, with minor variations, in the same direction as the earlier British leadership. In 1956 David Cole, one of the most widely known U.S. labor arbitrators, prepared a report at the request of the ILO on the role of collective bargaining in industrial relations. The Report

> stresses the need for minimizing the loss of productivity through strikes and lockouts, and therefore advocates a general system of

6   See H. A. Turner, *Wage Trends, Wage Policies, and Collective Bargaining: The Problems for Underdeveloped Countries* (Cambridge: Cambridge University Press, 1965), pp. 25ff., for a discussion of ILO policy.

7   The similarity of the arrangements proposed by the ILO, and the reasoning behind them, with those of the British Trade Boards Act of 1909 is striking.

collective bargaining in which parties show self-restraint and an overwhelming appreciation for the interests of the community. The Report professes the belief that adequate training in human relations will infuse the negotiating parties with reason and patience; if only they are given enough cold economic facts of a statistical nature, they will resolve their differences peacefully. Cole proposed that the ILO assume the task of furnishing these statistics as well as circulating model collective agreements and the text of important contracts previously negotiated. Thus he hopes to spare industrializing countries the strife and bitterness that accompanied the Industrial Revolution in the West.[8]

The conclusions of the Cole Report were duly endorsed ("more or less," according to Haas) by a committee of experts and two years later by the International Labor Conference, the highest authority of the organization.

If these and related statements are examined more closely, it emerges that it is not simply collective bargaining in the general sense, but a very specific form of collective bargaining—namely, that of Great Britain and the United States—which is silently or explicitly assumed to represent the generally applicable model. It is not the French system of that period, in which the role of the government is far more pronounced than in the Anglo-American model that is recommended; nor is it the German system that the ILO had in mind. German bargaining puts its emphasis on collectively negotiated minima for industries in entire regions to be supplemented by various other agreements, including individual arrangements, setting effective rates and conditions. It is quite clear from the literature and particularly from the resolutions of the International Labor Organization that it is the Anglo-American model, indeed, the Anglo-American model in a glorified or simplified version, which is supposed to be applicable to the whole world, including the underdeveloped countries.

REALITY AND THE MODEL

The Anglo-American model, especially in the post–World War II era, was thought of as a system of sectional collective bargaining carried on by independent and effective private organizations, with a minimum or total absence of government intervention. It is true

8 This summary is quoted from Ernst B. Haas, *Beyond the Nation-State: Functionalism and International Organization* (Stanford: Stanford University Press, 1964), p. 186.

that reality in both the United States and Great Britain has substantially departed from this ideal. Incomes policies and legal minimum standards are examples of such departures. Yet on the whole these were either regarded as exceptional measures to meet extraordinary situations or assistance to weak social groups, designed to help them until they, too, could develop the strength necessary for a full enjoyment of the blessings of collective bargaining.

If we compare this ideal with the reality in large parts of the contemporary world, we find a variety of departures and contrasts. Some relate to the centralization of the bargain—the level at which the agreement is concluded and the scope of its applicability. The Anglo-American model in its idealized form refers to sectional agreements. Elsewhere we find highly centralized understandings covering entire industries or vast regions. The model regards bargaining as a private process. In large parts of the world wages and working conditions are directly or indirectly determined by government. In some cases, while the appearance of a private bargain is being preserved, one or both of the contracting partners are in fact organs of the government. Looked at in a different way, such departures from the private nature of the agreement may be partial or intended to be temporary (as is the case for incomes policies in most Western countries); in large parts of the world, the entire industrial relations system is dominated, directly or indirectly, by the government. Some of these departures from the Anglo-American model may be the result of history and tradition: centralized industrial regulations have dominated the entire industrial history of the country. Other variations may result from the objective conditions on the labor market, as, for example, when long-term excess supplies of labor exist.

Examples for these propositions are not difficult to find. In the underdeveloped or developing nations collective bargaining continues to remain the exception rather than the rule in determining wages and working conditions.[9] Even some of the agreements that exist are either mere window-dressing or the result of powerful governmental pressure upon, most often, foreign-owned enterprises. In the advanced industrial nations various forms of incomes policies have introduced outside intervention—with varying degrees of success—into what was supposed to be a private agreement, independently arrived at by the partners to the agreement. In Belgium, France, and Italy new types of agreements have emerged at the con-

9   Walter Galenson, ed., *Labor and Economic Development* (New York: John Wiley and Sons, 1959), "Introduction," esp. p. 8.

federal or even inter-confederal level. Thus the rough counterparts to the AFL-CIO in these countries and some modified National Association of Manufacturers have concluded agreements on basic issues of the employment relationship. Most often the government has sponsored such agreements; but even in the absence of outside pressure, it is obvious that this development has little similarity to the sectional competitive bargaining system advocated almost as an article of faith in international and Anglo-American (especially American) documents.

The question thus arises as to the conditions under which a genuine collective bargaining system approximating the Anglo-American ideal may be expected to operate. Clearly one of the obvious conditions is the existence of a legal and political system permitting the existence and functioning of reasonably *free* labor organizations. Illegal or underground unions have existed in various places and at various times, and they most probably exist today in some parts of the world, but their activity is bound to aim at the creation of the conditions necessary for collective bargaining rather than at collective bargaining itself.

However, from this the inference should not be drawn that in the absence of legal restrictions workers would automatically turn toward collective bargaining. Such an idea would have appeared senseless to craftsmen of most of the older industrial nations in the early beginnings of the industrialization process. During that era, which in some countries coincided with the predominance of mercantilism and in others with cameralism, it was regarded as obvious that the earnings of craftsmen were to be determined by public authority rather than by the laws of the market. Thus since the middle of the sixteenth century the British Parliament accepted the responsibility for determining wages, and the famous "Statute of Artificers" embodied this principle. When Parliament reversed itself two centuries later, a tradition had been built up of workers' turning to Parliament for relief. It took several decades for the lesson of this reversal to sink in among the workers of Great Britain and to influence their industrial relations strategy. As a general proposition, we may suggest that a tradition of industrial relations regulation or absence thereof, once established for a long period, may last after the conditions giving rise to the creation of this tradition have ceased to exist.

A second prerequisite for the rise of collective bargaining is that unions be more or less stable, reasonably well organized, and fairly evenly matched with the employers in bargaining strength. This apparently simple proposition involves in fact a most complicated set of conditions.

Effective unions have rarely if ever been organized by "noncommitted" workers, i.e., casual workers who change jobs frequently, return periodically to their native village, and have no specific industrial skill, even of a very simple kind. Yet even fully committed industrial workers with little or no skill are capable of engaging in effective collective bargaining only under certain conditions which are rarely found. In most (though by no means all) newly industrializing countries, large excess supplies of common labor are available for nonagricultural work. Not only are unskilled workers rarely capable of forming unions of their own under such conditions; if they succeed in doing so, their unions have little or no bargaining power.

The difficulties confronting such workers in attempts at establishing unions to engage in bargaining on their behalf are well known. Poor and illiterate, common laborers depend on outside leadership which, if it is forthcoming, is more likely to lead them in political action than onto the economic battlefield. This is so, not simply because the outside leader expects more glory and personal advancement in politics, but also or even more because economic action holds out little promise of success. The pressure of excess supplies of common labor on the market reduces the bargaining power of a union limited to unskilled workers to almost zero. A strike is an ineffective weapon when both union and workers are extremely poor and when thousands of job-seekers wait at the factory gates, willing and eager to take the jobs of the striking workers.[10]

This applies not only to many of the countries now entering the era of industrialization. Where and when similar conditions prevailed in now highly industrialized nations, they witnessed the same phenomenon: collective bargaining was an effective weapon for skilled workers only, because they were the only ones in short supply and therefore difficult to replace.[11] Skilled workers are literate

10   Capital intensity of specific industries may moderate the harshness of this situation, as indicated below in the study of Argentina by Sanchez and Arnaudo.

11   As Hla Myint observes: "Many underdeveloped countries suffer from a greater shortage of skills than of material capital, so that they sometimes prefer more expensive machinery, which reduces repairs and maintenance, to cheaper or second-hand machinery which, although it might reduce the ratio of capital to unskilled labour, requires a larger amount of the scarcest factor, skilled labour . . ." (*The Economics of the Developing Countries* [London: Hutchinson & Co., 1964], p. 137). Moreover, as he adds, with training facilities in short supply, in the short run the supply elasticity of skilled labor is quite low. Indeed, skilled labor is to be regarded as a separate factor of production.

and reasonably well off—and thus able to support themselves for some time in the case of a strike, to set up stable organizations with at least a minimum staff, and to bolster them with mutual insurance institutions. Strikes then need not be simply demonstrations limited to short periods and mainly designed to arouse public opinion or to induce government intervention. The walkout serves to create the situation described in texts on bargaining, i.e., to inflict economic harm upon the employer to the point where concessions to the workers will be economically more acceptable for him than a prolongation of the conflict. This supposes that the demands are reasonable enough or modified by bargaining to the point that they can be met by the employer. Collective bargaining cannot serve as an instrument of basic social change in the way revolutionary movements do.

A further prerequisite for the existence of a long-term collective bargaining system is a balance of power. The power relationship at the bargaining table must be such that the outcome of a conflict is at least to some degree uncertain at the outset. If it is obvious that the employer holds all the winning cards, not simply on one occasion but systematically, then effective bargaining is impossible. Vice versa, if the workers are bound to win regardless of the size of their demands, and this situation prevails over extended periods, then collective bargaining is unlikely to survive as a private process in which outside forces such as the government do not intervene.

INDUSTRIALIZATION WITH SURPLUS LABOR

So far the discussion has been concerned mainly with industrializing nations possessing a large surplus of common labor. This is the model which Arthur Lewis presented in his two celebrated articles.[12] The reasoning outlined above was originally derived from his model of a two-sectoral growth process. Reasons to question its universal applicability even in countries with excess supplies of labor have been put forward in many recent publications. For the purposes of my reasoning we can avoid many of the disputed parts of the Lewis model.[13] It is sufficient to think of a highly elastic supply of common

12   W. A. Lewis, "Economic Development with Unlimited Supplies of Labor," *The Manchester School of Economic and Social Studies* (May, 1954), and "Unlimited Labor: Further Notes," *ibid.* (June, 1958). See also S. Enke, "Economic Development with Unlimited and Limited Supplies of Labor," *Oxford Economic Papers* (June, 1962).

13   Koji Taira, for instance, in his *Economic Development and the Labor Market in Japan* (New York: Columbia University Press, 1970), Ch. 4, restricts the validity of the model to the wage-paying sector of the country. Yhi-Min Ho.

labor available in the wage-paying sector of the economy or ready to move into that sector. The wage may be substantially above subsistence or per capita income in the pre-capitalistic, non-wage-paying sector as discussed below. This situation must prevail over a sufficiently long period—perhaps two decades or more—to have the effects on the labor movement described in this paper.

I believe that conditions of this kind or closely approximating it exist in many, though not all, of the underdeveloped countries today. While the industrialized nations show a different economic structure, the model helps to understand some phases in the history of now fully industrialized nations. If the conditions outlined above apply, we would expect labor movements in older countries to have confronted similar situations in their earlier history. If so, we could submit the hypotheses derived from these considerations to empirical tests.

Arthur Lewis argues that, given excess supplies of common labor, the industrializing or modernizing sector of the economy—the "capitalistic" sector, in his language—would be confronted with a perfectly elastic supply curve of common labor at a level corresponding to the average per capita income in the pre-capitalistic sector.[14] "Corresponding" does not mean "equal"; there may be a differential to compensate for the costs of transfer from one sector to another, differences in living costs, separation from the family and the relative security it offers, etc. On the management side, apart from occasional humanitarian considerations, there are sound economic reasons for offering wages above the subsistence level: improving the health of the employees so as to reduce absenteeism as well as turnover (such a reduction would tend to minimize training costs),

"Development with Suplus Population—the Case of Taiwan: A Critique of the Classical Two-Sector Model, à la Lewis," *Economic Development and Cultural Change* 20, no. 2 (January, 1972), departs from the Lewis model and its refined Fei-Ranis version by pointing out the possibility of labor absorption in agriculture. This does not seem to me a serious criticism of Lewis since a capitalistic agriculture, even with highly labor-intensive techniques, would clearly come under the heading of Lewis's modern sector. L. G. Reynolds's study of Puerto Rico ("Wages and Employment in the Labor-Surplus Economy," *American Economic Review* 55, no. 1 [March, 1965]: 19–39) explains the rapidly rising wages in nonagricultural activities by reference to rising legal minimum wages while "trade union organization in Puerto Rico is relatively weak." This is perfectly compatible with the scheme presented in the text. The question of whether expanded manufacturing with or without multiplier effect in generating employment in the service sector can absorb unemployment—as suggested by Walter Galenson, "Economic Development and the Sectoral Expansion of Employment," *International Labour Review* 88 (June, 1963)—can also be left unanswered for our immediate purposes.

14　Some facets of the process by which labor becomes a marketable item—so that we may speak of supply and demand—are treated in Hoselitz's paper.

retain a labor force used to industrial discipline and form a group from which candidates for training as skilled workers and foremen can be selected. This may establish some—perhaps loose—relationship between the earnings of skilled workers coming from the primitive sector and those of skilled wage-earners in the modern sector. Furthermore, while it is analytically convenient to speak of subsistence earnings in the primitive sector as if there were a uniform level of such earnings, there is considerable diversity in most cases between various areas and different functions. This in turn will affect the earnings which the modern sector—or at least some part of it—has to offer to attract and retain labor from the primitive sector. In combination, these factors may help explain the often considerable difference between the incomes of common labor in the two sectors. Other institutional factors that enter into the picture, such as those which enable wage-earners in the modern sector to use union tactics effectively under conditions of labor surplus, will be discussed later.

In any case, provided the marginal product of labor is sufficiently higher in the capitalistic sector to induce a transfer of labor from the traditional to the modern part of the economy, employment is determined by the supply of capital. In a closed economy and assuming that the transfer of labor proceeds faster than population growth in the pre-capitalistic parts of the economy, surplus labor is gradually being absorbed. Average incomes in the traditional economy grow in line with the change in the land-labor ratio; more work is done per head of the labor force and better nutrition enables better work performance. Output need not decline and may even increase as an aggregate and can be distributed among a smaller number of people. Thus the supply price of labor to the capitalistic sector increases until it reaches—perhaps still with a certain differential over income in the traditional sector—the level of marginal productivity in the capitalistic sector. This, in the meantime, has been subject to at least two contradictory influences: the impact of the influx of common labor, and qualitative improvements in capital and work performance. The incentive to increase the capital-labor ratio is rather weak as long as production can be expanded by widening rather than deepening capital investment. It would follow that marginal productivity in the capitalistic sector would remain relatively constant or slowly rising and that wages for common labor would be constant over a fairly long period. Similarly, the incentive for introducing labor-saving devices in the capitalistic sector during this period would be minor, and collective bargaining would play a limited role in wage-determination, i.e., limited at best to skilled workers.

Some of the essays in the volume to which this article serves as introduction touch upon these hypotheses. Peter Kilby and James Scoville apply them to the situations in Nigeria and Afghanistan, while Kawada and Komatsu use some of them to reinterpret Japanese industrial developments. I would like to review the British and American experience, where we encounter some interesting findings in the literature. While careful tests would require elaborate analysis, a few references may be of some interest.

For the period from 1815 to the 1840's in Great Britain, Habakkuk[15] points out:

> The supply of labour was increasing from the following five sources:
> (1) After 1815 a large number of men, some 400,000, were demobilised, and a substantial number must have been released from agricultural investment (especially enclosures) which was low from 1815 to the 1850's. "This surplus" [that is, of agricultural labour] said a Sussex farmer in 1837 "has been growing for years; but it commenced with the peace." The agricultural surplus in the southern counties was principally due to large families and a low level of agricultural investment. "The competition for work among the labourers is so great, that they underbid each other, and leave the bargain entirely at the discretions of the master."
> (2) Population was increasing very rapidly.
> (3) Capitalism was invading the labour reserves of domestic industry. Many of the textile factories, until well into the nineteenth century, drew their marginal labour from rural industry. The villages to the north and north-east of Coventry, for example, in the 1830's and '40's provided a reservoir of country weavers for the Coventry industry.
> (4) There was a large influx of labour from Ireland.
> (5) Technical changes in agriculture increased the supply of labour available to industry. Though it is true that landless labourers were so numerous in English villages before the main phase of the enclosure movement that the relative increase due to enclosure was slight, enclosure did make *some* difference; by reducing rights of common it tended to weaken the ties which bound the cottagers to the villages and so made them less reluctant to respond to the demand of the factories for labour.

15   H. J. Habakkuk, *American and British Technology in the Nineteenth Century* (Cambridge: Cambridge University Press, 1962), pp. 136–39 and *passim*. The quotation of the statement of a Sussex farmer is from A. Redford, *Labour Migration in England, 1800–1850* (Manchester, 1926), p. 70.

This is of course not precisely the situation underlying the Lewis propositions. Yet in the context of the inferences which we wish to draw from his model, the differences are of limited relevance. Thus, as Habakkuk further reports, "industry could obtain [between 1815 and the 1840's] additional labour from the reserve army of agricultural labourers on favourable terms; and because food was cheap, the wages, in terms of output, of the industrial workers were low."[16] There was

considerable underemployment of labour in England in the decades after 1815, particularly in the English countryside. There is direct evidence of this in the figures of able-bodied paupers, and also in the course of real wages. Whether there was an increase in real wages down to the 1840's is still in dispute but even on the more optimistic view it seems that any rise was not enjoyed by the great mass of unskilled workers.

From 1815 to the 1850's the English manufacturer, in comparison with the American manufacturer, had a very elastic supply of labour at the ruling wage. It need not be supposed that this was a physiological minimum wage; it included an addition for superior diligence and skill and the transport costs of movement into industry; and the employers' fear of social disorder as well as social conscience might maintain it at a higher level than strictly economic forces by themselves would have done. Moreover, long-term abundance of labour was compatible with complaints of shortages in particular industries and localities, with a favourable bargaining position for particular groups of workers, and even, on occasion, with a more general sense of shortage at the height of a boom. But in general the shortages were local and temporary.[17]

One of the results of this long-term situation was that

the abundant supply of labour in England and the low floor set to the industrial wage by agricultural earnings allowed capital accumulation to proceed without pressure from that side. . . . Considerable new additions were made to capacity—much larger additions absolutely than in other countries—and this allowed scope for the employment and testing of new methods. . . . From this point of view the abundance of labour in England was favourable to technical development, for by promoting a high rate of investment it afforded Englishmen plentiful opportunities of trying out new methods. On the other hand, it blunted the incentive to

16   *Ibid.,* p. 138.
17   *Ibid.*

invent labour-saving devices; and also the incentive to adopt those which were invented, when the price of saving labour was an increase in capital per unit of output. Abundance of labour favoured accumulation with existing techniques—widening rather than deepening of capital—even though the supply of capital might have permitted a technologically more advanced development.[18]

Moreover, labor was hostile to labor-saving inventions, especially to the reduction of piece-rates on more productive machines —in contrast to less restrictive attitudes on the part of labor in the United States.

How was this situation reflected in the evolution of the British labor movement? Prior to the Napoleonic wars, the main concern of the skilled craftsman in the towns was to protect himself against the "influx of pauper labor. His defence was to ask for the enforcement of the law relating to apprenticeship," as the Webbs report in their *History of Trade Unionism*.[19] They add in an interesting footnote that Lujo Brentano, the famous German trade union historian, asserted that British trade unions had their origin in the nonobservance of the Elizabethan Statute of Apprentices and "that their primary object was, in all cases, the enforcement of the law on the subject." They pinned their hopes on the government to protect them. It was the failure of the government to provide such protection which "brought all trades into line, and for the first time produced what can properly be called a Trade Union Movement."[20]

The lesson of the changed attitude of the government was driven home forcefully by the Combination Acts of 1799/1800 as well as by a decision of Parliament in 1808 refusing to fix a minimum rate of wages for the handloom weavers because this would not be practicable, and, if it were, "would be productive of the most fatal consequences." The one-sided application of the Acts—"there is no case on record," the Webbs report, "in which an employer was punished"[21]—added to the resentment of the workers. Yet while the Acts weighed heavily on some groups of workers, especially in the new textile industries, the laws failed to suppress the trade unions of the skilled handicraftsmen who formed a working-class aristocracy, based upon their short supply.[22] These groups frequently had

18   *Ibid.,* pp. 140–41.
19   Sidney and Beatrice Webb, *The History of Trade Unionism* (London: Longmans, Green, 1920), p. 47.
20   *Ibid.*
21   *Ibid.,* p. 73.
22   "The substantial fees demanded all through the eighteenth century for apprenticeship to the 'crafts' had secured to the members and their eldest sons a

the open or silent support of their employers in their efforts to maintain their standards, in exchange for supporting the interests of their masters against outsiders. Some forms of collective understanding on wages and working conditions thus survived even this dark period, but they were limited to craftsmen with skills in rare supply in relation to market demand.

For the great mass of the workers no form of collective bargaining, however concealed, was available; hence they turned toward other forms of action, ranging from violence to the organization of, or at least participation in, a large political movement. One outstanding example of the first was the Luddite movement of 1811–12, when workers destroyed machinery, especially textile machines, and sometimes entire factories. The great popular movement of the Chartists, the movement for electoral reform in 1831–32, and the Owenite movement (1833–34) were the instruments by which large parts of the working class sought to improve their desperate situation.

The utopian elements of these movements derive perhaps from the fact that, for the great mass of unskilled workers and the craftsmen whose skill was rendered obsolete by mechanization, collective bargaining held out no hope. Yet in the long run the revolutionary and romantic counter-revolutionary movements failed equally to hold the allegiance of the great majority of the workers. This resulted not only from a disillusionment with these movements, but also from a radical change in the economic situation.

The period from 1850 on saw more rapid and steady economic expansion than the preceding decades. Chartism dwindled and "New Model" unionism developed: "Trade Unionism obtained a financial strength, a trained staff of salaried officers, and a permanence of membership hitherto unknown."[23] National unions grew, as well as county organizations. These were exceedingly moderate unions opposed to radical slogans as well as to strikes. Their substitute weapon was, significantly, a restriction of the supply of the particular skill. The limitation of the number of apprentices, the abolition of overtime, and the encouragement of emigration came to the fore. The less effective emigration funds proved, the greater became the stress upon the restriction of the number of apprentices. This of course was applicable only to skilled trades. A high point

---

virtual monopoly. Even after the repeal of the laws requiring a formal apprenticeship some time had to elapse before the supply of this class of handicraftsmen overtook the growing demand" (*ibid.*, p. 83).

23 *Ibid.*, p. 181.

of this evolution was the formation of the Amalgamated Society of Engineers, which proceeded to raise specific demands with employers, such as the abolition of overtime and exclusion of "laborers and other 'illegal' men" from the machines.[24] Collective bargaining, though in a somewhat abbreviated form, resulted from the scarcity of certain skills and aimed at the perpetuation of scarcity. Even though the union suffered many defeats in its early stages, it continued to exist and even to expand. Its policy continued to be dominated by a spirit of exclusiveness for the protection of the "vested interests of the craftsman in his occupation."[25] The course of events thus corresponds to the hypotheses formulated at an earlier stage.

INDUSTRIALIZATION WITH SCARCE LABOR

Quite different is the evolution of industrial relations strategies in countries where industrialization begins under conditions of a relative labor shortage. The classic example is the United States. Regardless of whether the Turner hypothesis on the impact of the frontier is accepted in its rigorous interpretation, it appears plausible that "the abundance of Western land drew away many thousands of potential wage earners (from the hill towns of New England and from the exhausted farms of New York and Pennsylvania) who might otherwise have crowded into the factories."[26] This tended to set a floor for industrial wages, especially in the first fifty or sixty years of the nineteenth century, at a level related to what a small farmer could earn on a piece of land. That wages in the United States or even in colonial America ran high above those of contemporary British workers was pointed out by observers more than a century ago. It is easily understandable, in light of the fact that output per man on land in the United States was high.

Moreover, the supply elasticity of labor was low as long as the country depended mainly on the natural population increase for additional workers. This changed only when mass immigration set in during the latter half of the nineteenth century. We would expect, following the hypotheses set out earlier, that collective bargaining of some kind would find a fertile soil under conditions of labor scarcity and low elasticity of supply, but that its character would change substantially when the supply elasticity was greatly increased by mass immigration.

24   *Ibid.,* p. 214.
25   *Ibid.,* p. 217.
26   C. Goodrich and S. Davison, "The Wage-Earner in the Westward Movement," *Political Science Quarterly* 51 (1936): 115.

A brief look at American labor history would tend, on the whole, to confirm these expectations. Unions arose early along the east coast; they sought to obtain arrangements from their employers which would nowadays be labeled "closed shops," and they concluded some wage agreements or adopted on their own a scale of wages ("books of prices" or "price-lists") below which their members would not work. Employers reacted by invoking the common law doctrine of conspiracy. Nevertheless, during periods of prosperity unions also prospered and expanded. But prolonged depressions destroyed unions and directed working-class attention toward political objectives and political means of action.

So far the story reads pretty much like the British. Indeed, it is quite probable that, consciously or not, the British model influenced American developments for some time. Yet with the age of Jackson a basic difference begins to manifest itself. Property qualifications for suffrage had been removed in the early 1820's (1820 in Massachusetts, 1822 in New York), and the workers, proud of their newly won right, far ahead of their English brethren, used it to help install an administration friendly to the common man. Free universal schooling was one of the main demands of the workers. It was met in the East by the middle of the century. Manufacturers favored better education for the workers, since in a labor-scarce economy the efficient use of labor was an economic necessity and education contributed greatly to higher productivity of labor. This same set of circumstances also contributed to the ease with which inventions could be introduced in the United States, compared with Great Britain.

With voting rights obtained at an early stage and universal free elementary education on its way, the main impetus for political action came from demands for a legal limitation of the hours of work, since only a few crafts had been successful in achieving a ten-hour day by way of economic action.[27] This, too, was gradually achieved, with legislation passed in New Hampshire in 1847 and Maine and Pennsylvania following soon afterward.

From then on social reform plans emerged again and again with various utopian schemes taking hold at various times, but their appeal was limited to small groups of poorly paid workers whose ranks were swelled by heavy immigration in the 1840's and 1850's. The crafts continued to concentrate on "the closed shop, apprenticeship rules, ample strike funds, employment exchange offices,

[27] Herbert Harris, *American Labor* (New Haven: Yale University Press, 1939), p. 51.

minimum wage and hours standards, and all the other accouter-
ments of a 'pure and simple' trade unionism."[28] The only new development in this area was the growth of the national unions in the
wake of the development of national markets, a result of the rapid
growth of railroads.

THE ROLE OF IMMIGRATION

The growth of immigration—mainly of cheap unskilled labor—
coincided with increases in the cost of occupying new land. While
the supply of skilled labor remained short in relation to the demands
of more and more rapid industrialization, the pull of new land was
increasingly limited to skilled workers who could afford the higher
costs of occupation. Unskilled labor, German and Irish immigrants,
were not only available in larger numbers; their supply elasticity
increased when demand rose as immigration responded more and
more to the stages of the business cycle in the United States.[29]

The gap between skilled and unskilled workers expressed itself
in large skill differentials.[30] These divided the working class into
groups of very different living standards. Moreover, these divisions
most often coincided with ethnic distinctions, or at the least with a
difference between native-born and typically skilled workers and
unskilled immigrants. Even the latter need not despair. The lack of
any long-established class system permitted a high degree of social
mobility. Social prestige was achieved by material success rather
than by the accidents of birth. No hereditary aristocracy, not even
a powerful bureaucracy, existed; even the army did not bestow any
great prestige upon its members. The early abolition of class distinctions in voting rights and elementary education further weakened whatever feeling of class solidarity might have survived the
conditions created by economic evolution. Thus while occupational
solidarity caused the extension of unionism horizontally, on a national scale, inter-occupational solidarity failed to develop in any
significant measure.

The one cause that seemed able to call forth united labor action
in the political field was the legal introduction of the eight-hour day.
The Knights of Labor was the one organization of more than passing significance which, though acting as a national union, devoted

28   *Ibid.,* p. 57.
29   Habakkuk, *American and British Technology,* pp. 126ff.
30   Compare their size with those of French and British workers as presented
in Sellier's article in this volume.

itself also to the propaganda for a vast number of reforms. At various times it advocated the eight-hour day as well as public ownership of utilities, espoused the expansion of cooperatives, joined the Greenback opposition to the gold standard, and took part in many other passing fads. Its greatest triumph, however, was a series of victorious strikes in the 1880's, primarily on railroads including those owned by Jay Gould, the "wizard of Wall Street." Yet the victories were obtained by the skilled workers in its ranks; increasingly the skilled craftsmen, conscious of their bargaining power, turned away from the unskilled workers who formed the great mass of the Knights' membership. In 1881 the craft unions formed a new association, which grew into the American Federation of Labor. Two of their basic ideas were the exclusion of the unskilled from the unions and their concentration upon collective bargaining. "Pure and simple" trade unionism flourished while the Knights rapidly declined, weakened by anarchist groups that had forced their way into demonstrations arranged by the Knights, and deprived of the cutting edge which the skilled workers alone represented in a period of mass immigration.

While not refusing legislative or administrative support when it could be obtained, the AFL relied upon collective bargaining as its main, almost only, weapon. The unskilled workers, mainly immigrants from overseas, were left to fend for themselves.

The period from the early 1870's to about the middle of the 1890's was characterized by fairly long and sharp depressions and relatively weak and short recovery periods. Although, compared with Western Europe, the economic situation was far more favorable and industrialization progressed at a rapid pace, the growth of the volume of immigration coinciding with the relatively unfavorable economic situation created serious problems for the AFL. Immigration of Chinese workers in California was especially resented, partly for racial reasons, but even more because of the competition of the immigrants on the labor market, even for skilled workers.[31] For a time mass immigration acted somewhat like the unlimited supply of common labor in the Lewis model, with the major qualification that at least some of the immigrants could be easily trained to replace skilled native workers. Demands for the restriction of immigration on the part of AFL unions became more and more frequent and intense.[32] The same mixture of racial and economic

31   Philip Taft, *The AFL in the Time of Gompers* (New York: Harper and Brothers, 1957), p. 302ff.
32   The proposal to suspend immigration altogether for a year was rejected, however. *Ibid.*, p. 305.

motivations guided many unions in adopting restrictive clauses directed against black workers. Legislation restricting immigration was first passed in 1882; this was specifically directed against Chinese labor. Later informal agreements limited Japanese immigration.

The act of 1882 was the entering wedge of increasingly restrictive legislation, but it was only the legislation of 1917 which, by establishing a literacy test, generalized the restriction principle.[33] The dangers threatening collective bargaining from this angle were at least greatly diminished, if not entirely eliminated.

POLITICAL UNIONISM IN DEVELOPING COUNTRIES

Collective bargaining thus appears to be a far from universal method of labor action. Indeed, its effectiveness is restricted in general to situations or groups of workers whose supply is limited in relation to demand at prevailing wages and whose supply elasticity appears to be low. Yet we find collective agreements in situations and for groups that do not fit this description. Thus collective agreements have been concluded for workers with little or no skill in countries such as Mexico prior to World War I, in a situation of huge excess supplies of labor, or in a number of contemporary African countries. What is the explanation for this phenomenon?

If it is a passing phase, then we may be simply confronted with a case of international snobbery. Eager to be modern, a country may introduce a collective bargaining system regardless of whether the conditions for effective bargaining exist, simply because it is fitting for modern nations to do so. It is likely that in such cases collective bargaining will not long persist and that either government regulation or unilateral wage determination by employers will take its place. Examples of this kind can be found in many countries that became independent after World War II, including quite a few in which labor leaders played a leading role in the independence movement and in the new governments.

In other countries collective bargaining persisted, even though objective factors continue to operate against it. A few agreements in Africa, for instance, have had a long lease on life. In those cases, the explanation probably can be found in the fact that foreign-owned firms were involved, often also under foreign management. The workers may count upon the support of public opinion and of

33   Samuel Eliot Morison and Henry Steele Commager, *The Growth of the American Republic* (New York: Oxford University Press, 1942), vol. 2, pp. 184ff.

the government, and this may offset the strategic disadvantages under which unskilled workers (or workers with a specific, untransferable skill) suffer.[34]

There are other reasons why a government may wish to support a union or even a union-to-be. Eager to have organized mass support apart from that of the armed forces, the government may give a union or a union leader the privileges of a closed shop in a particular industry or range of industries and, perhaps, also the right to set itself up as a closed union. Ownership in jobs and improved wages are thus granted to a group of workers who, in the absence of such rights, might be either unemployed or have modest wages and poor working conditions. Withdrawal of these rights may destroy the union and bring a new leadership to the fore. Union members and union leaders are thus tied to the government, to which they give support in exchange for the privileges which they enjoy.[35]

Whether agreements concluded by such unions represent genuine collective bargaining or not may be a question of semantics. What matters is that this case is clearly different from the Anglo-American model. It is, in fact, some kind of mixture between political action and collective bargaining, and the proportions between the two may be subject to considerable fluctuations as political and economic conditions change.[36]

Complicating this example is the fact that occasionally a union thus established by government-created privileges manages to set up a firm power base and maintain itself under hostile governments. The outstanding example is the group of unions sponsored by Juan Peron in Argentina; they have successfully weathered the opposition of the anti-Peron governments since the overthrow of the Peronista regime. The impact of these unions upon the Argentine wage structure is the subject of one contribution in this volume.[37]

34   Thus a worker skilled in copper mining in a country that has only one copper-mining firm has an untransferable skill.

35   The unions may even be "integrated into the government party," as is the case in Mexico and many other countries.

36   In the words of Walter Galenson: "The outlook for non-political unionism in the newly developing countries is not bright. We may expect, rather, a highly political form of unionism, with a radical ideology. Indeed, so strong is the presumption that this will be the prevailing pattern that, where it is absent, we may draw the conclusion that unionism is, in fact, subordinated to the employer or to the state, i.e., that we are dealing either with company unionism or a labor front" (*Labor and Economic Development,* p. 8).

37   American observers may point at the New Deal support for the CIO unions as another example of government-sponsored growth of unionism and collective bargaining among semi-skilled and unskilled workers, admittedly under circumstances quite different from those in newly developing countries. In this

Political action of some systematic or unsystematic kind seems thus the most promising avenue for labor action under a whole series of conditions. The most obvious case is the one in which the survival of feudal institutions and those of "enlightened absolutism" almost forced labor into the political arena. Where open or barely concealed class distinctions prevail to "keep labor in its place" and legislation or courts prevent the workers from organizing effectively for the defense of their interests, the main thrust of any workers' movement will almost inevitably be directed at a basic change of the institutions, and the means available to the workers will be political: mass demonstrations, violence, sabotage, political strikes, etc. In the history of most Western labor movements, this was the "heroic" period in which the struggle for democracy combined with that for the advancement of the economic and social situation of the working class. The power of the Marxian appeal resided precisely in the combination of these two elements. Perhaps the main reason why the same ideology played a relatively minor part in the evolution of the American labor movement lies in the fact that political and social equality was given to the workers at an early stage of the development of the movement.[38]

In many of the newly developing countries, the struggle for national independence from colonial oppression appears to have served as a counterpart to the heroic age of Western labor. The advancement of the native working class was tied to the attainment of national liberation, in the minds of the intelligentsia and the workers; the labor movement became a part of the national liberation struggle, just as it had been an essential part of the movement for democracy in the West.[39]

Labor movements, thus formed, tend to have a heavy ideological freight from their beginnings. This has not prevented them from attempting to use economic action under the colonial regime, insofar as the government permitted; nor to develop it, once independence was attained, for those groups whose situation on the labor market was favorable for genuine collective bargaining. In essence, these were skilled workers, white-collar employees, and, as we just pointed out, the workers of foreign-owned enterprises. The fact that white-collar workers in many of the new countries were predominantly government employees often created special difficulties for

case, too, the institutions once firmly established (and, one might add in this particular case, favored by long periods of full employment) have survived in spite of considerably less friendly administrations.

38   I shall return to this issue below.

39   Kilby's paper summarizes this process in Nigeria.

this group. According to its inclinations, the government could grant or refuse bargaining rights to white-collar workers in general, or government employees in particular.

In most cases the urge for rapid industrialization has led the governments of new countries to turn against the unions—their former allies—and to impose wage restraints of some kind. Indeed, quite frequently the unions were either abolished or put under government control. Whatever modest beginnings of a collective bargaining system might have existed were thus destroyed. Moreover, the existence of a relatively well-developed system of fringe benefits, based upon legislation or administrative fiat, tended to make the wage component of total labor costs subject to collective bargaining relatively less important than in most developed countries.[40]

Another factor may blur the picture. The struggle for social and political equality or for national independence may forge such a powerful alliance between skilled and unskilled workers that even those groups which could rely upon their economic strength to obtain special advantages for themselves may refrain from doing so, or use it in behalf of their less-favored brethren as well. The feeling of class solidarity may be so strong that working-class opinion would not tolerate any special group obtaining privileges; therefore few such groups would be tempted to do so. A tradition of this kind, once established, may live far beyond the existence of the conditions that gave rise to it. Thus to this day "plant selfishness" (i.e., the achievement of wages and working conditions at levels above those of others in the same industry and occupational group) is frowned upon in West Germany, even though the main and most visible elements of the pre-1918 political and social discrimination against workers have been eliminated or greatly weakened. The longevity of ideology tends to make short-run predictions based upon the original hypotheses exceedingly difficult. For the long run, however, it is reasonable to expect that tradition will give way to methods more appropriate to new conditions. What we do not know, in the light of existing theory, is how long it takes for the "long run" to dominate the scene.[41]

LAGS AND ADAPTATIONS

Thus a lag exists between changes in the labor market situation or in the political and social status of workers and their strategies,

40   Turner, *Wage Trends,* p. 31.
41   Interesting studies of some variants of this problem are presented in this volume by Kawada and Komatsu, as well as by Taira.

organizational structure, ideology, etc. Traditions once established are not easily abandoned; in some cases traditional institutions have outlived even cataclysmic changes in the country's entire life.[42] Most interesting are cases in which attempts are made to adapt traditional features of an industrial relations system to a considerable change in the underlying conditions. Thus the boom and the labor shortages of the 1950's and 1960's have produced new features in collective bargaining in France, Italy, and Belgium which, I believe, can only be understood as experiments in the adaptation of the traditional features of the systems of these countries to greatly changed labor market conditions.[43]

Collective bargaining developed rather late in the countries mentioned above. In France it was not until the sitdown strikes and the Popular Front government in 1936 that bargaining began on a substantial scale; even then, the government played a key role in the process. World War II destroyed the system after it had barely gotten under way, and it was not until 1950 that a new departure was undertaken. In Italy the rise of Fascism destroyed the unions, and collective bargaining, which had begun to develop at the beginning of this century, did not start again until after World War II.[44] Most wages and working conditions were thus determined traditionally by the government or unilaterally by the employer. When in distress, workers turned to the government or the legislature for relief.

The 1950's produced an acute labor shortage in France, which became one of the main importers of foreign labor. In Italy the rapid industrialization of the north led to a shortage of skilled workers. The boom and the mass migration of Italian workers, including unskilled workers from the south, to West Germany, Switzerland, and France depleted even southern Italy of most of the excess supplies of unskilled workers which had been characteristic of that area for a century. Conditions were thus favorable for the growth of a collective bargaining system, the more so as the former sharp class distinctions and class discrimination were either elimi-

42   One example among many is the spontaneous reconstruction of Workers' Councils in Germany when the Nazi regime collapsed. It might have been far more appropriate for the new unified trade union movement to establish its own plant organization, but by the time the unions were firmly established the councils had already been formed and assumed essential functions in the industrial relations system.

43   Pen's paper reveals some aspects of this process in the Netherlands.

44   Daniel L. Horowitz, *The Italian Labor Movement* (Cambridge: Harvard University Press, 1963).

nated by the progress of democratic institutions or weakened by the impact of labor shortages.[45]

Yet the growth of collective bargaining has developed institutions in France, in Italy, and to a considerable extent in Belgium as well, which retain the spirit of the tradition while molding it to the new conditions. A special type of agreement has evolved whose partners are trade union confederations on one side and employers' confederations on the other, with the government acting openly or indirectly as a sponsor.

These "inter-professional" agreements on a national scale apply not just to the members represented by the organizations on both sides of the bargaining table, but to all workers defined in the agreement. Thus they have some of the characteristics of a law, though they emanate from an understanding between private organizations. While some earlier agreements of this kind in France (such as one about a fourth paid vacation week or another about compensation for partial unemployment) were essentially extensions of previous branch agreements of the conventional type, the upheaval of 1968 in France produced new types of agreement: new in the subject matter covered, as for example the monthly pay system for manual workers; new also because one of the most important agreements of this kind deals with vocational education and requires legislative action for its full implementation. The state thus becomes the executor of agreements concluded by the bargaining partners.

What makes this development particularly significant is the fact that it departs sharply from the kind of bargaining provided for in the past, especially by the legislation of 1950. Moreover, these national agreements are quite different from the nationwide basic agreements in Scandinavia. The latter set limits which individual branch agreements have to accept. The French and Italian agreements, on the contrary, provide additional rights for all workers, beyond those granted them under the different branch agreements.[46] The device represents a new stage in the evolution of collective bargaining under a system with a tradition of uniform regulation. Private organizations agree on rules which the government enforces.

45   No more effective device has yet been discovered to weaken or even remove class or racial discrimination than a labor shortage. U.S. experience coincides with that of Western and Central Europe.

46   Much of this is based upon an unpublished paper by Gerard Adam, Jean-Daniel Reynaud, and Jean-Maurice Verdier which Reynaud has kindly made available to me.

IDEOLOGY AND LABOR

So far, references to ideologies have been few and far between, unless the reader has been reading between the lines. In its most obvious meaning, "ideology" includes ideas as diverse as that collective bargaining is the best device for labor action, and the demand for revolutionary political action and the creation of a new social system. From the point of view of the American observer, "ideologies" are of course those of other nations;[47] for the American labor movement in its great majority, especially at this time, Marxist ideologies in their great variety—not all of which Marx would have recognized as his own—are the conspicuous and significant ideologies. Just as Werner Sombart at the beginning of this century raised the question of why the United States was almost alone among the industrial nations of the world in having no significant Socialist movement, American labor leaders have been asking again and again: why has European and Japanese labor (in fact, labor in all industrial nations outside the United States, even in neighboring Canada) been under significant Socialist influence of some kind? There is no doubt that ideologies—sometimes tied up with foreign "models"—have been of great importance in determining the types of labor organization developed, the relationship between various parts of the labor movement, its strategy, tactics, and objectives. The nature of the ideologies of the industrial relations system as a whole and of the labor movement in particular is thus a factor of considerable significance. Clark Kerr and his associates have explained the characteristics of industrial relations systems by relating them to the nature of the elite under which the nation enters the era of industrialization. They write: "The major characteristics of a national industrial relations system appear to be crystallized by the leading elite at a relatively early stage."[48]

There are both minor and major objections to this kind of analysis. A minor one refers to the entire concept of a "national" industrial relations system. One would have difficulty in analyzing

47   My ideology is no ideology; your ideology is an ideology!
48   Clark Kerr, John T. Dunlop, Frederick Harbison, and Charles A. Myers, *Industrialism and Industrial Man: The Problems of Labor and Management in Economic Growth* (Cambridge: Harvard University Press, 1960), p. 235; as John Windmuller has pointed out ("Model Industrial Relations Systems," *Proceedings* of the Sixteenth Annual Meeting, IRRA, December, 1963, p. 61, note 3), this idea has been suggested in almost exactly the same form by John T. Dunlop, *Industrial Relations Systems* (New York: Henry Holt, 1958).

the French and Italian systems—very different in terms of industry, occupation, and region—during most of the last century as if they were "national" systems. I doubt whether the Japanese or the contemporary Mexican industrial scene would lend itself to such unified analysis. More important, however, are other questions. How much explanatory value is there in the concept of the "leading elite"?[49] Do we not most often infer the character of that elite precisely from the nature of the industrial relations system that prevails during the early industrialization stage, rather than the reverse? Isn't the reference to the "leading elite" simply a shorthand description or a simplified classification system of the ideology of the industrial relations system? It would seem that there is a close connection between a country's political and social system (or systems) and the labor market conditions at the time of early industrialization and that country's leading elites. An explanation would thus take us to these objective factors, rather than to the ideological inclinations of the elites. I believe this kind of analysis has a further advantage in that it permits us to trace the evolution of industrial systems, which are by no means static, to the changes in the circumstances that occur, either autonomously or as a consequence of the industrialization process itself. True, such changes are frequently accompanied by changes in the composition of the leading elite; but, unless one wishes to regard these as ultimate independent variables, the question of why and how elites change will inevitably present itself. The answers to this question seem to offer far more insight than a static classification system.

Ideologies are offered to prospective "consumers" like dishes on a menu. While the choice of a dish may have considerable favorable or unfavorable impact on the health and the behavior of the customer, at least equally significant is the question as to why certain ideologies are adopted by certain groups at certain times and changed, dropped, or expanded at others. The hypotheses discussed in this essay and other papers referred to in it are attempts to offer some tentative answers to a few of these questions.

This is, however, far too large a topic to be treated in passing. Wise self-limitation requires restriction to what has been said above. Additional attention is paid to the subject in some of the essays that follow, especially Peter Lösche's article on Germany and the theoretical essay by Scoville.

49 One may question the entire concept of "the leading elite." There may be many different elites in a society in different contexts and rival elites in the same context.

MODELS

A few words need to be said on the impact of foreign models. At all times some labor movements and the industrial relations systems which they are aiming to establish or those in which they are operating have served as models for others. In earlier periods the importers were the main active part, although the originators of the model did not remain entirely passive: resolutions at international labor and Socialist congresses were designed to stimulate or guide others to follow the example of the "model." What is relatively new is the power of the urge to export one's own system and the willingness to bring sacrifices or use force for that purpose.[50] The intent is to use the export item to acquire friends and influence abroad.[51] In the case of the Soviet Union, the United States, the Histadrut, and most recently West Germany, this intention is fairly obvious. Foreign policy considerations then dominate the export policy, and the exporter uses his product as an instrument to influence the character of the leading elite in the import country.

The transfer of models from one country to another has played a large and frequently undesirable or even pernicious role in the evolution of labor movements.[52] It is unavoidable and desirable that people both in the labor movement and outside of it learn from the experiences of other nations or groups. But this process of learning is quite different from imitation on one hand and forced imposition of a foreign model on the other. In fact, both of these have occurred and indeed dominated the international labor scene at various times. Thus the German model influenced the evolution of many labor movements in Europe and elsewhere, especially prior to 1914. When the establishment of unions was permitted in the French and British colonies, it was almost axiomatic that they would be shaped, as closely as circumstances permitted, in the pattern of the movements in the respective mother countries; indeed,

50   Windmuller, "Model Industrial Relations Systems," where examples are given and some of the relevant literature is quoted. See also Charles A. Myers's excellent presidential address at the Fifteenth Annual IRRA meeting: "The American System of Industrial Relations: Is It Exportable?"

51   See Windmuller's interesting paper for a statement regarding Histadrut.

52   Whether, on balance, these efforts have been successful unless sustained by force remains open to doubt. One astute observer of African developments said some time ago: "Results have been meager. Few strong, self-sufficient unions exist. Political dividends have been slight; it is not even certain that foreign trade union operations have made more friends than enemies" (Elliot J. Berg, "The External Impact on Trade Unions in Developing Countries: The Record in Africa," *Proceedings* of the Sixteenth Annual Meeting, IRRA, December, 1963, p. 89).

in many cases they were simply branches of the unions in the colonial power.

The most obvious and historically significant attempt to impose particular brands of unionism (and consequently of industrial relations) on other countries is the one undertaken by the Bolsheviks after 1917. The model of union structure, relationship to other unions, and union strategy changed from time to time, following the external or domestic needs of the Soviet Union as perceived by its rulers. All these variations and fluctuations which Communist-inspired unions had to undergo were imposed upon them by the High Command in Moscow. Only lately have there been some signs of independent moves by one or two Communist-dominated unions in Western Europe. It is too early to judge whether these attempts will continue.

In very few cases of relatively free choice of a model is an entire system transferred and adopted. Moreover, adoption is followed by a process of assimilation or integration. One of the most promising avenues of international comparative research would deal with these processes and their results. Which parts were adopted? What change did they undergo after adoption? Did the choice affect the nature of the "leading elite"? Has the latter been transformed, enlarged, or reduced in size and thereby changed its character?

STRUCTURE OF THE LABOR FORCE

Various parts of earlier papers referred to in note 1 dealt with the impact which changes in the structure of the labor force have had upon the nature of the labor movement and, through it, upon the entire system. The American and British experiences in this respect are well known, and I have little to add to what was said earlier. It is obvious that the greater the degree of class consciousness and class solidarity in a labor movement, the greater will be its readiness to accept unskilled and semi-skilled workers in their organization. Indeed, since in the very same situation that gives rise to class consciousness the emphasis is normally on political action, the numerical growth of the organizations is likely to enhance their strength. Economic power is frequently derived from rarity, political power often from numbers. It is thus not surprising that the integration of large masses of unskilled and semi-skilled workers occurred with the least friction whenever political means of action were central to the strategy of the movement: in Europe, especially in those countries where the struggle for democracy was still to be won. Though the connection is a different and more complicated one, it is also no accident that in Britain the organization of unskilled workers was followed almost immediately by the establishment of the Labour party. Further studies of these connections seem the more timely, as we may currently be witnessing a reversal of the process. The achievement of at least basic political and social equality has weakened class feeling and solidarity in most Western labor movements. Recent changes in the structure of the labor force, the stagnation in the share of manual workers, the absolute and relative growth of the white-collar groups, especially of the professionals and technicians, have affected the character of trade unions, and their traditional relationship to labor and social democratic parties. In Britain, the tensions between unions and party at times have reached an intensity unknown since the unhappy days of Ramsay MacDonald's break with the party and the unions in the 1930's. In West Germany, the 1959 Congress of the Social Democratic party in Bad Godesberg proclaimed the transformation of the party from a class to a people's organization, thereby changing the traditional relationship between the SPD and the unions. The American industrial relations literature has so far shown few signs of having noted these momentous developments. It would also be most interesting to examine the extent to which the long period of tight labor markets in Western and Central Europe has contributed to this evolution by strengthening the unions and making them less dependent upon their political allies. The conclusion of the interprofessional agreements in France and other countries suggests that this could have been a contributory factor, and that our hypotheses may help in the analysis of these processes.

UNIONS IN A FULL-EMPLOYMENT SOCIETY

Other recent developments of fundamental significance are touched upon in Pen's challenging contribution to this volume. Bargaining power is derived from scarcity and low supply elasticity. How has the extreme and long-lasting scarcity of manpower of the post–World War II era in the West affected relative bargaining strength and thus the operations of the entire system? It is true that mass immigration has tended to reduce the scarcity of manpower and has increased the supply elasticity of common labor in several countries. There is no conclusive evidence as to the sequence of events in the wage-price spiral. However, there is little doubt that, in most industrialized nations during the post–World War II boom, average labor costs per unit of output have been rising in monetary terms. Wage (plus benefit) increases have been higher than productivity increases.[53]

Many countries have sought an answer to the problem of persistent inflation, lasting far into recession periods and departing significantly from the pattern established in the Phillips curve, in so-called incomes policies. This is a vague term covering a multitude of policy mixes designed to restrain the rise of prices and wages. The latter element in these policies is of particular interest to us. Wage restraint of a more or less permanent nature is likely to lead to a far-reaching reorientation of unions' role in capitalistic or mixed market economies committed to maintaining relatively full employment. The fundamentals of the problem were outlined as early as World War II, in Lord Beveridge's report on full employment in a free society. This was later supplemented by the Phillips curve, relating unemployment rates and their change to price increase. Recent developments, such as the combination of unemployment and inflation, have weakened the foundations on which the Phillips curve rests, but the basic problem still remains. Its solution may involve far-reaching changes in long-established institutions. However, before these can be tackled, further analysis of the data provided by experience and the development of new theoretical propositions will be required. Some of the studies in this volume, especially Pen's article,[54] make a major contribution to this discussion and thus prepare the ground for further insight into the evolution of industrial relations systems under the impact of economic and social change.

53   Causal explanation in this area is particularly difficult. An important factor in the rise of the cost of living has been the shift in consumer expenditures to services, e.g., medical care and entertainment, in which productivity increases are far more difficult to obtain than, for instance, in manufacturing.

54   Following upon several earlier papers of his and John P. Windmuller's book, *Labor Relations in the Netherlands* (Ithaca, N.Y.: Cornell University Press, 1969).

Bert F. Hoselitz

The Development of a Labor Market in the Process of Economic Growth

I

LABOR IS AN ACTIVITY of mankind which has existed since the beginning of the human race. In economic discussions the term "labor" is generally thought to designate the same kind of activity in both developed and underdeveloped countries. But this designation does not apply at present; there is a marked difference in the meaning of the word in developed and underdeveloped countries.

One of the most important aspects of economic development is the increasingly rational allocation of labor. But in order for this to occur societies have to develop mechanisms which will perform this function, and they have to perfect these mechanisms as their economies grow. One of the most efficient mechanisms for the allocation of resources ever invented by man is the market. Wherever it has come into use, it has been maintained (although it has lost a few times to pinpoints of state control); wherever it was adopted for a limited set of goods, it tended to increase in scope, and an ever growing number of commodities tended to become subject to market allocation. Even in societies in which the functioning of the market was temporarily limited or even eliminated for political or ideological reasons, it has become reestablished or market-like mechanisms have become common features. For example, various commodity markets which ceased to function during times of war and revolution were reestablished with new vigor after the emergency was over. Legal markets which had been eliminated for ideological reasons in countries under Soviet-style planning were either readmitted openly or cropped up in the form of black or gray markets. In developing countries where market transactions had been performed on a limited scale because many peasant households were virtually self-supporting, fairs and other seasonal markets have grown in size, scope, and comprehensiveness; but so have more regularized markets.

The efficiency of the market as an allocating mechanism is so well established, and markets as institutions for exchange and resource allocation are so ubiquitous, that we hardly ever question their scope and extension. In theoretical economics market exchange was tacitly assumed until alternative allocative mechanisms, e.g., rationing or direct allocation on the basis of production plans, had become realities in many situations. But even then the market mechanism was taken by economists as a standard, and alternative forms of allocation were judged in terms of the results that would be obtained on a market.[1]

But this unquestioned assumption of the ubiquity of markets, either as a mechanism or as an institution, is not warranted. There have been societies in which market exchange was unknown, and there are still some societies in which markets are an exceptional feature. Karl Polanyi, Conrad Arensburg, and their students have provided us with extensive descriptive analyses of various historical and contemporary societies in which trade and exchange relations of some magnitude prevailed, but which did not have regularly functioning markets. Many examples of marketless trade come easily to mind. The various patterns of what Polanyi calls reciprocity and redistribution, from the Kwakiutl potlatch to the Melanesian kula, and from the reciprocal gifts exchanged by the Homeric heroes to the tribute and counter-tribute paid by Indian rajas, are too well known to require extensive documentation.[2]

On the basis of materials such as these a "natural history" of the market could be written. This history could be organized by following one of two main principles of organization. It could center on the evaluation of forms of exchange in general, leading from the most simple and primitive types of gift exchange to the most

1   Wilbert E. Moore and Arnold S. Feldman, eds., *Labor Commitment and Social Change in Developing Areas* (New York: Social Science Research Council, 1960), pp. 136–236.
2   Karl Polanyi, Conrad M. Arensburg, and Harry W. Pearson, *Trade and Market in the Early Empires* (Glencoe, Ill.: The Free Press, 1957), *passim;* also, for the Homeric period in Greece, M. I. Finley, *The World of Odysseus* (New York: Meridian Books, 1959).

complex worldwide markets. This first type of analysis has usually been followed and underlies such classifications of economic stages as those of Karl Bücher and his followers.[3] It could also center on the gradual involvement of different kinds of commodities in the market matrix, i.e., the extension of markets as a mechanism and an institution for exchange, first of special, rare objects, and later of the most commonly found types of goods.

Descriptions of the evolution of exchange systems implicitly differentiate different kinds of services and commodities. The existence of a market, and even its common use, does not necessarily mean that all commodities which could be exchanged there are actually admitted to market exchange. This can most clearly be shown by the study of exchange relations in simple societies, as is exhibited, for example, by the research of Richard Salisbury among the Siane of New Guinea.[4] He found that in this society there existed three classes of goods which could be designated "free goods," "priced goods," and "ceremonial goods." For example, staple foods are free goods among the Siane, and though they require resources for production it would not enter anyone's mind that they therefore should be sold at a price. Similarly, ceremonial goods cannot be exchanged either against food (free goods) or priced goods (certain tools and special nonstaple foodstuffs, like salt), and any notion that human services rendered by one member of the community to others could be subject to exchange transactions is completely foreign to the conceptions of the Siane.

In Vunamami,[5] New Guinea, the use of labor in a much more sophisticated market more closely resembles the way the markets were developed in seventeenth-century Europe. This is especially clear from the fifth chapter of Salisbury's more recent book, which shows the historical development of the Vunamami marketplace in which free goods, priced goods, and ceremonial goods (which still existed in Siane) had completely disappeared. The market itself was not yet as impersonal as Western wholesale markets, but the prices of the commodities exported as compared with those locally consumed became increasingly controlled by less personal forces.

Whether or not special rules prevail with respect to certain exchange partners or the marketability of certain goods depends on

3   Karl Bücher, *Die Entstehung der Volkswirtschaft* (Tubingen, 1893).
4   Richard F. Salisbury, *From Stone to Steel* (Melbourne: University Press, 1962).
5   Richard F. Salisbury, *Vunamami* (Berkeley: University of California Press, 1970).

a complex set of institutional arrangements; it is extremely difficult to generalize on this subject. However, certain commodities may be found which become the object of market transactions more easily, and others less easily. In general, market exchanges are entered into more easily with strangers than with closely related persons. There is a certain parallel between the circle of persons with whom one will enter into market-centered exchange and those to whom one will loan money on interest. As Benjamin Nelson has shown so conclusively, in the Judeo-Christian tradition the rule of usury was interpreted in a very special way in that usury was not permissible in one's relation with one's brother and only in relations with what Nelson called the "generalized other."[6] Similarly, market-oriented trade is normally entered into with those whom one does not regard as one's brothers, whereas the exchanges with one's brothers are regulated typically by conditions of redistribution or some form of reciprocity. Here is another piece of evidence of Henry Maine's general rule of the gradual replacement of social interaction based on status relations by those based on contract.[7]

This relationship may also be stated in somewhat different terms by saying that, in social situations in which face-to-face relations prevail, contracts are uncommon and the definition of mutual rights and obligations is based predominantly on status considerations. Where these face-to-face relations are lacking (i.e., where individuals meet with strangers), men enter into contractual relations, since they feel the need for an objective definition of the relationship existing between them. Moreover, the contract clearly delimits the degree of involvement, and in the absence of any personal relationships between contrahents the description of their relationships by the contract is the only means of identifying the extent and form of interaction. It is therefore not surprising that in Western Europe the most extensive development of contractual relations was the work of merchants, primarily merchants who participated in the trade between the various regions of Europe. And Maitland was quite accurate when he designated the law merchant as "the private international law of the Middle Ages."[8]

6   Thomas O. Beidelman, *A Comparative Analysis of the Jajmani System,* (Locust Valley, N.Y.: J. J. Augustin, 1959).
7   Benjamin Nelson, *The Idea of Usury* (Princeton: Princeton University Press, 1949), esp. pp. 73ff.
8   W. Mitchell, *An Essay on the Early History of the Law Merchant* (Cambridge: Cambridge University Press, 1904), p. 21.

Rather than discuss the history of the labor market, I shall turn to its relationship to the problem of viewing labor as a marketable commodity. As Polanyi correctly pointed out, under the guild system of medieval Europe "as under any other system in previous history, the motives and circumstances of productive activities were imbedded in the general organization of society."[9] In fact, Polanyi's entire book, *The Great Transformation,* is devoted to an examination of the changes which took place in the socioeconomic relations of Western Europe after labor and land became ordinary marketable commodities. This peculiarity of labor being treated as a marketable commodity within a modern industrial context had already been noted by Marx. In fact, we may even say that he defines the capitalist mode of production as one which coincides with the development of a labor market:

> Capitalist production only then really begins, as we have already seen, when each individual capital employs simultaneously a comparatively large number of labourers; when consequently the labour-process is carried on on an extensive scale and yields, relatively, large quantities of products. A greater number of labourers working together, at the same time, in one place (or, if you will, in the same field of labour), in order to produce the same sort of commodity under the mastership of one capitalist, constitutes, both historically and logically, the starting point of capitalist production. With regard to the mode of production itself, manufacture, in its strict meaning, is hardly to be distinguished, in its earliest stages, from the handicraft trades of the guilds, otherwise than by the greater number of workmen simultaneously employed by one and the same individual capital. The workshop of the mediaeval master craftsman is simply enlarged.[10]

The entire content of Chapter 13 of *Capital* is a very careful analysis of the difference between the economy before and after the creation of a market for labor.

Another perhaps sharper explanation of the existence of a labor market is from the same book: "The historical conditions of its existence are by no means given with the mere circulation of money and commodities. It can spring into life, only when the owner of the means of production and subsistence meets in the market with

    9   Karl Polanyi, *The Great Transformation* (New York: Farrar and Rinehart, 1944), p. 70. In even more provocative terms the relationship Polanyi draws between the different socioeconomic functions of markets is expressed in *Primitive, Archaic and Modern Economics* (New York: Doubleday, 1968), esp. Chs. 4, 7.
    10   Karl Marx, *Capital* (Chicago: Charles H. Kerr and Co., 1906), p. 353.

the free labourer selling his labour-power. And this one historical condition comprises a world's history."[11]

Although they differ in terminology, Marx and Polanyi come to the same general conclusion: a labor market which functions upon the well-known principle of free markets is generally characteristic of a highly developed economy, one in which complex processes of economic organization have been elaborated and in which industry and large-scale enterprise, as well as urbanization and the growth of the secondary and tertiary sectors of production, have become characteristic features of the social landscape.

In contrast, simpler and less highly developed economies, though they may have well-functioning commodity markets, have labor markets either not at all or only in exceptional instances in which productive services are bought and sold in accordance with ordinary market characteristics.

This leads to the conclusion that one of the important institutional changes in the process of economic development is the elaboration of a labor market, both in the economic and the institutional sense. In other words, in the course of economic growth, there develops the general conception that the performance of productive services is based not on considerations of mutual rights and obligations growing out of aspects of social structure, but upon specific contractual relations pertaining to the productive services by themselves, divorced from the wider social existence of the persons or groups of persons who perform them, or on whose behalf these productive services are performed. At the same time, there develop institutions, e.g., labor exchanges, hiring halls, employment agencies, and, on a less complex level, various personal intermediaries, which bring together a seeker for a job and one who is building a labor force. In other words, the performance of productive services has become a special role which is, in principle, separable from other forms of social interaction of the individual who performs that role; this role then is the object of trade and exchange; it is the "entity" which is offered on the market.

This, at least, is the ideal situation. But in practice this transition from a society in which labor markets are unusual to one in which they are a common feature, not questioned by any one, is a long and difficult process which takes on different aspects in different societies. These differences are due to a number of factors —some to existing values and norms; some to the previously established social structure; some, and perhaps the most important ones,

11 *Ibid.*, p. 189.

to the existing pattern of economic activity and the relative abundance or scarcity of labor; and some to the level of economic organization and the technological and organizational sophistication of the population.

The impact of these variables upon the formation of the labor market in developing countries has, as yet, been little explored. Although we possess some empirical studies, on the whole they have been carried out without consideration of a general theoretical framework, either of the development of markets in general or specific markets for labor. These studies were usually motivated by the appearance of conflict situations, the growth of slums and the development of various aspects of social disorganization in the cities of developing countries, or by practical problems of improved allocation of manpower. Hence, in order to fill out the discussion of the varieties of market situations with respect to labor in developing societies, I shall not be able to refer in all cases to actual empirical data. In many instances, instead of proposing solutions of problems, queries will have to be raised, and I hope that the posing of these questions will provide an inducement for scholars to enter into a more systematic exploration of these very important problems.[12]

II

One approach to the study and evaluation of the development of labor markets as a feature of economic growth is through history. We can ask how labor markets developed in European societies in which economic growth gradually became accelerated so as to lead these societies to an industrial revolution and subsequent phase of rapid economic development, and we can perhaps derive from these historical experiences some conclusions concerning parallel processes in the countries which are now in the early stages of an industrial take-off. Superficially, the similarities appear considerable. Anyone perusing the works of Charles Booth, John A. Hob-

12   The problem of the development of labor markets both historically in the advanced countries and contemporaneously in the less advanced countries has been treated in many sources. It would be impossible to mention all of them, but several are Allen Spitz, *Developmental Change: An Annotated Bibliography*, (Lexington: University Press of Kentucky, 1969), pp. 58–134, and John Brode, *The Process of Modernization: An Annotated Bibliography on the Sociocultural Aspect of Development* (Cambridge: Harvard University Press, 1969), esp. pp. 73ff. A very challenging approach to the encounter with market economies is given by a collection of articles entitled "Marketing and the Farms," *Development Digest* 8, no. 4 (October, 1970): 65–106.

son, or some of their contemporaries who discuss the conditions of British labor during the last decades of the nineteenth century will be struck by the similarity in tone and emphasis of this literature with the descriptions of the condition of urban workers, especially unskilled workers, in the current literature on developing countries. Yet there was a considerable difference in the situation of labor in most European countries as compared to that existing now in many underdeveloped countries, especially in Asia and Africa. To begin with, it is very likely that during the nineteenth century the overall level of living in Europe was well above that of the less-developed countries today. In terms of Colin Clark's International Units, this difference may be suggested by his calculations that in the midnineteenth century output per man year in Western European countries (Great Britain, France, Germany, Sweden) ranged from 353 I.U. to 707 I.U., whereas in underdeveloped countries in the 1940's it was around 200 or less I.U. per man year.[13] The research on national income since the mid-nineteenth century has produced various studies on individual European and North American countries; these publications have been drawn together in two books by Simon Kuznets.[14] He summarizes the rapid growth of income during the last two hundred years in Europe and North America in the first few pages of his Chapter 2, "Growth of Population and Product," in *Modern Economic Growth: Rate, Structure, and Spread*. He says, for example: "In short, it is only relatively recently that mankind attained both the large numbers *and* the high rates of growth that are characteristic of the modern era. In this respect, as in many others, the modern era is unique; and much of what we learn from the premodern past must be qualified because of the smaller magnitudes involved."[15] He supports this in his discussion of the substantially higher growth rates in the last two hundred years compared with the years before 1750. This higher growth rate in modern times is widely acknowledged, although the reasons for it are in dispute.

Other measures lead to more or less the same conclusions. For example, there is good reason to believe that at a time when approximately one-third of the labor force in European countries was

13   Colin Clark, *The Conditions of Economic Progress*, 2nd ed. (London: Macmillan, 1951), pp. 63ff.

14   Simon Kuznets, *Modern Economic Growth: Rate, Structure, and Spread* (New Haven: Yale University Press, 1966), and *Economic Growth of Nations: Total Output and Production Structure* (Cambridge: Harvard University Press, 1971).

15   Kuznets, *Modern Economic Growth: Rate, Structure, and Spread*, p. 36.

in nonagricultural employment, as is now the case in some of the developing countries of Asia, the amount of capital per worker was between three and five times what it is now in South and Southeast Asia.[16] The consequences of this fact may be viewed in various ways. There was less pressure of population on nonhuman resources than is the case now in countries like India, Indonesia, or Egypt, and as was the case in Japan shortly after the Meiji restoration. It also means that, *mutatis mutandis,* the productivity of labor was higher, and that therefore, in spite of the frequent reports on poverty, the actual real income of workers then may have been higher than it is now in the countries mentioned. Finally, because of the relatively greater abundance of labor in relation to capital in currently developing countries, more labor-intensive production processes are better suited to their conditions than the processes which were developed in Europe. The equilibrium price for labor in Europe, except in periods of depression and slump, would thus have been higher, at least compared to the current situation in most underdeveloped countries.

On the whole, the economic history of much of European industrialization shows as a main characteristic that, in spite of temporary gluts, the market for labor was in relative equilibrium throughout the latter part of the nineteenth century at a wage which was considerably above the cost of minimum subsistence. This was made possible by the fact that capital investment, especially in the nonagricultural sector, proceeded fast enough to provide employment opportunities for the more or less constant increase of the urban labor force; it was made possible, moreover, by the fact that there were certain "safety valves" open to European countries if and when the supply of labor should become overly full, the chief of them being the possibility of emigration to North and South America, Oceania, and parts of Africa. Third, it was made possible by the fact that the development of industrial technology kept approximate step with the growth of the nonagricultural labor force and the demand for industrial products and the output of service industries. Since there was relatively little governmental regulation of markets and prices in most European countries during the major portion of their industrialization phase, capital allocation and the degree of labor intensity and capital intensity of productive methods was influenced closely by the relative prices of labor and capital. Hence, if there was a sudden rapid

16   Bert F. Hoselitz, *Sociological Aspects of Economic Growth* (Glencoe, Ill.: The Free Press, 1960), pp. 119ff.

upsurge of the supply of industrial labor, owing to unanticipated and apparently uncontrolled events, the introduction of labor-saving devices would be postponed until the supply of labor had returned to more "normal" dimensions. These temporary ups and downs in the relative price of labor, produced either on the supply side by sudden local migratory movements or on the demand side by new technological developments or a general decline in business activity, tended to be a common feature of all labor markets in Europe and the countries settled by European populations. But the fluctuations of the price of labor tended to cluster around an equilibrium price which displayed long-run tendency to rise secularly.

This economic characteristic of Western European labor markets is important to note, since it puts into sharp focus the social and political aspects of the contractual employment nexus. The stresses and strains which developed in the course of European industrialization were due not to secularly falling real income (though temporary setbacks did occur), but to the social process of proletarianization of the labor force. What are the characteristic and outstanding elements of this process?

Basic to this social relation is the existence of a class of persons who are, and essentially remain, without property. There is no question that from the social point of view Marx's original definition of the proletariat as composed of persons who have to sell their labor power, because they have no control of productive assets, is a correct description of the crucial social characteristics of the proletariat. But added to this is the fact that, since the worker must sell his labor, he participates in a process of commercialization of human attributes, the establishment of labor as a commodity, the "reification" of the social nexus implied in a process of production, and its conversion into a mere contract with some monetary value attached to it. In brief, the performance of labor which has become subjected to the mediation of the labor market has become a social category of its own, denuded of its earlier social and interpersonal context. The relationship between the wage worker and the employer is not normally a face-to-face relation, and the growing size of industrial plants frequently implies that the ultimate purchaser of labor and its seller are strangers and may never have seen each other.

If we interpret the labor contract within this social nexus, we may begin to understand the shock exerted by the urban industrial employment relation on a population as yet little accustomed to the impersonality and anonymity of the wage labor situation. But associated with this decline in the wider social meaning of the work relation is the decline of any ethical content of work. The situation in a society which does not know labor markets is very simple. The performance of services for others, if not based on the exercise of sheer force as in slavery, is founded upon moral sentiments of mutual obligation and responsibility. The particular moral content may vary, of course. It appears in one form in the ethics of the liberal professions in antiquity, and in a very different (but no less real) form in the paternalism of the guild master. But with the transformation of labor into a commodity, with the evaluation of a given "quantity" of labor in terms of money, any moral content of labor ceases and the relation between the buyer and the seller of labor becomes a morally neutral pure contract.[17]

This impact of the labor market has been described and recognized already by Marx in one of his earliest economic writings. In a manuscript composed in Paris in 1844, he describes the implications of the situation of the worker who sells his labor as a commodity as "alienation." He goes on to ask:

> What then, constitutes this alienation of labour? First the fact that labour is *external* to the worker, i.e., it does not belong to his essential being; that in his work, therefore, he does not affirm himself but denies himself, does not feel content but unhappy, does not develop freely his physical and mental energy but mortifies his body and ruins his mind. . . . Lastly the external character of labour for the worker appears in the fact that it is not his own, but someone else's, that it does not belong to him, that in it he belongs not to himself, but to another. . . . An immediate consequence . . . is the *estrangement of man* from *men*. . . . What applies to a man's relation to his work, to the product of his labour and to himself, also holds of a man's relation to the other man, and to the other man's labour and object of labour.[18]

Although Marx's terminology, which is derived from Hegel, may cause some difficulty, his meaning is clear. His error consists only

17 The discussion in this and the preceding paragraphs owes much to the excellent presentation of the nature and condition of the modern Western European proletariat by Goetz Briefs, "Das gewerbliche Proletariat," in *Grundriss der Sozialoekonomic,* IX, pt. I, *Die gesellschaftliche Schichtung im Kapitalismus* (Tubingen: J. C. B. Mohr, 1926), pp. 145ff., and Werner Sombart, *Das Proletariat* (Frankfurt: Rutten und Loening, 1906), *passim.*

18 Karl Marx, *The Economic and Philosophic Manuscripts of 1844* (New York: International Publishers, 1964), pp. 110–11, 114.

in that he attributes the condition of alienation to the system of capitalist production, whereas it is conditioned by the appearance of labor as a commodity on any more or less organized market. Hence we may encounter the same condition of alienation in the Soviet Union and other socialist countries, since there also the performance of labor is based on a contractual relation and the allocation of labor is achieved through market or quasi-market processes.

In citing Marx, we have omitted his extensive comments on the poverty of the laborer and the physical misery in which he lives. It is admitted that poverty, misery, and economic insecurity add to the social and psychological deprivation involved in alienation. But it is important to note that alienation is a condition which exerts its impact even if the general standard of comfort of the worker is adequate and even ample. It is the loss of self-control over the environment as a result of the sale of one's most private property, i.e., one's daily activity, at a price determined on an impersonal market (or, in Soviet-style economies, imposed by an impersonal authority) which contributes to alienation far more than the low physical standard of living.

In the late 1950's and early 1960's the degree of the labor force's commitment to industrialism was also considered a strong aspect of the social conditions of labor. As Moore and Feldman have explained so lucidly, a "fully committed worker . . . has internalized the norms of the new productive organization and social system."[19] This internalization of the norms of the new social and productive system implies that the persons committed to an industrial way of life tacitly accept the market as a mechanism by means of which labor, including their own labor, is allocated. Thus they accept a situation in which the work relationship has taken on an impersonal character, in which work is accepted not primarily because of its intrinsic characteristics, or because of the satisfaction it provides as an activity in itself, but because of its capacity to provide the worker with an income by means of which he may satisfy his other, more generalized needs. Moreover, this internalization of a new set of norms is associated with a new behavior pattern, with a new set of expectations and attitudes, possibly with a change in basic personality disposition. Most important from the viewpoint of role performance is the fact that workers, whether new entrants to the labor force or persons already long in employment, will make use of the labor market for their

19 Wilbert E. Moore, and Arnold S. Feldman, "Spheres of Commitment," in Moore and Feldman, eds., *Labor Commitment and Social Change,* p. 1.

own advantage. They use the competitive situation in the market to improve their own positions; they are motivated by self-interest rather than by loyalty or a sense of responsibility; in short, they imitate those who purchase labor and use the market as an instrument to serve their own personal goals. Collective bargaining may emerge as one of the devices by which workers manipulate the market mechanism in their favor.

To expect an agricultural worker who comes to the city for industrial labor to be committed to this new role would indeed be unrealistic. It is much more likely that such a laborer would experience alienation as a result of this change. In other words, it would be strange if persons who have recently come to urban areas from a purely rural existence, who have little or no experience with commodity markets, who have never offered their services on a labor market, and who have not yet internalized the norms and typical behavior patterns of an industrial social system, were not to experience serious ambiguity, shock, and confusion. Their behavior and their own definition of their role will be ambiguous, and they will often make ineffectual or erroneous choices. In fact, in extreme situations these persons may experience sentiments of profound *anomie* and of psychological estrangement or alienation which Marx has described.

The feeling of *anomie* or alienation is usually quite strong among those workers who come from rural society and are industrial workers for the first time in their lives. This feeling has been observed in many societies, in Europe during the nineteenth century, and in Africa, Latin America, and Asia only in recent times. The reason for *anomie* or alienation is the very complex situation of a new recruit on the labor market. Many observers have seen it and have given it different psychological interpretations. For example, Everett E. Hagen has written a whole chapter on what he calls "The Transition to Economic Growth."[20] Only the terminology is different; instead of using *anomie* or "alienation," he speaks of "retreatism," with the same meaning.

Newcomers to a labor market experience difficulties even in less extreme situations. They are less able to take advantage of opportunities offered on the market, since their contrahents are normally much more experienced in manipulating the conditions of a labor contract and in using price as a guide to conduct. They tend to seek intermediate solutions in which some elements of the former

20   Everett E. Hagen, *On the Theory of Social Change* (Homewood, Ill.: The Dorsey Press, 1962), pp. 185–258.

worker-employer relationship are preserved. In some cases they find that the only way to voice their frustration about the new situation is to engage in violent protest, either by themselves or through combination in some organized movement.[21] By finding that the new situations result in violent protest or in some organized movement, we are not far from interpreting this movement as political.

These developments are also discernible in the histories of European societies after the extensive introduction of labor markets in the course of urbanization and industrialization. The experiences with the machine-breakers and Luddites, and similar violent movements elsewhere, represent one part of the evidence. The duration of the cultural and social gap which persisted in the countries of immigration between persons coming from different parts of Europe is another. One of the most characteristic features of many of the immigrants from Southern and Eastern Europe to the United States —as compared with those from Western and Northern Europe— was their smaller capability for adjusting to the new life in an industrial environment, their prolonged seclusion in linguistically and ethnically separate groups, and the great retardation with which they entered the "melting pot" of American society.[22] The reason lies not in their linguistic difficulties, since these were experienced in a similar manner by the French, the Swedes, and the Germans, but in their lack of experience with a thoroughly market-oriented society and, above all, their ignorance of the customs and behavioral norms of a labor market.

Yet it is important to point out that the European populations,

21 On the forms and general pattern of worker protest under early industrialization and its changes in the course of growth of industrial society, see Clark Kerr, John T. Dunlop, Frederick Harbison, and Charles A. Myers, *Industrialism and Industrial Man* (Cambridge: Harvard University Press, 1960), pp. 193ff. Several of the books by the same authors which followed the book cited have substantiated this point of view. The same opinion on alienation versus commitment is emphasized by Richard D. Lambert, "The Modernization of the Labor Force," in Myron Weiner, ed., *Modernization* (New York: Basic Books, 1966), pp. 281–93. A somewhat different political development is described by Koji Taira, *Economic Development and the Labor Market in Japan* (New York: Columbia University Press, 1970), esp. Chs. 1, 4. A still different approach to the adjustment of the worker in an economically developing country is expressed by Adolf Sturmthal, "Economic Development and the Labour Movement," in Arthur M. Ross, ed., *Industrial Relations and Economic Development* (London: Macmillan, 1966), Ch. 8.

22 Perhaps the classic study on the adjustment problems of Eastern European immigrants is the work by W. I. Thomas and Florian Znaniecki, *The Polish Peasant in Europe and America* (Chicago: University of Chicago Press, 1918), vols. 1–3.

especially those of Western and Northern Europe, faced fewer problems of adjustment to a social system in which the allocation of labor took place principally through the market. Historically, they had gone through certain collective experiences which made this adjustment easier. In the first place, they were already quite familiar with commodity markets, since extensive markets, even for the ordinary products of daily existence, had been quite common in European countries since the Middle Ages. Second, they even experienced, in a more limited sense, transactions involving labor contracts. Although neither the guild system nor the manorial economy had a properly functioning labor market, there were many instances, even in medieval Europe, in which workers were hired as day laborers for ordinary wages. The records of large enterprises—e.g., the building of cathedrals, castles, or other public works—from the twelfth century on show that various contractual relations pertaining to the performance of certain labor services were not uncommon. Moreover, the putting-out system in many instances quite clearly implied wage relationships, though they were hidden externally as relationships involving a form of subcontracting.

Another important peculiarity of European societies which made the introduction of labor markets easier was the long prevalence of the nuclear family, especially among the lower classes of society. Patterns of reciprocity and redistribution require some socio-structural substratum on which to base claims and counter-claims; this substratum is usually provided by some kinship or quasi-kinship institution, normally some form of the extended family. (We are concerned in this context not with commensality or intermarriage, i.e., the more purely "family" aspects of the extended family, but with the family as an economic entity.) There is a good deal of evidence that in Europe the nuclear family was a fairly common institution among the lower classes, especially in the urban areas, long before labor markets became common.[23] But if a poor family is small and depends for its livelihood upon the earnings of its head, it may often become imperative for this person to enter into a work relationship which is very close to a wage contract. Although most poor families living in the predominantly pre-industrial period in Europe cannot be regarded as "proletarian" in the Marxian sense, many of them at least occasionally passed through epi-

23   William J. Goode, "Industrialization and Family Change," in Bert F. Hoselitz and Wilbert E. Moore, eds., *Industrialization and Society*, 2nd ed. (Paris: UNESCO-Mouton, 1966), pp. 237–55.

sodes which greatly resembled the typical life experiences of the labor proletariat.[24]

III

The variables discussed in the preceding section may explain why labor markets first developed on a sizeable scale in Western Europe, and why the populations of Western Europe became adjusted to this new form of relating workers and employers with relatively little resistance and difficulty. In the developing countries of Asia and Africa the situation appears to be fundamentally different. Not only are there cultural differences which have their expression in different religious beliefs and social values, but even the more proximate factors determining the facility with which a labor market can function are present only in a strongly modified form.

Among these factors which influenced the development of labor markets in Europe were the relatively high productivity of labor, the fairly high degree of mobility of labor made possible by internal and overseas migration, the rapid growth of nonagricultural capital which supported geographical and occupational mobility of labor on the one hand and, on the other, made available over the long run adequately paid employment opportunities outside agriculture for a growing number of persons, the ubiquity of commodity markets and related institutions, the frequent practice of day work and other contractual relations pertaining to the laborer-employer relationship, and the widespread institution of the nuclear family among the lower classes.

The countries which have accepted these values are primarily developed countries which originally had higher national incomes and other advantages. For example, education consisting of reading, writing, and simple arithmetic to at least fourteen years of age became quite widely accepted in the course of the nineteenth century. In almost all developed countries an education of this sort was guaranteed by the state, and there was no question that all workers could at least grasp the simple directions which their work required. This was not so in almost all the underdeveloped coun-

24   The importance of alienation as a factor even in modern, well-developed capitalistic societies is made clear by Robert Blauner, *Alienation and Freedom* (Chicago: University of Chicago Press, 1964). In his footnotes to the first chapter he gives a number of references to authors who also are concerned with the problem of alienation in modern industry. From all this it should be obvious that alienation rather than any other form of socialization is a guiding principle in the modern approach to economic development.

tries. Not only were there many illiterates; while their percentage decreased during the last decade, the absolute number of illiterates increased.

Also, in most developing countries where agricultural densities are high, the process of capital accumulation outside agriculture is apparently not sufficient to absorb all the new entrants to the labor force who cannot be employed in the already labor-saturated agricultural sector.[25]

According to a survey of urban employment and unemployment conducted by the National Sample Survey organization in India from September, 1957, to May, 1958, in towns with a population of 50,000 or more the underemployed in India constituted 11.38 percent of the gainfully occupied persons.[26] In another survey embracing both the urban and rural sectors it was found that 26.69 million persons (14.36 percent of the gainfully employed) worked with less than full intensity, and that among them 16.02 million persons (8.62 percent of the gainfully employed) worked with the intensity of a quarter or less. Out of the rural underemployed of 19.65 millions, 14.53 millions worked less than four hours a day.[27]

Economic growth consists largely of the transition from traditional to modern productive processes; in addition to different skills, organizational talent, entrepreneurial activity, and technological know-how, it requires above all the investment of capital. But capital markets in developing countries are highly imperfect and fractionalized, and the accumulation of large "chunks" of capital is often not possible by anyone other than governments or a few wealthy individuals. Hence, even where new investments are made, the amount of capital available for them is small and the resulting kinds of enterprises tend to adopt many "traditional" features on the technological and organizational level. The productivity of labor is low, especially in traditional occupations, and there is a tremendous gap between productivity in "traditional" and in "modern" occupations.[28]

25   Adolf Sturmthal, "Economic Development and the Labour Movement," pp. 172–74.
26   *Tables with Notes on Employment and Unemployment in Urban Areas,* The National Sample Survey, Thirteenth Round: September, 1957–May, 1958, no. 63, issued by the Cabinet Secretariat, Government of India (Calcutta: Eka Press, 1962).
27   *Report on Employment and Unemployment,* The National Sample Survey, Ninth Round: Supplementary to Report no. 16, May–November, 1955, no. 62, issued by the Cabinet Secretariat, Government of India (Calcutta: Eka Press, 1962), p. 19.
28   Adolf Sturmthal, "Economic Development and the Labour Movement," p. 180.

Although in some Southeast Asian countries the nuclear family has been common for many decades, and even centuries, in other countries the family structure, even among the lower social classes, rests firmly on the extended family and derived kin-groups, such as castes, tribal groups, or village communities.

The prevalence of tribalism in many underdeveloped areas, most pronounced in various African countries, impedes progress toward industrialization. When European colonialism and capitalism were introduced in Africa, the rural African did not have the motivation of the rational economic man he encountered. His actions were still guided by tribal customs which stressed the supreme importance of a moral community and granted advancement in status through accomplishments that did not include economic profit. These Africans did not consider wage labor the wherewithal of human existence but merely a form of exchange for certain desirable European commodities. To an ethnocentric Western observer, the willingness to engage in wage labor displays economic rationality, but to an African it might simply appear as a new activity motivated by traditional values.[29]

In a recently published article C. M. Elliot has described the African society as "rational" in a way which is different from the "rationality" of the Western economic man. The majority of African labor is still agricultural. At present even industrial workers return to the land periodically, and there is a tendency on the part of most workers to retain their "rational" values. These values in this time of African economic development are quite different from those of Europeans at the same time in history, and the creation of a proletarian class and the impetus toward organization of labor unions in Europe occurred under conditions totally different from those in Africa at present, where laborers devote their leisure time to important activities which are an integral part of their life style. In Elliot's words:

> Leisure is not merely the absence of work, a vacuous residual which betokens a large reservoir of potential labour. This primitive view, the unimaginative product of cross-cultural transference, has survived too long in much economic literature. Detailed studies of how farmers actually spend their time, particularly in seasons in which the demand for agricultural labour is lower, reveal that although they may then be economically unproductive they are socially

29 Simon Rottenberg, "The Immobility of Labour in Underdeveloped Areas," *South African Journal of Economics* 19, no. 4 (December, 1951): 404–8.

maintaining kinship bonds, giving and receiving status gifts, trans-
acting legal proceedings, and generally servicing the intricate fabric
of their society. This social expenditure of labour time has, of
course, an economic product, insofar as in many tribes farmers are
dependent upon labour from relatives and clan relations for help
in the harvest. But that is a subsidiary issue in the sense that social
bonds are maintained for their own ends and not for economic
purposes. Any discussion of "labor abundant economies" must be
heavily qualified by the awareness that the labour abundance is in
some ways more apparent than real. A simplistic calculation that
relates total labour time productively employed to total labour time
potentially available oversimplifies the time commitments of the
individual farmer. A high leisure preference does not necessarily
imply idleness. Nor does it necessarily imply the more liberal interpretations of idleness, as a result of ill health, malnutrition, or
deficient motivation. Leisure may be accorded a high preference
because without it the bonds of society would atrophy and the
whole social organization would thus disintegrate.[30]

In fact, in addition to dividing his time between labor and leisure,
an African worker has an additional challenge to his stability,
namely, risk. For him, work in factories or work on new crops is
not yet seen as his submission to the economic system, because he
does not work all the time in factories, and when he plants a new
crop he does not entirely give up the old one. An African worker,
like many Asians, has a very complicated scheme of dividing his
time; the way he works in the new capitalistic enterprise is a result
of the "rational" labor he performs.

This rationale of the various classes of workers who divide their
time between labor, leisure, and risk paints an ideal picture. In
certain occupations such workers devote only a short time to a
more profitable enterprise, because it is too risky or demands too
much labor activity. They also return the use of their land from a
high-productive new crop to a previously grown low-productive
crop if the risk of getting a good result with the new crop is too
high. In Africa and Asia examples of this are common, such as
the failure of the introduction of cotton crops in Kenya, the return to traditional rice crops in India, and the well-known ground-
nut scheme in Africa.

What does all this mean for the development and functioning of

30   C. M. Elliot, "Agriculture and Economic Development in Africa: Theory
and Experience, 1880–1914," in E. L. Jones and S. J. Woolf, *Agrarian Change
and Economic Development* (London: Methuen & Co., 1969), pp. 124–25.

labor markets? The most important result of the combination of these factors—especially the abundance of labor, the threat or actuality of unemployment, and the highly imperfect capital markets —is a fractionalization of the labor market. I have described this feature elsewhere and need not repeat it here in detail.[31] The main points this discussion brings out are that in the heavily populated developing countries uniform labor markets do not develop, that certain informal social barriers to the free mobility of labor are erected, and that there tend to develop among the laborers sets of noncompeting groups, i.e., special labor markets on which "privileged" individuals compete with one another, and other markets on which the remainder of the jobseekers compete. However, the privileged group of workers does not exist as a result of its special skills, knowledge, or other personal characteristics, but merely because for some reason it has access to the more highly organized market, while others are effectively prevented from competing as a consequence of certain informal, but nevertheless effective, barriers which prevent access to the privileged market.

We do not always know what these barriers are and can only guess what some might be. The situation may best be visualized if we imagine the instance of an employer who is confronted with a perfectly horizontal supply curve of labor. The existence of such a supply curve in many developing countries was suggested by W. A. Lewis.[32] Translated into more commonsense language, it merely means that the employer has more applicants (of apparently equal qualifications) at the wage offered than he has jobs to fill. How will he select among these applicants? Remember that I am merely depicting the actual facts as they occur nearly every day in front of the factory gates of almost any plant in a densely populated developing country (e.g., Egypt or India), particularly when rumor has it that the factory is adding to its working force.

It is quite clear that in the case described the factory manager must use certain noneconomic criteria to select among the applicants. He may choose those who already have relatives or friends in the factory, and he often does this since the employed friends and relatives will recommend certain workers. If he is a labor boss or hiring agent, he may use criteria for selection which have their

31   Bert F. Hoselitz, "The Market Matrix," in Moore and Feldman, eds., *Labor Commitment and Social Change*, pp. 224ff.

32   W. A. Lewis, "Economic Development with Unlimited Supplies of Labour," in A. N. Agarwala and S. P. Singh, eds., *The Economics of Underdevelopment* (Bombay: Oxford University Press, 1968), pp. 400ff.

basis in the "traditional" system of action—i.e., he may choose persons related to him either by kinship ties or familiar to him as stemming from the same locality. He may accept those who offer or promise bribes and reject others who cannot or will not do this, and he may employ still other criteria (such as race or religion) for selection. We know little about them; it would be helpful to determine on what basis selections to the labor force on different levels of skill are made, and, in particular, to what extent achievement criteria tend to replace ascriptive criteria in selection.

It must be admitted that similar choices often did, and still do, confront persons selecting employees in economically advanced countries. But whereas in Asia a gap in remuneration, working conditions, and technological equipment of different work groups has developed which is likely to persist in the long run because of the continuing pressure of population, social and occupational mobility and the creation of constantly new employment opportunities mitigated and, on the whole, eliminated the fractionalization of the labor market in the economically advanced countries of the West, and in many instances prevented the market from ever becoming fractionalized. Noncompeting groups existed in Western labor markets, and they still do. Some are also the result of racial or religious prejudice, but, as Cairnes already pointed out, most frequently the members of the different groups are endowed with different skills—i.e., they are distinguished by achievement criteria. In the Asian countries, however, the members of different noncompeting groups apparently are distinguished principally by ascriptive criteria.[33]

In many developing countries the multiplicity of labor markets is supported wittingly or unwittingly by the labor and social legislation of the government. It prescribes certain procedures for the larger, modern enterprises which do not apply to the smaller, "traditional" ones, and it imposes certain additions to real wages in the form of social services for workers in some labor markets and not in others. What I am discussing here is not the same thing as Boeke's dual economy, though there are certain similarities between the two situations. Boeke describes a division in the society and economy of a developing country due to differences in the

---

33 A discussion of the concepts of ascription and achievement orientation, which are derived from Talcott Parsons, and their application to economic growth may be found in Hoselitz, *Sociological Aspects of Economic Growth*, pp. 23ff. The original definition and description of noncompeting groups was presented in 1875 by J. E. Cairnes, *Some Leading Principles of Political Economy Newly Expounded* (New York: Harper, n.d.), pp. 65ff.

underlying values on which social and economic action is based in the traditional and modern sectors.[34] I am not concerned with values, but with restraints to mobility, the norms on the basis of which persons are selected for certain occupational roles, and the mechanisms by which labor is allocated as between different occupations and different enterprises. In fact, I suspect that Boeke's analysis of the dual economy could quite easily fit into the scheme presented here, especially if the fractionalization of the labor market is extended by analogy to other markets as well.

In considering the problem discussed in the preceding paragraphs, the question arises whether the fractionalization of the labor market may not be regarded primarily as a transitional phenomenon through which most developing societies must pass. In a sense this question may be answered affirmatively, though it must be admitted that for some of the more densely populated countries of Asia and Africa this period of transition may last for several decades, and possibly even centuries. Hence it becomes partly a matter of definition whether this phase should be considered transitional. At the same time, the longer the division in the labor market lasts, the more strongly it operates as an impediment to economic development, for it strengthens informal social control mechanisms which are opposed to free social and occupational mobility and which support misallocation of productive resources.

Thus we find that one of the profound differences between the development of labor markets during the industrialization phase in Western Europe and in Asia and Africa is the variation in the organization, comprehensiveness, and openness of the labor market. But there is a further difference which lies in the greater remoteness of Asian and African populations, especially Asian and African peasants, from the market as an institution in and of itself. We have seen earlier that even during the medieval period labor contracts in Western Europe were not uncommon, although there were few people who ever experienced the actual operation of a reasonably well functioning market for labor services.

34 J. H. Boeke, *Indishce Economie*, vol. 1 (Haarlem: Tjeenk Willink and Zoon, 1947). Boeke's theory has been widely discussed, among others by Benjamin Higgins, "The Dualistic Theory of Underdeveloped Countries," *Economic Development and Cultural Change* 4, no. 2 (January, 1956): 99–115. The concept of dualism has become very important in the last ten years. An alternative to Boeke's way of using it was first used by J. S. Furnivall in *Colonial Policy and Practice: A Comparative Study of Burma and the Netherlands India* (Cambridge: University Press, 1948). His approach has been summarized in Benjamin Higgins, *Economic Development, Problems, Principles, and Policies,* rev. ed. (New York: W. W. Norton, 1968), pp. 227–41.

In Asia and Africa many of the newly industrialized populations have not had much experience even with commodity markets. Above all, they have been accustomed to social relations involving the performance of labor services in which judgments are made not in terms of wages and overall earnings, but in terms of the meta-economic responsibilities and obligations arising out of the performance of these services. To this must be added the sense of alienation which all newly industrialized wage workers experience and which played an important role in the early phase of industrial-urban developments in Western Europe. But here again the involvement in extended families and similar kinship relations increases the gap which the worker in developing countries must overcome to make a transition from a traditional to a modern sector.

The relationship between employer and worker may often be anonymous. From this follows the probability that the psychological conditions encountered by a job-seeker on the labor market of a developing country are fundamentally different from those prevailing in his traditional environment, and the shock of the impact of the new impersonal system of allocation is profound. But the reaction to this changed situation, which is reinforced by the loneliness and anonymity experienced in the urban environment, is the development of sentiments of *anomie* on the personal level, or the joining up with similarly situated individuals in various political and quasi-political movements which often lead to violence and other forms of political instability.

This difference in the degree of receptiveness with relation to one's economic role in traditional and modern types of employment situations may also be one factor explaining the maintenance of barriers against free mobility which are a characteristic of the labor markets in densely populated developing countries. Since these barriers are largely informal, i.e., based not on legislative prescription but on forms of voluntary collective behavior, the reasons for their existence must be explained by their filling some need on the part of a large number of persons.

In part, as appears from an analysis of such a situation in Japan, they are due to the functioning of a set of actions related to the "boss-henchman" system, which some Japanese scholars designate as a feudal survival in modern Japan.[35] But these barriers may also

35   On the "boss-henchman" system, see, for example, John W. Bennet, "Economic Aspects of a Boss-Henchman System in the Japanese Forestry Industry," *Economic Development and Cultural Change* 7, no. 1 (October, 1958): 13–20.

be partly due to the reluctance of a considerable number of workers to leave the more highly personal environment of traditional small-scale production, and to expose themselves to the harsh winds of a labor market, where (ideally, at least) full competition prevails. Hence, although it is probably more accurate to look for the origin of the barriers to mobility on the side of the more highly organized industry and services, some of them may be erected in the nonmodern sector and may consist basically in a reluctance to leave the warm personal ties which still exist even in many traditional types of nonagricultural employment. But with progressive urbanization and rationalization of production, these barriers may be expected to weaken and the workers in the technologically more backward sectors are likely to swell the crowd whose propensity toward political violence and instability is such a prominent feature of the social life of developing countries.[36]

It would be a gross exaggeration to maintain that all these changes are the result only, or even primarily, of the growth of a market for labor and the institutions associated with it. The growth of labor markets is the concomitant of other developments in the economic and social sphere. We have made frequent references to such characteristic features of economic development as industrialization, rationalization, urbanization, and technological change. The ultimate change is one of culture in which a predominantly nonindustrial system tends to be replaced by an industrial one. But to speculate or to theorize about these ultimate changes is of little operational significance. It seems more fruitful to investigate the more proximate institutions through which the ultimate cultural changes manifest themselves in social behavior and attitudes. On this level the study of developing labor markets, the emergence of organizations of those seeking jobs by way of the market, and their impact on related social institutions, motivations, and forms of social action is of the utmost importance.

36 Barriers such as closed shop exist even in industrially advanced countries as devices to allocate jobs, especially when labor surpluses exist.

James G. Scoville

Some Determinants of the Structure of Labor Movements

A COMMON THEME of this volume is the interaction of institutions with economic and political forces in changing societies. It may now be appropriate to build upon those findings and expand beyond them in a more general discussion of the factors which shape the functions and structures of the institutions which comprise the labor movement. What are the major determinants of the several organizational structures that arise from inchoate worker protest and dissatisfaction? How are these structures related to and influenced by the goals and problems toward which the newly born organizations direct themselves? Can we suggest hypotheses dealing with the continuing interrelationship between the purposes and the structures of labor movements?

It may be worthwhile to restate and emphasize with more concrete examples those three general questions which will serve as the focus for this essay. What factors shape the relationships within the broader labor movement between the workers' party and the trade union organizations? Why do craft unions arise in some places and eras and industrial unions in others? Why are these two principles of organization the ones which survive (with mutations like British "general unions"), while a most common basis at the outset of industrialization—geographical organizations of all workers—seems incapable of survival? Finally, is it not possible to develop a conceptual framework in which the Anglo-American experience is partially relieved of its status as a special case?

Scholars have largely neglected these narrower structural questions in favor of periodic debates on whether we can have *a* theory of *the* labor movement. This seems unfortunate, as implicit assumptions about the answers to these questions must lie behind customary comparative discussions of labor history and institutions.[1] How else is one to understand the differing institutional structures of various modern and developing labor movements?

I

The literature on the subject is not only limited; its most important treatment is also impaired by neglecting the other components of labor movements in favor of emphasis on the trade union sector alone. With respect to the shapes and purposes of labor organizations (particularly at their inception), only one line of thought has generated comprehensive hypotheses. The first relevant discussion of factors shaping the emergence of trade unions appears in John Dunlop's "The Development of Labor Organization: Some Theoretical Observations."[2] Using concepts which were later refined to those of *Industrial Relations Systems,* Dunlop explored the circumstances which lead to the birth and prosperity of union organizations in some sectors of the economy, and to their failure elsewhere. Technology, market structures, and prevailing social philosophies and ideologies define the places where labor action is both possible and acceptable. This analysis was carried forward in *Industrial Relations Systems* (Chapter 8) and *Industrialism and Industrial Man* (Chapter 8) to the point where some general hypotheses were suggested concerning the organizational structure of labor movements, and trade unions in particular, in relationship to the nature of the industrializing elite of the particular society.[3]

Two facets of Dunlop's formulation merit further discussion. Sturmthal's earlier work and his essay in this volume make it abundantly clear that we should not confine our attention to trade unions alone. Union organizations and workers' political institutions are clearly interrelated; their respective functions and importance clearly influence one another. We must not fall victim to the American tunnel vision which identifies trade unionism and the labor movement.

1 Some recognition of this problem is shown by Robert H. Bates, "Approaches to the Study of Unions and Development," *Industrial Relations,* October, 1970.
2 In R. Lester and J. Shister, *Insights into Labor Issues* (New York: Macmillan, 1948).
3 See, for example, J. T. Dunlop, *Industrial Relations System* (New York: Holt, 1958), pp. 323–24.

Moreover, if we are to develop a richer model, there must be some attempt to move beyond the virtual inclusion of the formers and shapers of labor organizations within the industrializing elite. Elites are not necessarily a useful analytical device, for one thing, and even were the device appropriate to discussion of newly developing countries in a world of conscious imitation of others' models, it may not be the appropriate concept for a more wide-ranging historical study.

It may be useful to dwell a bit more on this point. In *Industrial Relations Systems,* Dunlop has generally dealt with cases of mature, developed systems of industrial relations.[4] In these situations, well-articulated management and workers' institutions exist, government agencies have established a variety of interests in labor markets and industrial relations, while economic history and social policies have established a generally solid power and ideological basis to shape and constrain the parties' behavior. At the outset of industrialization it is clear that few, if any, of these conditions are present. Although by no means the only one, the most obvious missing part of the system is likely to be the organizations representing workers in both the plant and the polity. How do such organizations arise? Perhaps more important, what is the best approach toward incorporation of these phenomena into a general framework?

The line that is taken in *Industrialism and Industrial Man* comes very close to asserting that labor organizations will be those desired, or even designed, by the industrializing elite. Thus, "It should be understood that each of these elite groups may have associated with it or indeed may be composed of several elements—political leaders, industrial managers, military officers, religious figures, top civil servants, leaders of labor organizations, associated intellectuals. . . . Each of [the five] elite groups has a strategy by which it seeks to order the surrounding society in a consistent and compatible fashion."[5]

To be quite fair, the authors admit that analysis of labor relations questions during industrialization by means of a set of elites is only a first step toward understanding the processes at work.[6] From a rough survey of journal reviews of *Industrialism and Indus-*

---

4 A possible exception: Yugoslavia. Yet this case is one where an "industrializing elite" can most clearly be seen at work.

5 J. T. Dunlop, Clark Kerr, Frederick Harbison, and Charles A. Myers, *Industrialism and Industrial Man* (Cambridge: Harvard University Press, 1960), p. 50.

6 *Ibid.,* p. 51.

trial Man, I gather that most writers in the field are agreed on this. Unfortunately, insofar as it relates to the development of labor organizations, it is quite possible that analysis in terms of types of elites may actually obscure factors and processes of great importance. In principle, it may be desirable to break out the labor organizers (at least) from the bundle of groups composing the elite; in practice, it may be essential to do so for analysis of earlier historical periods when the desirability of industrialization was not inherent in the common ideology of the society.

II

In the pages that follow, an attempt is first made to assess the social and economic features of various societies during the early stages of industrialization which bring one or another protest group to prominence and which concurrently mold the structures of labor organizations. This might be called the "initial solution." In the second stage, I have attempted to suggest the nature of the forces working on and with these institutions to shape the course of their further evolution.

The Menu of Goals and Means

Before launching into a discussion of the preferences and choices for action by the various parts of the labor movement, it will be useful to spell out the general dimensions to which subsequent remarks will apply. We begin with the fundamental dichotomy of political and economic objectives, central to Sturmthal's earlier discussions. In most cases, the meaning of this time-honored distinction will be clear—the right to vote is a clear example of one type, while extraction of an increased wage from the employer exemplifies the other. There are undoubtedly a number of fuzzy areas; demands for improved and extended general education would probably be termed political, while similar demands relating to vocational training might be regarded as economic. But whatever the problems in classifying particular cases, this basic distinction about goals appears analytically useful.

A similar political-economic categorization can be and has been applied (by Sturmthal, for example) to description of the means by which objectives are pursued. However, it may be more valuable to make another distinction before applying the political-economic labels. We may distinguish between those groups or individuals who would effect changes through traditional means and those who would utilize nontraditional means. In today's terminology, we might consider the former as "working within the system," while the latter may be (but are not necessarily) "revolutionary" in approach. My contention is that the factors shaping the outcome of the decision[7] about approach will illuminate the subsequent selection of political or economic goals or means.

This "within the system/outside the system" dichotomy is often (perhaps tediously) used to characterize political actions, but it has been less often applied to actions of an economic nature. It is therefore clear that, if this conceptual distinction is to have any value, we must present examples where *economic* means for the advancement of labor (or mankind) have been proposed which lay outside the accepted *economic* framework. One fairly straightforward example would seem to be the various cooperative workshop movements stemming from rejection of "the wage system" and insistence upon its destruction.

Protest Groups and the Labor Movement

In the course of industrialization certain focal points of protest, conflict, or disagreement regarding the nature of society seem to develop. The groups in which this disagreement is concentrated appear to follow stable historical patterns. In the first place, there are groups which center on workers, and which may be organized and led by workers themselves. Second, middle-class reform groups have often appeared, as individuals in this class find their economic advancement is not paralleled by similar developments in the political arena. Finally, groups of intellectuals (perhaps also disenfranchised) are formed in concern and protest at the distributions of gains and burdens of industrialization, which they may perceive as inequitable. A number of other types of protest foci also develop—in agriculture, for instance—but these three are of primary concern to our analysis. In various combinations, they constitute "the labor movement" as embraced by the more general European parlance. Yet it is critical (especially for Americans) to recognize that this movement is in fact composed of diverse parts. The relationships among these constituent groups in the early stages of industrialization, against a background of social, political, and economic factors, shape the particular forms which the labor movement and trade union organizations will assume.

7   This "decision" may be so constrained by social, political, and economic factors that it becomes involuntary—there is no real choice to be made, and one outcome appears inevitable.

In the usual labor histories, importance is given to two prominent subsets of industrializing society which are commonly supposed to have particular impact on the shape of the labor movement. These ideal types are middle-class reformers on the one hand,
and revolutionary intellectuals on the other.[8] These groups share a
common trait: disapproval of the way some part of the society is
working or of the goals toward which it is aimed. The activities
of both groups are related to the choice of purposes by the labor
movement and, at least in some cases, their political preferences
may have impacts on the structure of workers' organizations. Thus
one can trace the impact of the middle-class reformers who began
and sustained the Chartist movement in England, their gropings
for support among the workers and relationships with the trade
unions in their struggle for survival in a hostile environment. This
process was forerunner to the development of the Labour party as
the political instrument of the trade union and reformer groups.

Alternatively, consider the results when the intellectuals, following one variant of the Marxian prescription, assume management of
worker protest at the outset of industrialization. In this case the intellectuals will tend to influence or control labor organizations
through the machinery of their own pre-existing organization, usually the party, so that the relationship between the two organized
groups is the reverse of the British pattern. This type of party-union
relationship appears quite clearly in the beginnings in Germany,
with separate trade union centers growing up as results of party
schisms or new political forces.[9] Even with the virtual disappearance of one political faction (Communist) and reunification of the
trade union movement after World War II, the historical impact
of party dominance over trade union organizations remains evident
in the relative weakness of the DGB in comparison with its affiliated
bodies. In France, where the party "captured" a pre-existing organization with strong traditions of independence from the party, the
situation is somewhat altered. Although the nature of interconnec-
tions between the French Communist party and the CGT is clear,
the CGT has retained a greater degree of formal control over its
subordinate bodies than the DGB possesses.

The role of middle-class reformers and intellectuals in alliance
or cooperation with workers' organizations needs to be considered

---

8   The terms are Dunlop's, but the concept of these two general groupings can
be found throughout the literature, by whatever name. The terms are approximate
—some individuals defy classification or appear, for example, as rude workers in
a group generally denoted intellectual.

9   See Lösche's paper in this volume for treatment of these events.

in more detail. Which of the two groups exercises the most influence upon burgeoning labor organizations seems to reflect social and political conditions in the society. Thus the early national union movements of England and the United States were associated with an aggregation of reformers: the Chartists as noted in England; temperance, suffragist, educational, and other reformers in the United States. Robert Owen's Grand National Consolidated Trades Union and the Knights of Labor, as well as earlier groups, had memberships broader than the working class, encompassing diverse reform interests. On the Continent the feebleness of the middle class, in contrast to government by upper-class or military groups, generally left philosophical leadership of the nascent unions to persons of an intellectual bent. This leadership was either external (in the case of the Marxists) or internal (the anarcho-syndicalists) to the group of workers involved. Labor organizations, specifically those of a formal, on-going sort, do not seem to arise by spontaneous generation; hence, we must attach considerable importance to these two groups with respect to the formation, and particularly the goal selection, of early labor movements. It is also essential to separate these two groups quite clearly from our conceptions of whatever "elite" is guiding the society at the time.

Formation of the Goals of the Labor Movement

Two major influences seem to shape the initial goals of the labor movement and of its collaborating group. The international migration of ideas, as treated by Sturmthal in his 1966 essay, is of importance in shaping the way various groups (particularly the intellectuals) view their society and its functioning, as well as occasionally producing anomalous responses to social conditions. New means of communication (such as cheap radios) may reinforce and modify the nature of this migration process. Currents in labor and politics around the world can now be widely disseminated without having to pass through the heads of intellectuals in the society importing the ideas. Again, as suggested by the Sturmthal thesis, social and political conditions in the society seem to be the second major influence shaping labor's goals.[10] I shall concentrate on the second point.

10   Sturmthal stresses the point that political action may naturally be selected, since the typically loose labor markets at the outset of economic development take the bite out of economic activities. Parallel with that conclusion is the fact that economic theory from the wages fund to the doctrines of W. A. Lewis has continually taught the educated collaborators of the labor movement that this is so.

Why is it that the political characteristics and dimensions of a society appear to be decisive in the labor movement's choice from a menu of possible objectives? In the first place, repressive political structures generally exercise similar restraints upon collective economic actions. In such a situation political change is a necessary prerequisite to economic activity by the labor movement. Second, under such circumstances political goals may have greater appeal to the audience being organized. Between the predilections of the collaborators and the practical requirements of the situation, political questions can hardly avoid being of greater relative importance at the outset of labor movements. As Sturmthal observes, such a pattern characterizes nineteenth-century Europe as well as twentieth-century colonial territories.[11]

Two major aspects of a nation's political framework seem to affect the relative importance of political goals to the nascent labor movement. (Needless to say, the initial choice of objectives also influences the persistence of political activity in the subsequent history of the movement.) The first factor revolves around the class structure of the society and the associated distribution of political power. Insofar as power is concentrated in the hands of a few, the labor movement places more stress on its redistribution. Such an emphasis is augmented by the number of allies the labor movement has, which should be more or less in proportion to the degree of disenfranchisement across the society. Britain in the first half of the nineteenth century would be a case in point. Chartists, trade unions, and middle-class liberals worked together—until the early reforms diluted the concentration of power and appeased some of the allied groups. The bulk of the trade unions, imbued with liberal middle-class ideas and leaders, then made the transition from political to economic concerns of the narrowest sort. The "physical force" Chartists and the more political labor groups were left behind for the time being. Eventually this course of events led to sufficient neglect of the industrial population that the game was substantially replayed. With a modified collaborating group of Socialist bent, the

11   An empirical measure of this "greater relative importance" would be highly desirable. One direct approach would be to seek out data on political strikes in contrast to economic ones, and to trace the course of their relative sizes and frequencies. Unfortunately, neither nineteenth nor twentieth-century governments appear to have collected their data on this basis or on a basis that is convertible. Other approaches have their drawbacks as well. One might look at the pronouncements of trade union centers or of national unions in an attempt to assay the political-economic balance of their concern. Yet such comparisons over time or between places are meaningless without some measure of the power these bodies have in the respective spheres.

New Unionism developed, spawned the Labour party, and combined with other forces to produce another set of political reforms (1918).[12]

The second major characteristic of a political system which influences the nascent labor movement revolves about that system's responsiveness and sheer ability to change. The more responsive and flexible the system, the less likely is a political tradition to build up in the labor movement. We might here distinguish between the long-run impacts of the willingness (or cunning) to grant social and economic programs benefiting labor (viz. Bismarck) and an accommodation to labor's representational objectives. Representation in the United States, coupled with social programs that could hardly be considered progressive, yielded the least amount of pure political interest; in Germany, relatively generous social legislation without representation was associated with highly political unionism. These influences operated together in Finland before 1906—nonrepresentation in a system of foreign rule by an inflexible government with no inclination to meet labor's objectives —producing the Finnish labor movement's renown for its political inclinations and activity.[13]

In this context it is pertinent to observe that the labor movement's representational objectives are not confined solely to matters of parliamentary enfranchisement. In the colonial world this objective takes the form of participation in movements for independence or national liberation. The intersection of the colonialist-nationalist conflict with that between employers and workers is large indeed, rooted as the membership of both groupings is in historical patterns of social and economic development. The two conflicts often have the same sets of individuals arrayed against each other, depending simply on which hat they are wearing at the time. Confronted with conditions resembling those in czarist Finland, it is no accident that labor movements in many colonial states have been extremely political in their orientation.

Goals and Structures

The conditions and forces that influence the relative orientation of labor movements and of their organizers indirectly affect the or-

12   One can apply a similar paradigm to the rise of the CIO; looking forward, it might even be applicable to the possible rise of the ALA, although the staying power of this wave of new activity is uncertain.

13   See Carl E. Knoellinger, *Labor in Finland* (Cambridge: Harvard University Press, 1960), for discussion.

ganizational structures that develop. After all, political objectives and activities imply a need for an organization which is effective in the political sphere. Entirely different mechanisms may be required for economic effectiveness. In the realm of political action, various patterns appear to have evolved. If the group allied with labor is basically middle-class and reformist, the route followed toward political action has often stressed education. The end result in mind is to make one's laboring allies ready for enfranchisement on the one hand, while rendering them deserving of it in the eyes of the public. Such workers' education, pursued in small local groups, results in a decentralized base for the trade union movement, as was the case in England. Organizational strength and membership loyalties are thus developed at the lower levels of the movement. Although educational activities are not precluded, if leadership of the labor movement has fallen to the revolutionary camp, more direct forms of manifestation of workers' political strength may be chosen. Numerous examples can be found in Sellier's chapter. Effective management of such activities requires a mass organization under centralized control. Powerful central bodies thus tend to arise, paying little or no attention to craft distinctions, often with considerable strength at the regional (*not* plant) level. This latter trend has been based in part on the tendency of intellectual-led, politically committed movements to fractionate periodically between heretics and true believers. In such situations each contending leader requires a solid geographic base in either a city or region; the Italian labor movement before World War I provides excellent illustrations of this phenomenon. The tendency toward divisiveness further encourages centralization of the multiple confederations that result, the better to compete with rival federations as well as to control the internal workings of one's own group. All tendencies move power and control away from the workplace.

Let us further note that for the revolutionary, unlike the middle-class reformer, workers' protests and participation do not require "legitimization" through educational advancement or appeals to public opinion. The revolutionary-intellectuals' theory provides sufficient legitimization for their actions. This point is of limited importance in discussing history, but it can usefully be applied to the situation in a colonialist state. Although the underlying theory is somewhat different, the need to establish a basis of legitimacy is absent there as well. The right of peoples to run their own society is accepted today as a truism; neither the right to protest nor to participate in governance need be based on a demonstration of competence or ability. This "automatic legitimacy" removes the need for low-level educational work and strengthens both the political and the centralist tendencies of labor movements in backward colonial areas.

Thus we might summarize in the diagram below our hypotheses about the interaction of political conditions and the collaborating protest group.

| | | Political Conditions | |
		Open and Responsive	Repressive, Unresponsive
Collaborating Group	Middle class	Emphasis on education, representation; important local units	Unsuccessful attempts, typified by Hirsch-Duncker unions in Germany
	Revolutionists	Highly political Easily fractionated Ineffective Highly centralized	Direct political action Most centralized Highly political

With this argument in the background, that the interaction of an elite group with the political environment of the labor movement shapes major portions of that movement's purpose and structure, let us proceed to an examination of some other factors which will influence the shape of labor's organizations.

Social and Educational Conditions

Here two factors, social mobility and literacy, will be given primary consideration, although it is clear that they are to some extent intertwined and related to political characteristics of the society. Social mobility, given a political and economic system, reduces the clarity and permanence of class lines, thereby mitigating the grievances of labor as a group, as well perhaps as those of a middle-class collaborating group. Moreover, such mobility operates to weaken the lower levels of worker organization. Good leaders will either leave the ranks of labor or rise to higher positions in the movement at either national or federation levels. High degrees of mobility at the local level impede the retention of members and the collection of dues. The combination of these factors exerts a push toward centralization while focusing union attention on economic matters.

The levels and ubiquity of education clearly play a role in the selection of leaders and the relationship between workers' organizations and the collaborating protesters. The more pervasive is illiteracy, the more dependent will workers be upon external sources for leadership and managerial talents. From Russian workers around the turn of the century to present student-worker agitation in Afghanistan, this effect of labor illiteracy can be clearly observed. The reverse case, engendering minimal external influence upon labor organizations, can be seen in the United States.

Lack of literacy has a two-fold impact on the organizational structures of the labor movement—centralization and increase of leaders' power relative to workers-members at all levels. An associated by-product is likely to be the importation of an ideological cast to the trade union movement via the literate leadership. Moreover, the balance is likely to be tipped toward more radical, political action–oriented leaders from the revolutionary group, as those inclined toward "bread and butter" viewpoints will be in great demand to fill better-paying managerial posts.[14] A contrast between the AFL and CIO in the 1930's is suggestive of the importance of these forces: the typical CIO union member was less educated than his AFL counterpart, while precisely the reverse was true of their leadership echelons. Consider again the impacts of illiteracy and other factors impeding communication with the rest of society upon the structure, outlook, etc., of the Farm Workers Organizing Committee, with particular emphasis on the role of intellectuals. A counter-example reveals the way in which devious governments can use these natural dynamic forces to frustrate trade unionism: the Egyptian requirement that union officers must work full-time at their trade (in the 1950's), when placed on an ill-educated work force, led to virtual paralysis of the union movement.

The Role of the Family and of Rural Society Generally

The characteristics and functioning of the family unit and of the background rural or traditional society influence the development of labor organizations through their competition with the economic functions frequently associated with guilds or trade unions. The re-

14 See Kilby's chapter in this volume for examples of this phenomenon in Nigeria.

lationship between the industrial worker and the traditional agricultural society has often been summarized by placing him somewhere on a spectrum of "committedness." Part of that relationship (or definition, as you prefer) resides in the ease with which the worker can transfer himself and his skills back to traditional sector employment. For the early years of industrialization in most currently developed countries, agriculture reabsorbed some of those thrown out of industrial work in business fluctuations. Such flexibility clearly diminishes the need for economic action by trade unions—the more reversible the application of a worker's skills to industry, the less need for economic action, particularly in the areas of job security and fringe benefits. The lack of reversibility which grows as the industrial work force matures increases the union interest in programs to deal with its effects. In those countries where marginal and average products are low in agriculture, the stage of irreversibility may precede the development of a "committed" industrial labor force.

The nature and structure of the family also impinge upon the process of adjustment of the industrial work force to hazards of unemployment, but there are broader impacts as well. Moreover, the functions and responsibility of the family in areas of economic insecurity have persisted longer in the process of economic development than the possibility of moving back to the traditional sector. Insofar as social security, unemployment insurance, and even workman's compensation are functions assumed by the family, pressures on labor organizations to produce comparable results are lessened.

Two general effects are to be noted. Strong links to rural job opportunities and/or extended family systems weaken attachments to labor organizations at the local level, thereby strengthening tendencies toward centralization of authority in the labor movement. These same factors reduce the pressure for economic action by trade unions, thus guiding them toward policies with a higher political content.

THE STRUCTURE OF INDUSTRY

The first aspect of industrial structure I will consider is one central to the study of industry propensities to strike by Kerr and Siegel type of industry.[15] A variety of other sociological, historical, and

15   C. Kerr and A. Siegel, "The Interindustry Propensity to Strike—An International Comparison," in A. Kornhauser, R. Dubin, and A. M. Ross, *Industrial Conflict* (New York: McGraw-Hill, 1954).

psychological studies could be cited in which attempts have been made to go even further in explaining workers' behavior and outlook as functions of the technology with which they work. Industries typified by isolated, arduous, dangerous, or repetitive work may produce higher levels of labor-management conflict or greater worker radicalism. The distribution of a country's employment among various industries may thus influence the shape (and perhaps the goals)[16] of the nascent trade union movement. For reasons similar to those expressed in the AFL's Scranton Declaration of 1902, certain industries (most notably, mining) are particularly suited for organizations covering all the workers at the particular workplace. By extension, this implies industrial-type labor organizations. Where unions of miners and similar workers arise early in the process of development and lead in the formation of national trade union centers, one expects a greater preference for this organizational type, in contrast with the antipathy which developed in the United States.

A second dimension of industrial structure affecting the nature of labor organizations can be found in the size distribution of enterprises, particularly in manufacturing. This effect will be felt at a relatively advanced stage of the industrialization process, when mechanization or skill dilution has destroyed the handicraft enterprises of an earlier stage. Small industrial plants with few persons in each type of job provide an insecure base for organizations structured along craft lines. Unless some sort of mediating body (for example, works councils) exists to unify workers' representation at the workplace, a reliance on industrial organizations will ensue. As a consequence of either pattern, the power and authority of the local trade union will be relatively small in comparison with the national union.

The size distribution of plants will also affect the overall strength of the trade union movement, most directly through the financial resources which organization of the large plant represents to a union. Small plants are customarily the least organized in any industry, a result of rational allocation of scarce organizational and dues-collecting talents.[17]

16   The nature of the industry may affect the relative appeal of various ideas, political or economic, and hence the goals of the movement.
17   This raises a more general question about the influence on structure of the source of funding. We will expect more centralized movements where lump-sum government grants are the primary source (as in some African nations). Grants to local trade unions based on their membership would produce an entirely different structure.

Finally, the average-sized plant in an industry or economy may reflect conditions of entry into an industry. Coupled with the fact that easy entry and exit by firms inhibit successful plant-level unionization, small plant sizes will reinforce the tendency toward centralized, industrial-type unions.

A third industrial factor affecting the structuring of labor organizations can be identified, although it is clearly related to type of industry and size of plants. This is the nature and structure of the employers' organizations to be found in the industry or society. Centralization of employers' organizations will encourage, and perhaps necessitate, greater centralization in the trade union movement. A similar effect at the industry level derives from high levels of concentration; for a nation, the union response to such centripetal pulls can be seen in the forces and responses active in the restructuring of the Swedish labor federation at the end of the 1930's. A fragmented movement could not fight or even cooperate with a highly centralized set of employers' organizations.

Market Structure

Beyond the narrow impact of concentration in particular industries mentioned above, the overall structure and competitiveness of a nation's product and factor markets influences the shape of labor organizations. One crucial aspect of market structure is the transportation and communications network of the country. This variable is of added importance as it experiences greater changes over the industrialization process than other variables (like family structure) which are typically more stable or sluggish in their evolution.

The poorer and less complete is the transport-communications system, the weaker is competition in product and factor markets. To the extent that local communities are isolated from each other, moderate quantities of monopoly power accrue to labor and managements. It is thus natural that organs arise intended to influence labor's lot in localities protected by transport barriers. As mobility of men and materials increases, such organizations are weakened or destroyed. Ulman's *Rise of the National Trade Union* provides numerous examples from American labor history: the attempts of city central labor unions to create local monopoloid structures and the struggles of the national unions to control nomadic members of their trade are sufficient to show the processes at work. Continuing advances in transport and communications have made one form of national labor federation—a federation of all-inclusive local monopoly unions—incapable of long-term survival.[18] Labor and capital mobility, plus improved transport facilities, weaken such geographically based local labor organizations in their competition with organizational structures based on control of either craft or industry.

Finally, the stronger is the competitive nature of domestic markets, the more centralized will power be within the national trade unions. Again we cite Ulman for examples. A corollary of this rule would appear to indicate that increased levels of competition from the outside world exert a tendency toward mergers or cooperation among rival trade union federations, as in Sweden and the Netherlands, respectively.

Aspects of the Labor Market

As suggested by Sturmthal, a general superfluity of labor should increase the relative efficacy of political (as opposed to economic) action by the trade union movement.[19] A number of the contributions to this volume have given general support to this hypothesis (Taira, Sanchez-Arnaudo, and others) or the basic Lewis assumptions (my paper on Afghanistan). However, even with overall excess labor a variety of factors limit the pervasiveness of labor market looseness. Where the familiar Marshallian conditions for economic success are applicable, organizations arise with a capability in this sphere. Consider the trade union interest in lengthy and complicated apprenticeship programs in India, a country which might be deemed to have abundantly loose labor markets. A further example can be seen in Kilby's study of Nigeria, where personal considerations of economic security generate apprenticeship systems even in the nonunion part of the labor market, reflecting an effort to raise barriers to entry where capital costs are too low to do the job.

Other factors may also be operating to create, within a nation, separate labor markets between which movement may be difficult.

18   The attempted formation of the International Industrial Assembly of North America (1864) by city central labor unions is an example. Elements of this type of organizing principle are also to be found in the Knights of Labor, and in syndicalist organizations in France, Italy, and elsewhere. See Lloyd Ulman, *The Rise of the National Trade Union* (Cambridge: Harvard University Press, 1968).

19   This political action can be aimed toward government grants of economic power (via the closed shop, etc.). In this case, a basically political organization of the labor movement, constructed to produce votes or mobs for the government, will be modified by the creation of organs to exercise their economic powers. Yet that which governments grant they can revoke, so the basic objective of the labor organizations will remain political.

Caste systems or other forms of discrimination are among these barriers to homogeneity of tightness across all labor markets. Ethnic patterns of distribution of certain jobs to certain groups of workers are by no means rare—one can cite large areas of Asia, Africa, and the Caribbean where racial group and occupation have long been associated. Where labor markets are thus split up, it is likely that evolution of workers' organizations may follow divergent patterns within a single country. Whether economic actions are in fact less effective than political ones will depend on a variety of variables peculiar to each of the separate markets. Among these are differences in the rate of growth of labor demand *and* supply, differences in rates of productivity change, and the social and economic station of the people in the submarkets.

III

The Initial Solution and Evolution

The preceding pages have sketched a detailed view of the forces and factors shaping the labor movement in the initial stages of industrialization. In mathematical jargon, we have been exploring the parameters which determine the "initial solution"[20] to our problem of labor organization. When we turn to the course of labor history after the initial solution, two principal ideas are to be considered. In the first place, as the parameters which shaped the first stage change with progressing industrialization, the labor movement's goals and structure will respond to these modifications in its environment. Second, the initial structure of the labor movement exercises an impact on the future course of its evolution. Several causes explain this: the persistence of ideology formed at the beginning, the survival imperative of institutions, and the forces which the labor movement may exert to shape the evolution of the "external" parameters.[21]

Of the first class of evolving external influences upon the labor movement, it is likely that alterations in industrial and market structure are of foremost importance. The appropriate form of organization, and a host of allied characteristics, change as the society's economy evolves. Moving from the initial period of industrialization, a number of common patterns of evolution appear

20   This is a very crude analogy; the formative process is not static, and may well occupy a long time span.

21   The chapters by Pen and Kawada-Komatsu illustrate several aspects of responses to market and technological change.

in the historical record. The first stage of this process appears to involve increasing importance of manufacturing employment, and a trend toward the mass-production industries. This process has in the past posed a variety of problems for the then-existing labor movement. In movements characterized by "jurisdictions" new forms of organization arise, usually accompanied by a struggle between them and that older form of organization. As the areas of new organization appear typically to have been subject to political as well as trade union neglect, this shift has frequently been accompanied by marked political differences between the labor groups in the different industrial areas. We see examples in the conflicts between the new and old unionisms in Great Britain, the Communists and anarcho-syndicalists in France, and the CIO and AFL.

The second stage of evolution appears to involve a reduction in the relative importance of extractive and manufacturing activity, along with an expansion in the importance of service employments of all types. Not only does this transformation in the economy's job content lead to a relative shrinkage of the traditional base of the labor movement (which poses certain problems), but there occurs at the same time a shift in the predominant type of employer in areas of new job creation. Nonprofit institutions, governments, and *small* private enterprises in the service area increasingly characterize the expanding sector of the labor market. If the labor movement is to adapt to the shriveling of its base and continue to grow, it must adjust to bring the new types of work and workers under its control. The need to negotiate with types of employers different from the usual large-scale private industrial firm (or industry association) further conditions the evolution of the labor movement.

The final stage, if we are to believe the wisest prognosticators of Santa Barbara, California, will be the erosion of work itself as a foundation of modern human life.[22] It is to be expected that, depending on the ideologies which they have fashioned (and their own procedures in the labor market), the reactions of the various labor movements to such a development will be rather different. The U.S. labor movement, with its ideology of work and the control of work or job rights, and with numerous areas in which this control is a reality, will presumably respond to such radical reduction of needed levels of human effort through programs of spreading the work—reducing the work week, longer holidays, etc. On the

22 I should make it clear that I see little evidence for the imminence of such a development.

other hand, European movements would more swiftly (and more readily, given their political weaponry and inclinations) abandon the link between work and income so dear to Americans, and move to assure that the final distribution of income was relatively even and independent of the sweat of one's brow. I suspect that this discussion need detain us no longer, as it looks further into an improbable future than a historical paper must.

Turning to the influence of the original structuring of the labor movement on the course of its future evolution, particular attention must be paid to the role of ideology. The central notions which characterize the thinking of leaders of the labor movement, and particularly of the trade unions, are quite diverse when viewed in comparative fashion. One such set of basic ideas involves the proper relationship among the various components of the labor movement. Early experiences and developments in the relationships between party and union groups will often produce a set of unwritten laws or ideology on this subject. What roles politicians or intellectuals shall play in the trade union movement are questions which preoccupied the French anarcho-syndicalists and German unionists, respectively. The ideologies developed may be inconsistent with the long-run survival of the organization in societies undergoing social and political change. Thus, the anarcho-syndicalists' rejection of political action within the mechanisms of the system in part explains their long-run defunction.

As observed above, the objectives chosen by the labor movement, combined with the logical structure of organization, will yield a reliance on certain types of weapons. Not by coincidence do these weapons themselves enter into the ideology of the labor movement, shaping both its future actions and its course of evolution. Thus political objectives will lead to an emphasis on fundamental political organization and the use of essentially political weapons. One of these, perhaps the most likely to succeed in placing immediate pressures on the surrounding society, is the general strike. It should be clear, though, that the general strike is not just another weapon in the hands of labor (like a union shop or a union label), but one with a peculiar flair and flavor of its own which enters into the ideology of the labor movement as both symbol and unifying force. Surrounded by mystical qualities, the general strike may survive into the era where political action ceases to be the primary focus of labor's discontent. Its survival into the period when economic aims are most important may well lead to a labor movement which relies on the wrong weapons for the adjustment of labor's myriad interests in a complex economy. The trade union movement as part of the "revolution" of May, 1968, was able to extract from the French government an increase in the minimum wage. This does little for the mass of workers, and almost nothing about wage inequities, working conditions, and the like. The general strike is clearly a very crude tool to employ in an advanced, largely private economy.[23] Yet it survives as part of ideology and threatens to render anachronistic the movement that lives by that ideology.

A host of other factors shape and condition the evolution of labor movements. Changes in the political arena alter the rules under which trade unions, other labor organizations, and managements are to operate. Legacies of the colonial era affect the structuring and functions of labor movements in the developing world. The political and economic integration of nations will undoubtedly have impacts on the pre-existing organizations of labor. Naming these few cases is only suggestive of all the possibilities which should be considered in a more definitive treatment of the subject.

IV

This essay has attempted to sketch out in general terms a model of the development and evolution of labor organizations, with particular emphasis on their goals and institutional structures. As such, it is a response to a challenging topic suggested in one of the sessions at the Second Congress of the IIRA: "Political Systems and Industrial Relations." At that session, B. C. Roberts concluded that, at a fairly high level of theoretical aggregation, "political systems have a decisive influence on the basic characteristics of industrial relations systems . . . [although] . . . economic and technological factors influence the interaction between [them]."[24] I have sought to carry the analysis further and to deal with finer variations in political and industrial relations arrangements by spelling out additional social and political conditions shaping the course of events and the emergence of institutions. To claim that the task is

23   The fact that this picture is overdrawn, that the real result of May, 1968, has been to stimulate a great deal more collective bargaining, only supports the contention in the text. No one would suggest, however, that the general strike in France has become a ritualistic dance preliminary to serious bargaining.

24   B. C. Roberts, "Political Systems and Industrial Relations Systems in Western Europe and North America," presented to Second World Congress, International Industrial Relations Association, Geneva, September, 1970. Quoted from pp. 37–38.

complete would be foolish indeed, but the more detailed hypotheses advanced above have brought us closer to a unifying model of the social and economic factors behind the diverse patterns of development of labor movements.

François Sellier

The French Workers' Movement and Political Unionism

THE RISE of a general movement of industrial workers in France is difficult to pinpoint. It is possible to place its emergence in the years following the Napoleonic wars, with the 1831 uprising of the Lyon silk workers of particular significance. Although unions were legally forbidden until 1884 and strikes were considered a criminal offense as late as 1864, a large number of friendly societies and illegal associations had developed in the early days of the nineteenth century.

From February to June, 1848, the common action of the bourgeoisie and workers led to a revolution against the king. A radical government was installed, but after a short period of social reforms, fierce street fighting put an end to the cooperation of the Republic with the workers. Not long afterward, Napoleon III was elected. Until 1860 labor's every attempt to organize was strongly repressed, but in the second decade of his reign, the regime was progressively liberalized. The government authorized the sending of a delegation of workers to the London World's Exhibition of 1862. The First "International"[1] was founded in 1864, and French workers' associations were tolerated in practice.

After 1871 and the tragedy of the Paris Commune, workers' friendly societies and cooperatives grew again. They became more influenced by socialist ideas after 1880. From 1880 until 1906 two

1 An international association of various national radical groups and trade unions set up in London, at first strongly influenced by Marx, later increasingly dominated by syndicalists.

distinct and divergent viewpoints characterized the movement's ideology. Their inclination toward political action (with an alliance between the socialist party and unions) and their orientation toward economic as well as political aims (and consequent opposition to party politics) balanced each other in workers' meetings. The second tendency took the lead at the Amiens Congress of 1906, but not for long. World War I, the foundation of the Soviet Union, the rise of the Communist party—all these factors brought radical changes in the delicate equilibrium between political and economic aims on one side, and political and economic weapons on the other.

According to one of the best-known writers on French unionism, Val R. Lorwin, "The French workers have, with a few interesting exceptions (notably the printers) . . . placed a low value on organization. Perhaps the weakness and decentralization of union structure are in part a reaction to the overorganization and over-centralization of the political state. At any rate, the French have achieved a combination of strong class consciousness and weak class organization in unions."[2]

The focus of this chapter is an attempt to disentangle the factors which explain, in the French case, the choice between political and economic objectives, and the choice—resulting only in part from the former—between political and economic weapons. I shall point out that the tendency toward craft unionism, a strong basis for workers' organization, has been hampered in France by the lack of a manpower surplus due to the early decline of birth rates. Only when great, across-the-board manpower surpluses exist, endangering the position of skilled and craft workers, do the latter tend to form strong organizations of their own to control entrance to the trades. Even when this condition is satisfied, civil inequality and aversion to class society may be such that these workers aim instead at political objectives for the whole working class.

These latter factors were important in the French case. The ideals of "republicanism," defined by hostility against aristocratic society and Catholic church traditions, favoring egalitatian ideas, had been, all through the second half of the nineteenth century, progressively diffused among the children of the working-class elite through the spread of primary education and the influence of republican teachers. Parallel with these developments, however, the hopes and ideals of the French Revolution were frustrated by right-wing governments almost until 1876.

---

2   "Reflections on the History of the French and American Labor Movements," *Journal of Economic History,* March, 1957.

With rapid industrial growth and the flow of workers into industry restrained by agricultural protectionism, wage differentials for skilled craft workers ceased to be large, relative to the well-paid workers of mass industry. This leveling of their economic situation also favored the tendency toward general unionism, although the diversity of political orientations of the workers' elite has hampered until now the unification of the movement.

POLITICAL AND SOCIAL STATUS OF THE WORKING CLASS

Voting Rights

The French were the first in Europe to obtain universal suffrage, excluding any voting tax (*cens*). The 1791 constitution granted citizenship to all men of French nationality, but not all were entitled to vote, since "active" citizens had to pay a direct tax at least equal to three days' labor. Nonetheless, there were at this time 4,300,000 "active citizens" (one-sixth of the French population, as against one-fourth in 1940, while the proportion of young people and children was much larger in 1791). In 1792 the voting tax was abandoned, but it was reestablished in 1795. Thereafter a variety of restrictions were adopted to curb the franchise. Only with the Republic of 1848 were voting taxes and other restrictions abolished.

However, the early conquest of these rights caused political frustration with their temporary suppressions or numerous violations, especially after 1795 and after 1848. Such frustration may have enhanced the interest in political struggle, nourished as it was by buoyant party activities, especially between 1876 and 1898, the period of the "Conquest of the Republic by the Republicans." From 1877 to 1954, election results show a "deeply divided public opinion"[3] between two opposing groups, one oriented toward the ideals of the 1789 Revolution (the Republicans) and the other oriented toward the institutions and values of the *ancien régime*. To a considerable extent, this division follows the regional lines observed in development of modern industry.

The "radical dynamism"[4] of 1871 to 1901 developed at first along the Mediterranean coast, the Rhone Valley (its eastern part, mainly), and in the districts of Lyon, Macon, Nevers, Bourges, and Besançon. In the northeast region, Dijon, Châlons, and Amiens

3 Maurice Duverger, *Institutions politiques et droit constitutionnel,* 11th ed. (Paris: Presses Universitaires de France), p. 575.
4 René Rémond et al., *Atlas historique de la France contemporaine* (Paris: Colin, 1966), pp. 116–18.

rapidly became Republican. Just before World War I, the Socialist districts were those of Lille, Arras, Mezières (extreme east and north), Paris, Moulins, Bourges, Vesoul, Grenoble, Toulon, Marseille, Nîmes, Montpellier, Narbonne, Albi, and Toulouse. The development of socialism was not limited to great urban regions; it extended to many rural areas, whether industrial centers or not. The workers' militancy, the peasants' discontent, and the early decline of church influence[5] combine to explain the rise of the Socialist party.

Unionism and strikes had developed long before political voting power, but statistics[6] are available only after 1884, when union activity was legalized. Before World War I, seven cities or regions had more than five labor chambers (*bourses du travail*): North (Lille-Roubaix-Tourcoing), Rouen, Paris, Bourges, Lyon–St. Etienne, Toulon, and Montpellier. In 1890, six years after their legal recognition, 1,000 workers' unions (locals) were registered (as many as employers' associations), with 140,000 members. There were 400,000 by 1893 (2,000 locals), 500,000 in 1900 (2,700 locals), 1,000,000 in 1911 (5,300 locals), and 1,600,000 members in 1920. Such is the record of growth of the first CGT (General Confederation of Labor, officially founded in 1895) until it was split by the rise of the Communist party in 1921.

Industrial and Urban Population

Regional and industrial patterns of population growth have affected the development of French unionism.[7] Thus in 1845 the main coal fields were located at St. Etienne, near Lyon.[8] Although the bulk of production had shifted to the north by 1890, there could be some relation, however slight, between the development of the first coal fields near the Saône-Rhone Valley or in the south (Creusot, Cevennes, Aveyron, Herauld) and the rise of radicalism and socialism. Other small coal fields, existing since 1850, should be noted in this respect: Commentry, in the center, Ronchamps, Vosges, Creuse, Decazeville. Some of them were sources of socialist influence. The development of foundries reinforced the regional patterns prevailing in the coal mines.[9]

5 C. Willard, *Les Guesdistes* (Paris: Editions Sociales, 1966), Introduction and pp. 219ff.

6 INSEE, *Annuaire statistique,* 1946, p. 75 (rounded numbers).

7 J. C. Toutain, "La Population de la France de 1700 à 1959," *Cahiers de l'Institut de Science économique appliquée,* January, 1963, Supplément no. 133, Sér. AF, no. 3 (ISEA, Paris), pp. 79, 138.

8 Rémond et al., *Atlas historique,* p. 83.

9 *Ibid.,* p. 96.

From 1836 to 1851 towns of 20,000 to 50,000 grew faster than those of 10,000 to 20,000, an indication of rapid urbanization. From 1851 to 1881 the larger the towns, the faster they grew.

Despite this accelerated urbanization, the total labor force grew faster between 1789 and 1856 than later on (1856–1954). In these two periods the difference in growth rates was even greater for the industrial labor force, as is shown in Table 1.

Table 1.   Long Period Growth Rates

	1789–1856	*1856–1954*
Total population	0.44	0.17
Industrial labor force	1.99	0.60
Total labor force	0.52–0.56	0.39

SOURCE: J. C. Toutain, "La Population de la France de 1700 à 1959," *Cahiers de l'Institut de Science économique appliquée*, January, 1963, Supplément no. 133, Série AF, no. 3 (ISEA, Paris), p. 130.

It should be remembered that the number of births decreased regularly after 1870, from 1,000,000 births per year in 1860 to 600,000 in 1939. In fact, the birth rate began to decline slowly long before 1870, dropping by 50 percent between 1830 and 1938.

The labor force was already rather large before 1800 in textiles, but growth was much more rapid between 1810 and 1850 in mining, metal, building, and wood and paper than in textiles, where a decline was observed after 1856 and especially after 1896. After 1866 the highest and steadiest growth rates until 1926 were to be observed in metal manufacturing, the dress industry, mining, chemicals, and printing.

In spite of high growth in some industries (approximately 80 percent in metal manufacturing from 1866 to 1906, for example) the growth rate in the same period for the total labor force was below 25 percent.

Toutain has estimated a series covering the evolution of the number of workers (manual workers) and of self-employed or employers (patrons) in industry from 1866 to 1931, shown in Table 2. The most striking feature of this series is the long-term stability of the fraction of workers in the total. From 1876 to 1906 the percentage of manual workers remained at 72 percent.

More detailed data, available only for certain regions, allow us to give a more precise account of the evolution of the social status

Table 2.　Workers in Industry

	Workers (000) (1)	Employers (000) (2)	Total (000) (3)	Workers to total: percent (4)
1866	2,738	1,511	4,250	64
1876	3,151	1,126	4,277	72
1881	3,032	1,169	4,201	72
1886	3,056	1,007	4,063	74
1891	3,303	1,047	4,350	73.5
1906	3,385	778	4,163	72
1921	3,892	666	4,558	85
1926	4,794	714	5,508	82
1931	4,803	699	5,502	82

Source: J. C. Toutain, "La Population de la France de 1700 à 1959," *Cahiers de l'Institut de Science économique appliquée*, January, 1963, Supplément no. 133, Série AF, no. 3 (ISEA, Paris), pp. 101–3.

of workers.[10] For example, in one of the two districts of Alsace (Bas-Rhin), the number of craftsmen (artisans), counting employers, workers, and apprentices together, declined by a quarter (from 40,000 to about 30,000) from 1807 to 1861.

In 1852 in the total industrial and craft population, the proportion of workers and apprentices to employers was 64 percent. F. Hordern has divided this total population into four parts: small craft shops (establishments of less than five people), small industry (less than one hundred people), big industry (more than one hundred), and cottage industry.

Table 3 shows the main characteristics of the social status in the craft and other industries, as well as the great relative importance (in 1852) of handicrafts.

Table 3.　Composition of Industrial Population in the District of Bas-Rhin (1852)

Proportion of:	Craft shop	Small industry	Big industry	Home industry	All industry
Employers	51.6	13.5	2.4	0.5	30.5
Workers	38.7	83.1	94.5	95.1	62.6
Apprentices	9.7	3.4	3.1	4.4	6.9
Shares of total industrial labor force	55.5	9.2	25.6	9.0	100.0

Source: François Hordern, "L'Évolution de la condition individuelle et collective des travailleurs en Alsace au XIXème siècle (1800–1870)," thèse (Paris, 1970), Vol. II, p. 18.

10　For example, Pierre Pierrard, *La Vie ouvrière à Lille sous le second empire* (Paris: Bloud et Gay, 1965), pp. 313ff. François Hordern, "L'Evolution de la condition individuelle et collective des travailleurs en Alsace au XIXème siècle (1800–1870)," thèse (Paris, 1970), Chs. 2, 5.

According to Table 2, the proletarization of the industrial population took place mainly before 1876 and after 1906, with the 1876–1906 period showing a relative stabilization of the average social status.

However, crude statistical observations cannot fully describe the more subtle evolution of big industry. According to a police report of the textile population of Colmar (Haut-Rhin, Alsace) analyzed by Hordern, the greater part of the industrial population was composed of low-wage workers: nonpermanent workers (*ouvriers flottants,* floating workers fired as soon as industry slackened), women, children, and other unskilled people.[11] Semi-skilled workers were another important part of the population but, according to the report, they formed the quiet element—less dangerous, very much attached to their town, their plant, and their village. The report concludes that a relatively small group of highly paid skilled workers, moving frequently from one place to another and interested in political and social problems, was the subversive element of the working class. Economic evolution partially deprived this upper echelon of their high wage differentials and reinforced their aggressiveness.

Public Education

Under the *ancien régime,* some tuition-free education was offered to the poor by church schools. General public education spread very swiftly after 1789. Under Minister Guizot in 1833 the principle of at least one school in every municipality was enforced; a special education tax was automatically added to the municipality's budget if it was not voluntarily accepted by the local authorities themselves.[12]

One-third of all primary school pupils were admitted free of charge in 1837, 40 percent in 1850–60, and 60 percent in 1880. In 1881 Victor Duruy firmly established the principle of free primary schools as a public service under state control. Illiteracy rates as registered during military service decreased steadily, from 50 percent in 1835 to 40 percent in 1850, 20 percent in 1870, 10 percent in 1890, and 4 percent in 1910. This progress was linked to and partly caused by lively political and religious competition between church and local authorities. As Prost put it, the 1881 and 1882 laws "profoundly divided the country"; the free public primary school was a political victory for the republic. "The achieve-

11 Hordern, "L'Evolution de la condition," I, p. 194.
12 A. Prost, *L'Enseignement en France, 1800–1967* (Paris: Colin, 1968).

ment of the republicans, with Jules Ferry at their head, was not only that they established primary schools, but also that it was a republican primary school system."[13]

Related to this point, the important part played by the state in the training of school teachers should be emphasized, especially in view of the spread of the ideas of progress and of loyalty to the republican state derived from the 1789 revolution: "Democracy and the Republic are the very heart of the liberal and rationalistic ideals of school teachers."[14] These ideals were generally very far from the collectivism and Marxism advocated by Jules Guesde after 1880. But they were completely opposed to the principles of authority upon which the conservatives and the mass of Catholics insisted.

Nevertheless, the above-quoted number should not obscure the fact that there were great interregional and sex differences in the spread of education. School attendance was much less frequent in rural areas than in towns, where schoolteachers were generally more competent. Northeast France (north of a line linking St. Malo to Geneva) was ahead of the rest of the country, where a "school desert" was often to be found. Faster progress took place in the southeast than in the southwest. Nevertheless, in France (excluding the central and northwestern regions, Vendée, and Bretagne) during the period 1871–75, 80 percent to 90 percent of registered young soldiers could read and write. As early as 1827–29 more than 70 percent of them could read and write in the Rhône districts, most of the eastern districts, and in the area extending from Orléans to Calais.

However, the poverty of workers, child labor in manufacturing, and unsatisfactory school facilities explain why few workers' children achieved secondary schooling. The great majority of them attended school for only two or three years; historians have noted the frequent reluctance of parents to send children to school. Only a very small percentage of children from workers' families entered higher schools or colleges. When they did, such an advance of the workers' "elite" often led them to leave their original social class; moreover, the movement of "mutual schools," in which most advanced pupils were required to help the teacher by taking charge of a small group of younger pupils, helped develop an elite among the working-class pupils themselves. "We should not be surprised," writes Georges Duveau, "to meet in union halls, in public meetings,

13   *Ibid.,* p. 105.
14   *Ibid.,* p. 385.

or in the meetings of the International many workers who look like teachers."[15]

These facts should be related to the early importance of political propaganda, political organization, and militancy. In explaining how the Republican party directed itself more and more toward the workers, Dolléans and Dehove insist on the part played very early by reading and lecturing. For example, "In 1833, in three months time six million leaflets were printed. Lectures were organized by the Association for Independent and Free Education of the People (*Association pour l'instruction libre et gratuite du peuple*); 2,500 workers followed 46 lectures in July 1833."[16] When Guesde came on the scene in 1880 and Marxist ideas began to spread, the working classes had long been educated in political ideas. This training had been mainly oriented toward progress and republican socialism, against conservatism and authority, but with a strong accent on liberty and liberalism.

THE SPREADING OF UNION PRACTICES AND THE CHOICE OF WEAPONS

With such socioeconomic status and such an ideological basis, how did the working class choose between economic and political weapons before World War I?

General voting rights had been obtained, and political action could be expressed either through voting power and political participation or through violence. It should be noted that violence in strikes, when specifically trade union in nature (professional), is classified among economic rather than political actions. Economic action could be carried on through the formation of associations, bargaining, and striking.

Social history often makes it difficult to disentangle the nature of weapons and that of objectives. However, even if political action was important throughout this period, it seems that economic action dominated the daily practice of the workers' life. But, as we shall see, the early development of political institutions involved in labor questions made it impossible to isolate completely the one from the other.

15 Georges Duveau, *La Vie ouvière en France sous le Second Empire* (Paris: Gallimard, 1946), p. 451.

16 E. Dolléans and G. Dehove, *Histoire du travail en France,* I (Paris: Domat-Montchrestien, 1953), pp. 194ff.

Objectives and Weapons of Earlier Associations

Collective economic action has existed for a long time in France. Maxim Leroy in his *La Coutume ouvrière* has studied, on the basis of workers' papers and associations' constitutions, numerous union rules founded upon long traditions. Among unionists' duties are "the duty to follow the union tariff, not to work on piece-rates, not to perform work at home, to report cases of violation of union rules, to bring to the union all professional demands . . . to limit births . . . and . . . the hours worked, to inform the union before deciding on a strike . . . etc."

"Sometimes," he writes, "mutual societies departed from their legal status and became fighting trade union ('professional') organizations against employers, as in Lyon, during the revolutionary battles of 1831–1834. But when mutual societies did not exist, others were founded, bereft of any legal basis, almost without constitution and in spite of laws prohibiting any workers' associations."[17] Although organizations specifically union in nature date back only to the workers' movement founded by the Workers' International Association (1865), these organizations inherited their rules and forms from much older structures.[18]

The reports of the government's Office du Travail make it possible to distinguish before 1884 or even 1864 the traditional craft associations (i.e., jewelers, woodworkers) from the associations in the new industries of coal and iron, and in textiles.[19] These reports, written by workers or drawn from their memories, clearly show not only that mutual societies dealt with problems of wages, employment, and hours but also that associations of very different kinds, and often of very short lives, appeared when conflicts arose and disappeared when they were settled. Finally, they show that some bargaining, at least of a tentative nature, took place frequently. Such was probably the case very often before World War I. Unionism was frequently a latent phenomenon and the strike a substitute for regular bargaining. According to the model of the modern Anglo-American theory of collective bargaining, the strike is either a breach of contract or the basis for a new one. Instead, an observation of facts will often show, at least in some continental countries of Europe, that the real terms and conditions of work are not specified by contract, and that their modifications are gen-

17　Maxim Leroy, *La Coutume ouvrière* (Paris: Giard, 1913), p. 42.
18　*Ibid.,* p. 45.
19　Office du Travail, *Les Associations professionelles ouvrières* (Paris, 1901).

erally due to the occurrence of strikes rather than to the normal termination of contract and the reopening of bargaining, as is the custom in Anglo-American countries.[20]

Contracting, defined as an encounter between two actors who agree to compromise, frequently occurred only by way of strikes. In many instances found in the reports of the Office du Travail, when an agreement was concluded or demands were satisfied after a strike, pre-agreement conditions (lower wages, longer hours) were often reestablished as soon as unemployment reappeared or as soon as the risk of strike disappeared.

Such behavior needs explanation. First of all, the workers' intentions to bargain on wages and conditions were firmly established in France. In mutual societies or other associations, as soon as wages were expected to be or had been effectively lowered, or when there was hope of stabilizing them at a satisfactory level, some action, often peaceful, was planned. We find such examples in the textiles of Lyon after the 1789 revolution, in 1817–18,[21] in the Limoges porcelain industry in 1833,[22] among the weavers of Vienne (Rhône) in 1861 (where machine weaving had been substituted for hand weaving and workers expected wage reductions, against which they decided to organize with a strike fund, established in 1865). This last was a secret society, without formal constitution, under the direction of a committee receiving the dues. Twelve hundred workers joined. Many meetings were held to prepare a revision of rates and, in February, 1867, a letter was sent to the employers to ask them for a wage increase. Without any answer from them the workers decided to strike. After five weeks a compromise was obtained. In January, 1868, a new strike occurred among the weavers; it ended in April with a new tariff and a new piece-rate system.

Among miners, long before the well-known "Arras bargain" (1891), associations and mutual societies tried to influence work and wage conditions. In Anzin in 1824 and 1830 strikes were opposed to rate reductions. Riots occurred in 1833; workers were arrested but released by the court.[23] From 1880 to 1890, many additional bargaining attempts by workers may also be found in the Office du Travail reports and in a study by Jean Néré.[24]

20   G. Giugni, "L'Autonno caldo," *Il Mulino*, 1970, p. 27.
21   Office du Travail, *Les Associations*, II, pp. 242–44.
22   *Ibid.*, p. 523.
23   *Ibid.*, I, pp. 373–74.
24   J. Néré, "Aspect du déroulement des grèves en France durant la periode 1883–1889," *Revue d'histoire économique et sociale*, 1956, no. 3, pp. 282–302.

The State Actor

From the observation of all these actions emerges a very important fact which appears repeatedly: the efforts of workers to bargain with employers often evoke the intervention (either on their behalf or not) of a third actor: the prefect, the inspector of labor, the mayor, or the local deputy to the National Assembly. Néré writes in this respect: "Public authorities intervene in many strikes under different forms and conditions." Of course, such public action is often favorable to employers, but "in fact, the permanent preoccupation of the prefects is to protect the industrial prosperity of their district, not only by controlling strikes but also by trying to find as satisfactory a solution as possible. Some of them have, of course, a very conservative bias and are very cautious towards workers' demands."[25] But many of them, especially in those districts where industry is fairly well developed, pay close attention to workers' conditions. "Whatever may be their own ideas or political inclinations, all try to bring the parties to a compromise, either by facilitating negotiations or—very often—by conducting them themselves. Not infrequently they are invited to engage in such action by the workers themselves."[26]

The prefect or the inspector of labor often played a part in matters of wages. Where working conditions were at stake, the workers would often turn to the deputy or the mayor. Sometimes they even tried to influence the legislators' action, as in the following example. In 1862 the Paris leatherworkers' association declared: "As the employers intend to return to the eleven-hour day of labor in winter, we ask that the working day be definitely fixed at ten hours by law." In 1865 the miners of Gier tried to get certain pits reopened. The local union federation sent one of its members to the Assembly in Paris.

A systematic study of all the facts would demonstrate not only the great activity of workers' associations in economic matters, but also the great difficulties which they encountered in establishing peaceful bargaining with their employers. Those facts put into light what is probably a specific trait of the French industrial relations system of those times, and one which is perhaps still valid: the systematic intervention of state or public authorities. Of course,

25 For example, in 1884, in the textile industry of Lyon, the prefect admonished the inspector of labor (*inspecteur du travail*) for having incited workers to resistance; *ibid.*, p. 298.
26 *Ibid.*, p. 296.

police or troop interventions are not specifically French. In every country such interventions have occurred frequently. But public intervention in order to invite the employers to bargain or to improve wages or conditions has probably been more frequent in France than anywhere else. From this point of view, the great conflicts, riots, and general strikes which often occupy the historian's center stage do not give the whole story. We should not overlook the many ordinary conflicts which public authorities tried to end by compromise. Such a situation creates its own logic, especially from the employers' side: with a public actor always in the wings, whose action works sometimes in favor of the employers and sometimes for the workers, according to the government's interests of the moment, it always pays to await the workers' (or government's) initiative.

Foundation of the Industrial Relations System

A pattern of strategies tended to establish itself. Workers showed great interest in economic action, but a link had to be established between willingness to act and effective bargaining. In fact, the link was often the intervention of state authorities.

Such a situation stresses the importance of the distinction between objectives and weapons. The objective is mainly economic, but economic action leads necessarily to political intervention and, through this, to political action. The importance of public opinion and of pressures on the public authorities is emphasized by Néré.[27] This kind of action is generally quite independent of political objectives. Its form, insofar as it may be termed political, does not so much result from the ideological orientation of the workers—although such orientations may accompany it and are in fact often denounced by prefects and police officers, even as early as in the 1830's—as from the structure of political power—centralized in Paris but reaching directly and actively into the detailed affairs of every community.

It may be said that in France until 1914 economic objectives were aimed at by workers, both through economic and political action, this last one being largely a result of the political organization of the state. For the workers, no choice between the two kinds of weapons was open. Economic action for economic objectives cannot help without some measure of political action. Political action in the form of riots and violence (instead of simple

27 Néré shows that in many cases of strikes leading to unemployment, shopkeepers were very sympathetic to the workers.

pressures on political authorities) also took place, but probably no more than in other countries. The state itself, by its very organization, tends to politicize every economic action. But the existence of other elements of politicization cannot be denied. Dolléans and Dehove, for example, having described the anti-worker reaction which succeeded the revolutionary events of 1830, observe that "after the days of 1830, they [the workers] became aware of the importance of the role they had just played. They understood that they had been necessary, that without them Charles X would still be there. The bourgeois newspapers recognized [these facts]. The Parisian workers derived from this a strong spirit of pride, to the point of imagining that the political destiny of the country was in their hands."

Later, after recalling the development of Republican propaganda between 1830 and 1848, the socialist experiences of the Second Republic (February–June, 1848), and the new anti-worker reaction that put an end to it, the authors write: "A sudden thrust, a rapid rise of the workers on the social scene [the Second Republic], was nothing but a bonfire followed by a reaction which was the more implacable as the fears of the bourgeoisie had become stronger. . . . Thus, the political evolution appears clearly to us as a determining factor in the birth and development of the labor movement. . . ."[28]

We have already called attention to Dolleans and Dehove's comments about the early and rapidly growing importance of workers' papers and leaflets, and to the active propaganda not only of worker militants but also of radical and socialist leaders. But often political and economic action and demands appear to have been complementary. Most workers' "brochures" (by Grignon, Leroux, Efrahem, and Louis Blanc) at the same time insisted upon the "class feeling, need for professional organization, willingness of class community for positive action."[29] Until the 1880's nonrecognition of union rights and the risk of strike action more often than not pushed to riots and violence, but until World War I political and economic action were intertwined by way of the intervention of public authorities.

At the same time the early progress of republicanism and socialism in vote-gathering, and especially in Parliament, helped develop confidence in the efficiency of legislative action. Calling on Parliament remains even today a specific trait of the system of industrial

28   Dolléans and Dehove, *Histoire du travail*, p. 209.
29   *Ibid.*, pp. 216–17.

relations in France. Calling in local authorities has probably diminished in frequency, owing to the development of centralized unions and collective bargaining institutions.

More than any other factor, the early centralization of the state explains the important part played, even before World War I, by public authorities and the use of political weapons for economic objectives. This tends to qualify the process described by Sturmthal. Economic *objectives* seem to have been dominant in the workers' movement before 1914, but their *action* seems to have been as much political as economic. The early conquest of political rights, coupled with the early development of a centralized but wide-ranging state organization, have been the main factors, according to this analysis; but in order to evaluate the part played by labor market forces, it is now necessary to turn to the study of economic factors.

THE COMBINATION OF ECONOMIC
AND POLITICAL FACTORS

According to Sturmthal, when a surplus of unskilled labor prevails, skilled workers tend to organize in craft unions as long as unskilled workers fail to have effective power in collective bargaining. However, if civic inequality and class society predominate, it may be that the advantage to be obtained from political action, even for skilled workers, carries more weight than the economic advantages to be gained from craft unionism.

If the labor surplus is small, as in the French case, economic action through industrial unionism should rapidly appear; this occurred, in fact. But broad-based industrial unionism favors political action. This relationship between the tendency toward industrial unionism (or an organization of the whole working class) and the tendency toward political action is characteristic of the French situation.

The Role of Economic Factors in the Size and the Wages of the Industrial Working Class

During the period under consideration industrial overpopulation was felt only during crisis years, in the occurrence of heavy urban unemployment. Some evidence of this general labor market tightness can be seen in the absorption of foreign workers. Popular feeling against such workers has existed in France, as in other countries; during the crisis of 1848, the republican government (invoking the Revolutionary principles of liberty) issued a proclamation inviting workers to moderate their hostile feelings toward foreigners. Despite such animosity the number of foreigners grew, whereas the local labor force remained quite stable (Table 4). The

Table 4. Total Working-Age (15–69) Population Compared with All Foreign Persons Residing in France

	1851	1861	1876	1881	1901	1911	1921	1931
Total working-age population (millions)	24.7	25.8	25.2	25.6	26.5	27.1	27.8	29.4
All foreign persons (thousands)	280	500	800	1,000	1,000	1,160	1,500	2,700

SOURCE: Line 1—J. C. Toutain, "La Population de la France de 1700 à 1959," *Cahiers de l'Institut de Science économique appliquée*, January, 1963, Supplément no. 133, Série AF, no. 3 (ISEA, Paris), p. 123. Line 2—*Annuaire Statistique de la France*, 1966, pp. 61–62.

absolute numbers of these workers may be less important than their relationship to the degree of tightness in the labor market. Thus there is no net inflow during the years of economic slack at the end of the nineteenth century.

Further evidence for our hypothesis is seen in the pattern of migration from rural areas. According to the infinite elasticity of labor supply hypothesis, as formulated by W. A. Lewis, working conditions and income levels in rural areas do not alter the rural-industrial wage differentials; these differentials represent only the excess of cost of living conditions in urban over rural areas. Although such a hypothesis, developed for underdeveloped countries, is not perfectly applicable to the beginnings of European industrialization, it can nevertheless be used as an indirect means of evaluation, to measure the effect of the elasticity of labor supply on wages. In France from 1850 to 1890 industrial wages rose relative to agricultural wages, and interregional differentials increased for agricultural wages.[30] After 1890 industrial wages decreased relative to agricultural wages, while inter-regional differentials of agricultural wages diminished as well.

In the earlier period, according to Goreux, the distance between emigration and development centers was the determining factor. Migration was limited, and the needs of industrial manpower were barely met. Low agricultural wages had little influence on industrial

30   L. M. Goreux, "Les Migrations agricoles en France depuis un siècle et leur relation avec certains facteurs économiques," in *Etudes et conjoncture*, 1956, no. 4, p. 327.

wages. In the second period general economic progress, and especially industrial efficiency, positively influenced agricultural wages. We might add that agricultural protection measures adopted at that time may also have had an effect.

The Goreux statistical model does not confirm any hypothesis of pressure from the subsistence sector on wages of the industrial sector. Perhaps industrial manpower has been relatively more scarce in France than elsewhere, in particular because emigration from rural areas has always been relatively slow.[31] Under such conditions, the problem of choice between the use of political action (to promote laws economically favoring the working class) and economic action of the craft union kind (to protect skilled workers against the masses of unskilled) was not as vital as in other countries. Perhaps the lack of population pressure on labor markets permitted the workers' movement to pursue simultaneously the objective of common political advantages for the whole working class and the economic defense of craft as well as industry people.

The Effect of Economic and Political Factors on the Structure of the Working Class

However, two special factors ought to be added as important elements in the evolution of the French labor movement: rapid decline of differentials between skilled and unskilled wages, and the early development of political ideas among workers' leaders.

Craft workers in small industry had the oldest traditions of economic action through associations, strikes, apprenticeship control, etc. This action permitted them to benefit for some time from much higher wages than the workers of the new industries. But quite early these differentials were reduced, and traditionally well-off skilled workers began to lose their economic advantage.[32] From 1830 to 1848 wages increased much more for unskilled or semi-skilled than for skilled workers.[33] From 1845 to 1865 this movement continued, especially in favor of textile and metal workers; however, mine workers in rural areas were at a disadvantage in this evolution.

Wages of the least-paid occupations in 1864 climbed to the

31 G. Dupeux, *La Société française 1789–1960* (Paris: Colin, 1964), pp. 22.
32 G. Weill, "Le Rôle des facteurs structurels dans l'évolution des rénumérations salariales au XIXᵉ siècle," *Revue Economique*, March, 1959, pp. 236–63. My data are drawn from "Statistiques des prix et des salaires en France" (Paris: Imprimerie Nationale, 1864), and from inquiries of the Office du Travail collected in the past from employees.
33 J. Vuillemin, "Les Syndicats ouvrièrs et les salaires," *Economie Appliquée*, ISEA, 1952, pp. 262–336. See also Weill, "Le Rôle," p. 250.

average wage of that time by 1896, and the workers of the new industries were on the same level as the workers of the well-paid traditional crafts. The compression of wage structure suggests that craft unionism had lost its economic efficacy while the leveling of differentials profoundly changed the social structure of the working class.

Some other evidence of this transition can be seen in data for the building trades in France, as compared with Great Britain and the United States. These figures take advantage of the relative stability of the work involved until World War I, and the fact that building jobs were quite similar in the three countries. The data of Chart 1 show that the decline in differentials came earlier, was

Chart 1. Average Relative Wages of Skilled to Unskilled in France, Great Britain, and United States—Building Trades

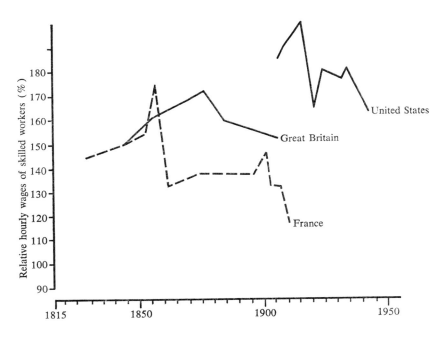

Source: E. H. Phelps Brown and Sheila Hopkins, "Seven Centuries of Building Wages," *Economica*, August, 1955, p. 195; Table I, p. 205. For Great Britain, the line has been drawn through the middle of the lines representing the average relative wage of each period according to Table I in the Phelps Brown–Hopkins paper. M. Parodi, *Croissance économique et nivellement hiérarchique des salaires ouvrièrs* (Paris: Riviere, 1962), p. 24. Harry Ober, "Occupational Wage Differentials, 1907–1947," *Monthly Labor Review*, August, 1948, p. 130.

more rapid, and reduced differentials the most in France. Moreover, for the period where most of the change occurred (1856–62), the compression of differentials is due entirely to a rise in unskilled wages (see Table 5).

Table 5. Average Hourly Wages (in francs and centimes)

	Skilled (macon)	Unskilled (terrassier)	$\frac{\text{Skilled}}{\text{Unskilled}} \times 100$
1852	0.43	0.28	150
1856	0.53	0.30	177
1862	0.53	0.40	137
1873	0.55	0.40	137
1906	0.80	0.60	133

SOURCE: Statistiques des Conseils de Prudhommes in *Annuaire Statistique de la France*, 1956, 2e partie, p. 60, or *Annuaire Statistique de la France*, 1961, p. 422.

However, the flow of semi-skilled and unskilled people to the new concentrated industries changed this social structure less rapidly in Paris, where small craft industries predominated until World War I, than in towns or regions of a dominant single industry (textiles in Lyon, and in the north) or in the developing metal industry regions of the center or the Rhone Valley. Nevertheless, sooner or later the old working-class elite was no longer economically advantaged everywhere.

It is thus perhaps true that the aversion against the class society takes the lead relative to the economic advantages which could be obtained by a small part of the working class. This aversion has been enhanced, among the older elite, by the process of "proletarianization"[34] of the skilled workers, resulting from the relative rises in wages of the unskilled. We can probably find here the very roots of the formation of the industrial working class and of class consciousness. Mass unionism became the only rational type of action as soon as high differentials had been lowered by a general scarcity of labor. But after the rapid destruction of the basis of craft unionism many militant and well-educated workers remained and became the leaders of the new mass unionism. However, because of its very diversity this old elite in a new movement sowed the seeds of terrible divisions.

Early general education, early political life, and strong traditions of workers' associations led to a proliferation of ideas and ideals,

34 Weill, "Le Rôle," p. 250.

and to a similar proliferation of workers' leaders. At the very time (1895) when the French workers' movement was uniting into one large organization, the CGT, the divisions continued to be as strong as ever. They have given rise to a great need for unity among rank and file workers. The foundation of the local union confederations (*bourses du travail*) and of the CGT itself were the two union responses to this demand.

Both of these responses were rather superficial, however. Paradoxically, some of the most ideologically oriented leaders, the anarchists, were the first (1894) to launch the motto "No Politics in Unions," as J. Maitron reports.[35] In 1898 no less than five socialist groups or parties were competing for the workers' support. Facing these divisions, Pelloutier asked with some success not only for the unification of the movement by way of local union confederations (Labor Chambers), but also for its centralization as a means of providing efficiency, although he himself was anarchist-oriented. But at the Congress of Amiens (1906) only an appearance of unity was established; in the end, it turned against him and against the anarcho-syndicalists. French labor, deprived of the opportunity for genuine union action by constant state intervention and the weak bargaining propensity of employers, but rich in unemployed leaders of high intellectual value, was inclined toward political action for both economic and political objectives.

The Political Way to "Unity"

Jules Guesde had already stressed the importance of political propaganda instead of the "confusion and pluralism" which was visible in workers' meetings.[36] After all, divisions among leaders were more easily hidden in electoral struggles, where the objective is simple and the enemy clearly defined, than in union meetings. Socialist successes at the 1896 municipal elections (Lille, Roubaix, Marseille, and in many small towns) led to the conclusion that workers had greater capacity to build a united political force in Parliament than to build a really united unionism among themselves. The importance traditionally given to law and to political pressure on public authorities reinforced such a belief.

The great changes brought about by World War I accentuated these tendencies. First, Paris itself became a great industrial city,

35   J. Maitron, *Histoire du mouvement anarchiste en France, 1880–1914* (Paris: Société Universitaire d'Editions et de Librarie, 1951), pp. 284ff.

36   Cf. Claude Willard, *Le Mouvement socialiste en France: Les Guesdistes* (Paris: Editions Sociales, 1966), pp. 219ff.

with vast modern plants which it had lacked before.[37] Second, the political division resulting from the war and from the emergence of Soviet power definitely prevented any effort toward durable unity. The leading place of craft unionism had, even before the war, disappeared in favor of industrial unionism. After the war this form of organization became dominant in every respect. It might have been possible for industrial organizations to have promoted collective bargaining. But two factors induced a counter-effect: first, the vast scope of labor legislation deprived collective bargaining at the industry level of many of its advantages; second, employers and governments—even those most favorable to the workers—were too afraid of revolutionary ideologies, and of the development of a decentralized union movement at the plant level, to encourage effective unionization at that level. But only in the plants could collective negotiations have appeared advantageous to workers.

Thus the unsatisfied need of the rank and file workers for unity in the labor movement, along with the obstacles they faced to the attainment of economic objectives through union action, necessarily led to the emergence of a strong political organization of workers.

This need for a united direction and a centralized organization explains, at least in part, the attraction toward and the success of the Communist party. The belief that political action of the whole working class is more efficient than the economic advantages which could be obtained by a small part of the working class, which stems from an orientation toward broad social action, added to the Party's success.

But it is difficult to say whether the aversion to class society helped determine such action, or whether this class consciousness is the result of the long-felt efficacy of political action. Parliamentary or governmental intervention, pushed by the workers' political and economic actions, has produced important results, both in the field of social security and, more recently, in the field of employment stability.

CONCLUSION

The French case illustrates a combination of strong aversion to class society (resulting from the simultaneous existence of the Revolutionary ideals of 1789 and an autocratic and hierarchical

37 A. Kriegel, *Aux origines du communisme français, 1914–1920* (The Hague: Mouton, 1964).

society) and relatively tight labor markets (resulting from the early decline of birth rates and pervasive agricultural protectionism). This last factor should have helped general collective bargaining to develop. And it seems, in fact, that such development did take place rather early, with a predominance of economic conflicts. But two main events reversed this trend.

First, there was ubiquitous expansion of state power, represented in each of the ninety departments by a prefect, nominated and strictly controlled by the central government, in charge of all political and administrative affairs. Every social conflict which might have led to political unrest was immediately arbitrated.

Second, following from the relative tightness of labor markets, craft and skilled workers lost their economic advantages rather early. Perhaps such advantages could have been maintained longer than they were through some sort of craft unionism. But the political radicalism of the skilled workers' elite—reinforced by the prevalence of a class society and by the strength of right-wing forces in parliamentary life—led them to consider unionism as a means of diffusion of political ideals, as well as of general economic defense.

Perhaps a better case for an investigation of the conditions giving rise to an emphasis on collective bargaining or on political action is one in which aversion to class society is combined with a large manpower surplus, flowing to industry in the main period of industrialization. Even so, we must explain why craft unionism lost its vigor so early in France. The answer may lie in the strength, in the minds of the workers' elite, of the ideals of the French Revolution, maintained until the political victory of the Republican party some one hundred years later.

Peter Lösche

Stages in the Evolution
of the German Labor Movement

CAN WE IMPOSE some order upon the apparent chaos of various types of labor movements that have appeared on the stage of history?[1] Here I will try to apply the model outlined in the introductory chapter to German labor history.[2] The objective of such a model is to indicate the key variables that must be examined in an analysis of labor history and in a prediction of labor behavior. In principle such a model is intended to be universal in its geographic scope and in its application over time. However, this paper deals only with the German labor movement; furthermore, it excludes labor's experience in the German Democratic Republic (East Germany) and in the Third Reich. Quite obviously the model is applicable only to capitalist countries with a certain amount of freedom fundamental for the development of at least a relatively autonomous labor movement. Independent labor organizations were suppressed under Nazi and Stalinist dictatorships.

Four independent variables are investigated: the pattern of labor objectives, the long-term situation on the labor market, the structure of the labor force, and international migration of ideas and models. Two dependent variables are emphasized: economic and political action. In this context a general methodological remark must be made. Here I am dealing not with a model, but at most with

1 Adolf Sturmthal, "Economic Development and the Labour Movement," in Arthur M. Ross, ed., *Industrial Relations and Economic Development* (London: Macmillan, 1966), p. 165.
2 *Ibid.*, p. 169.

a scheme of key variables, or even more clearly with some fundamental conditions of labor history. Key variables would have to be defined more precisely by concrete criteria, and determined empirically, if possible, in order to be operational. The "migration of ideas" factor, for example the influence of German Social Democracy on the American labor movement, could be quantified through a content analysis of programmatic declarations and speeches of labor leaders and through the position and frequency of (German emigrant) socialists in the labor hierarchy. Furthermore, within a model the significance of each variable for a labor movement would have to be defined, as well as the importance of other variables which were excluded from the model for the sake of structural analysis. At this point the methodological approach of applying a model might become questionable, and one could ask whether or not the traditional way of developing a typology of labor history might be more comprehensive. In this paper these methodological considerations will be set aside and the different variables will be examined.

Look at the confusing use of terms like "political weapons" and "economic weapons" in the labor movement and in its literature. This confusing use of language is a consequence of the problem itself. Even if it were possible to distinguish both terms in an abstract and formal way, to differentiate between them in social reality is impossible. It is almost too banal to state that all economic decisions will have political effects and that, conversely, all political acts imply an economic importance. Theoretically, collective bargaining could result in the redistribution of income and, possibly, wealth in a given society, almost automatically changing its social structure as well as its political system. However, a redistribution of wealth could take place by political means, through legislative or administrative measures or through revolution. The formal separation of the terms "political" and "economic" threatens to result in a one-dimensional analysis.

Still, a model in which economic and political action would be determined in their historical and social dimensions would be operational. "Political action" refers to activities which are designed to influence legislation or administration, including the weapons of voting power, persuasion, lobbying, rebellion, and violence. "Economic action" means collective bargaining or, in some peculiar situations, the simple use of collective negotiations—in other words, the use of power on the labor market. "Labor movement" embraces various types of organizations, parties as well as trade unions and, in the German case, cultural organizations. Of course, this scheme must be seen against the background of German economic development, one aspect of which is the progressive rise in the capital-labor ratio.[3]

Historically, the development of organized labor in Germany[4] generally follows the continental European pattern:[5] in the nineteenth century equal political rights, participation in decision-making in political, economic, and social life, social recognition, and access to educational facilities for workers comprised the main demands of the Socialist and, to a lesser degree, the Christian labor movement. At the same time higher wages, better working conditions, and social security were demands dominated by the more political objectives. The more organized labor gained in political power and social status, and the more educational institutions were opened for workers (although even today German high schools and universities are quite hostile to workers' children), the more important economic demands and collective bargaining became. Nevertheless, in the Weimar Republic not only the parties of the Socialist labor movement (Social Democratic party, SPD; Independent Social Democratic party, USPD; Communist party, KPD) but the Free Trade Union Federation (ADGB) as well, intended a fundamental change of the capitalistic system, to judge by their stated claims. Yet, in spite of its ideological stand, organized labor did not develop the strategy and tactics of radical social change. Even today in the Federal Republic the German Trade Union Federation (DGB), a merger of the Social Democratic, liberal, and Christian unions that had existed in the Weimar Republic, regards

3   For definitions and objectives of the model, see *ibid.,* pp. 167–69.

4   The amount of literature on German labor history is growing steadily. For the best introduction, see Helga Grebing, *Geschichte der deutschen Arbeiterbewegung: Ein Überblick* (Munich, 1966). This book will be available in English soon. Written from a critical point of view are Wolfgang Abendroth, *Aufstieg und Krise der deutschen Sozialdemokratie* (Frankfurt, 1964), and *Sozialgeschichte der europäischen Arbeiterbewegung* (Frankfurt, 1965). Containing a multitude of facts but, as a semi-official Communist publication, biased and therefore to be used with critical distance: Institut für Marxismus-Leninismus beim ZK der SED, *Geschichte der deutschen Arbeiterbewegung,* 8 vols. (Berlin, 1965–66). Excellent for facts and data: Franz Osteroth and Dieter Schuster, *Chronik der deutschen Sozialdemokratie* (Hannover, 1963), and Institut für Marxismus-Leninismus beim ZK der SED, *Geschichte der deutschen Arbeiterbewegung: Chronik,* 3 vols. (Berlin, 1965–67). For information on research in progress and on archival holdings in regard to German labor history, see *Internationale wissenschaftliche Korrespondenz zur Geischichte der deutschen Arbeiterbewegung,* ed. Historische Kommission zu Berlin since 1965.

5   Sturmthal, "Economic Development and the Labour Movement," pp. 169–70.

itself not only as an economic pressure group, but also as a political organization.

The experience of the DGB merits mention here. It is difficult to say whether in the eyes of its leading officers the federation is more an organ for political battle or an economic interest group. Since its founding in 1949 the DGB has on several occasions intervened actively in political issues: it opposed German rearmament, the arming of the federal army (Bundeswehr) with atomic weapons, and the emergency laws passed by the parliament (Bundestag) in 1968. In several instances the DGB participated in election campaigns, e.g., in 1953 by fighting for co-determination and a change of the Works' Constitution Law (Betriebsverfassungsgesetz). The industrial unions of the federation resisted the revival of right-wing parties in the early 1950's (the Socialist Reichs party, SRP under Remer) and in the late 1960's (National Democratic Party of Germany, NPD) much more strongly than did the democratic parties. Altogether, it sometimes seemed as if the DGB had taken over some of the functions of a political party and had transcended the role of a single-purpose movement. In the debate over the emergency laws some of the industrial unions, including the more radical IG Metall and the IG Chemie, participated in organizing the "extraparliamentary" opposition against the united front of the parties of the grand coalition, the Christian Democratic Union (CDU) and the SPD. Thus, not for the first time in German postwar history, the DGB found itself in opposition to the Social Democrats.

Since the 1950's this traditional party of the German labor movement tried to attract more electoral support from the lower and upper-middle classes by presenting itself as a "people's party" and no longer as a working-class party. The consequence was that such an "omnibus party" could no longer refer to a relatively homogenous social basis; it claimed to represent the unemployed as well as millionaires. After the adoption of the Godesberg reform program of 1959, the social composition of the party membership has come more and more to resemble the social structure of the Federal Republic, continuing developments which had started well before that year. Because of the competing social and economic interests within the party, its concept of social change became increasingly diffused and less committed to qualitative social reform. In contrast to the SPD, the DGB has a socially more homogenous membership. In terms of both its economic and its general political demands, the DGB has preserved more fully the traditions of the German labor movement than has the SPD, which today is a liberal party.

Although the political ambition of the Trade Union Federation may have been unduly stressed here, there is no doubt that German trade unions—compared to their sister organizations in non-Communist industrial countries (perhaps with the exception of Italy and France)—are still to some extent political and do not resemble the bread-and-butter union type we know in other countries.[6] Why is this? This question can only be answered historically.

The first Socialist organizations not only emphasized equal political rights, social recognition of the workers, and access to educational facilities for labor; they were internationalist and aimed at achieving social, economic, and political equality for all mankind, realizing the full potential of man. One could say that German organized labor started off as a movement for universal emancipation. Marx formulated it this way: "In Germany, no brand of serfdom can be extirpated without extirpating every kind of serfdom. Fundamentally, Germany cannot be revolutionized without a revolution in its basis. The emancipation of Germans is the emancipation of mankind."[7] As an ideology, this demand for universal emancipation was transmitted in the different types of Marxist interpretation down to the end of the Weimar Republic, although it was never translated into a concrete strategy of labor.

The political orientation of German labor, more pronounced than that of most other national labor movements, can only be explained by its universal emancipatory origin. This is also the key to the analysis of DGB policies when compared to trade union federations of other nations. To be sure, the organizations of the German labor movement have by now relinquished their socialism, the verbalism of universal emancipatory demands—the SPD with its Godesberg Program of 1959, and the DGB with its program of

6   However, in historical German perspective there was continuous progress from a political to an economic pattern of labor objectives, also in the early 1950's. Thus it seems as if Hans Böckler, the president of the DGB from 1949 to 1951, finally obtained a truce agreement between the trade union federation and the federal government: he accepted German rearmament and the West integration of the Federal Republic; Chancellor Adenauer accepted co-determination in the steel industry and the coal mines. See Arnulf Baring, *Aussenpolitik in Adenauers Kanzlerdemokratie* (Munich and Vienna, 1969), pp. 193–204. For the failure of the post-war trade unions to bring about a fundamental change of the economic structure, see Eberhard Schmidt, *Die verhinderte Neuordnung: Zur Auseinandersetzung um die Demokratisierung der Wirtschaft in den westlichen Besatzungszonen und in der Bundesrepublik Deutschland* (Frankfurt, 1970).

7   Karl Marx, "A Criticism of the Hegelian Philosophy of Right," trans. by H. J. Stenning, *Selected Essays by Karl Marx* (New York, 1926), p. 38.

1963. The Godesberg Program contains no theoretical analysis of the present historical stage of social and economic development; in this respect it is different from its predecessors and contrary to all Marxist policies. It flatly states: "The Social Democratic Party . . . is a community of men holding different beliefs and ideas. Their agreement is based on the moral principles and political aims they have in common." Instead of analyzing the economic structure and aiming at its change, the program employs a slogan: "As much competition as possible—as much planning as necessary!" Finally, what was socialism before is reduced to a general liberal belief: "Freedom, justice, and solidarity, the mutual obligations which arise out of the common bonds [of men] are the basic values of socialism . . . socialism is a lasting task."[8] Similarly, the 1963 DGB program emphasizes the "inalienable rights of man, among them liberty and self-determination," and demands the realization of the Declaration of Human Rights adopted by the United Nations. However, some remnants of the former Socialist analysis of society survive; while the concentration of capital continues to grow, the DGB program states, the employees, who represent a majority of the population, are still excluded from ownership and control of the means of production. Therefore, for the DGB, co-determination is the key to social and economic change in order to enable more and more citizens to become participants both politically and economically, in the shops, factories, and offices.[9]

Socialist labor's departure from its original objectives, universal emancipatory demands, originated in the 1890's with the debate on Eduard Bernstein's revisionism, with the pragmatism of the Executive Council (Generalkommission) of the Free Trade Union Federation, and with the successes of the reformists in southern German local and state politics. This process continued during the Weimar Republic and came to conclusion in 1969, when a liberal SPD, having dropped all concepts of fundamental social reform,

8 Translations of the Godesberg Program are taken from Douglas A. Chalmers, *The Social Democratic Party of Germany: From Working Class Movement to Modern Political Party* (New Haven, 1964), pp. 67, 85, 87. For further readings on the post-war SPD, see David Childs, *From Schumacher to Brandt: The Story of German Socialism 1945–1965* (Oxford, 1966); Harold Kent Schellenger, Jr., *The SPD in the Bonn Republic: A Socialist Party Modernizes* (The Hague, 1968); and—criticizing the politics of the party—Theo Pirker, *Die SPD nach Hitler: Die Geschichte der SPD 1945–1964* (Munich, 1965). A semi-official interpretation of the Godesberg Program is given by Fritz Sanger, *Grundsatzprogram der SPD: Kommentar* (Berlin and Hannover, 1960).

9 For the full text, see Deutscher Gewerkschaftsbund, Bundesvorstand, *Grundsatzprogramm des DGB* (Dusseldorf, 1968).

elected a Socialist chancellor for the first time in the history of the Federal Republic.

The organizations of the German labor movement have passed through several phases on their way from rigid isolation from society and its political system to social and political integration. While it was their original goal to jump in one step from a state of total alienation in capitalist misery to socialism with its self-realization of the individual in society, such was not their actual itinerary. After gaining civil liberties and a parliamentary form of government in the revolution of 1918–19, the Social Democrats as well as the trade unionists restricted their political objectives to the necessities of the next day. The demand for the Socialist revolution (whatever one might have understood by this term) was maintained by the SPD and ADGB, the Free Trade Union Federation, in a declamatory and perfunctory manner throughout the Weimar Republic—but, especially in the trade union movement, economic objectives and demands for a better system of social security dominated its actions. It became obvious in these years that verbal demands and actual politics had been divorced, the result of a process which had begun earlier. While the ADGB in 1920 was still able to resist the right-wing Kapp Putsch, it was not strong enough to oppose the Nazis at the end of Weimar; instead it was prepared to dissolve its close connections with the SPD and to arrange a compromise with the NSDAP for the sake of organizational survival. The free trade unions as well as the liberal and Christian unions failed to defend the first German parliamentary democracy against its enemies. Because of the strong pressure of the free trade union federation, which rigidly opposed an unimportant change in the unemployment insurance system, the last democratic coalition government under the Social Democratic chancellor Hermann Müller had to resign in the spring of 1930; this paved the way for the autocratic regime of Brüning-Hindenburg. Shortly before the Nazis seized power, the president of the ADGB, Theodor Leipart, negotiated with General von Schleicher about a coalition of the army (Reichswehr) and trade unions against Hitler, accepting by implication the establishment of an authoritarian government in Germany.

The catastrophe of 1933 is the main reason why the political orientation of the German trade unions persisted to some degree after 1945. The foundation of the DGB was based deliberately upon the Socialist origins of the German labor movement; the capitalist society which had produced fascism had to be overcome.

In 1949 the first DGB convention adopted a program which de-manded the socialization of banks and key industries such as mining, steel, chemistry, and transportation. A planned economy was pro-posed. Democracy was not to be restricted to the political area but expanded to the economy.[10] As late as 1954, Victor Agartz, at that time chief economic theoretician of the DGB, convinced the trade union congress to adopt his policy of "union radicalism": the fundamental industries should be decentralized and run by organi-zations similar to workers' councils, and co-determination should be expanded by way of a general economic council for the Federal Republic.

Two years later, in 1956, Otto Brenner, president of the Metal-workers Industrial Union (IG Metall), made one last unsuccessful attempt to reorganize industry along more democratic lines by reviving the Agartz plan. These proposals for fundamental eco-nomic and social reform were not the exclusive property of former Socialists but were presented also by former liberal and Christian trade union leaders. The outstanding example among them was Jakob Kaiser, a business agent of the Christian trade union council in Nuremberg during the Weimar Republic and after World War II one of the founders of the Christian Democratic Union in Berlin, the party of Konrad Adenauer. Going back to the social teachings of the Catholic church, Kaiser proposed a "Christian socialism" which included the nationalization of some important industries as well as a planned economy.[11] The economic development of the Federal Republic and the international situation compelled DGB[12] and SPD to abandon their demands for fundamental social change. A last remnant of universal emancipatory hopes can sometimes still be felt at the bargaining table when one of the more radical unions endeavors to achieve a redistribution of wealth through collective bargaining in order to establish greater equality.

It is quite obvious that a large number of the workers in the

10   For an analysis of the DGB's inability to perform according to its own program, see Schmidt, *Die verhinderte Neuordnung*.

11   For Kaiser's Christian socialism, see Werner Conze, *Jakob Kaiser*, vol. 3: *Politiker zwischen Ost und West, 1945–1949* (Stuttgart, 1969).

12   Numerically, the DGB gained influence as an economic interest group because different political groups of the Weimar Republic were united in one union federation. Today it is quite obvious that the different political groupings within the DGB—among others, one group is tending more toward the Christian Democratic Union, another more toward the SPD—have to compromise already within the federation and therefore neutralize each other politically. This has accelerated the process in which economic demands increasingly prevail over political objectives.

shops are dissatisfied with the trade union leadership because the unions have not been able to deliver as they were expected to. Wildcat strikes in the fall of 1969 were directed not only against management, but against the unions as well. Thus a divergence in the attitudes and behavior of the rank and file in the shops and the national union leadership has emerged. While workers are frustrated by the dullness and emptiness of their jobs, their low wages compared to growing—and manipulated—needs, and the increasing importance of local issues, union leaders at the shop level do not take full account of these grievances. Moreover, national union leaders have not transformed these complaints into political action. They failed to use the pressure of their members in order to obtain legislation which could provide for improved nationwide working rules. Instead, they often remained concerned with the framework of traditional social security policies. The economic demands of the rank and file became more and more urgent. It appears inevitable that union leadership will emphasize these issues if it does not wish to lose support in the shops.[13]

The radical origin of organized labor as expressed in the formulation of a philosophy of universal emancipation explains what in a comparative view looks like an almost unique phenomenon of German labor history, one which does not appear in the typical bread-and-butter unions: the rise of a Socialist subculture. Against the Prussian state the Socialist labor movement created, so to speak, a counter-world of its own which permeated the daily life of the workers in all its aspects. Organizationally, this was expressed in all kinds of workers' sports clubs, the theater organization Freie Volksbühne, consumer cooperatives, special organizations for children, teenagers, and women, the free-thinker organizations (Freidenkerverband) which provided for funeral services of their members, hiking clubs, and many other organizations. Ideologically, the Social Democrats and Free Trade Unionists secluded themselves by promoting their own brand of Marxism, called Kautskyanism after its best-known theoretician, Karl Kautsky. An autonomous

---

13　I would even say that, because of the political activities and orientation of the trade union leadership, the economic interests of the rank and file have been neglected. The most striking example in this regard occurred when, in the recession of 1966–67, DGB leaders agreed to follow governmental wage guidelines (as part of the so-called concerted action which under the formerly Social Democratic minister of economics, Karl Schiller, was supposed to harmonize the different economic interest groups) in collective bargaining agreements, which ran for two or three years. In 1968–69 industry boomed and corporation profits went beyond any expectations, but the unions were bound to contracts; wildcat strikes resulted.

Socialist literature developed. From birth to death the party member was surrounded and absorbed by the organizations of the labor movement. The internationalism of the SPD and of other Socialist parties of the Second International was the extroverted face of this subculture.[14]

For the analysis of this phenomenon I suggest the following hypothesis: only labor movements which, for reasons to be discussed later, in their period of organization aimed at fundamental social change through political (in the German case, revolutionary) means, developed a Socialist subculture. The longer and the more intensely the objective of universal emancipation was preserved, the more colorful and diverse a network of cultural organizations developed, and the longer the Socialist subculture continued. Until the end of the Weimar Republic these organizations existed within the orbit of the Social Democratic party, and to a lesser degree even within the Christian trade union movement. Our hypothesis rests not only on evidence from German labor history. Quite similar to the German case, the labor movements of Austria-Hungary and later the successor states of the Habsburg Empire developed universal emancipatory objectives as well as a Socialist subculture. To a lesser degree this is also true for Italy and France. On the other hand, the more economically oriented British trade unions and the Labour party, and even more clearly the unideological American unions of the AFL or the CIO (which were politicized for a short period only), may have sometimes linked cultural or sports organizations to their movement, but they were never developed into a subculture.

The radical political origin of Socialist labor organizations also elucidates the division of German labor into different political and ideological organizations. The universal emancipatory demands of Socialist labor led them to exclude all groups which because of

14 For the subcultural element of German socialism, see Erich Matthias, "Kautsky und der Kautskyanismus," in *Marxismusstudien II* (Tubingen, 1957); Gerhard A. Ritter, *Die Arbeiterbewegung im Wilhelminischen Reich* (Berlin, 1959); Guenther Roth, *The Social Democrats in Imperial Germany* (Totowa, N.J., 1963); Peter Lösche, *Der Bolschewismus im Urteil der deutschen Sozialdemokratie 1903–1920* (Berlin, 1967), and "Arbeiterbewengung und Wilhelminismus: Sozialdemokratie zwischen Anpassung und Spaltung," in *Geschichte in Wissenschaft und Unterricht* 20 (1969); Hans-Josef Steinberg, *Marxismus und deutsche Sozialdemokratie* (Hannover, 1967). For data about Socialist organizations and publications, see Dieter Fricke, *Die deutsche Arbeiterbewegung 1869–1890* (Leipzig, 1964), and *Zur Organisation und Tatigkeit der deutschen Sozialdemokratie 1890–1914* (Leipzig, 1962).

their religious beliefs expected the final realization of their existence beyond our world (the Christian trade unions), or which in principle were opposed to political actions of organized labor (the Hirsch-Duncker trade union federation before 1914). Quite often anti-Socialism, the rejection of the concept and ideology of universal emancipation as put forward by the Socialists, was the only factor which the Christian trade unions had in common while they were organizationally weak and undecided as to which methods should be used to achieve their aims. A permanent struggle was carried on within the Christian trade union federation on the issue of decentralization within the federation, the autonomy of the individual union, and, among Catholics, whether or not Protestants should be admitted to the union.

Whereas no compromise was possible regarding ideological objectives, the different wings of organized labor agreed much more easily on some of their immediate political objectives: until 1930 the Catholics in the Christian trade union federation, the Hirsch-Duncker trade union federation, and the ADGB all supported the policies of the parties of the so-called Weimar coalition (the SPD, the Catholic Center party, and the Democratic party, DDP) with their emphasis on the defense of the parliamentary system of government, although at the same time sections of the Protestant wing of the Christian trade union federation and the conservative white-collar salaried employee union, Deutschnationaler Handlungsgehilfenverband (DHV), opposed the democratic system. The different organizations of the trade union movement corresponded to political parties:[15] the ADGB to the SPD; the Catholics in the Christian trade union federation to the Catholic Center party; the Protestants in the Christian trade union federation and the Hirsch-Dunckersche trade unionists to the German Democratic party; and, toward the end of the Weimar Republic, the Communist trade union opposition to the KPD, and to some degree the DHV to the NSDAP. This symbiosis between trade unions and parties was paralleled to some extent by a similar relationship of employers'

15   For the representation of union members and officers in the Reichstag (the German lower house), see Max Schwarz, *MdR, Biographisches Handbuch der deutschen Reichstage* (Hannover, 1965). It is an indication of the impact of the Socialist subculture that up to 1933 almost all members of the Social Democratic Reichstag faction were members of one or the other union affiliated with the Free Trade Union Federation. In the Weimar Republic, the most powerful group in the Social Democratic faction of the Prussian Diet was the trade union officers. Even today most of the SPD Bundestag members have union cards in their pockets.

organizations to liberal—in the European meaning of the word—and conservative parties.[16]

The economic interests and objectives of the different trade union federations were almost identical; collective bargaining agreements were negotiated and signed jointly, and social legislation was influenced in a common effort. The German labor movement was thus divided on ideological grounds. Politically the labor organizations were spilt into opposing camps; yet economically they were bound together by the same interests.

The second variable of the scheme, the long-term situation in the labor market, can be applied without modification to German labor history. We are dealing here with one of the most important factors when analyzing the change of German labor organizations from a movement for universal emancipation to a pragmatic, mainly economic, institution. However, we want to underline that the pace of this change depends not only on economic determinants, but on ideological and political ones as well.

The German labor movement was organized in a period of excess supply of labor. In the last decade of the nineteenth century it entered a phase where the excess was absorbed. For the Federal Republic (i.e., the period since World War II) a third phase can be added, a period of extreme labor scarcity. The first period, lasting approximately to 1887, is characterized by rapid industrialization and excess supply of labor. Industrialization started in the 1830's and was accelerated by the following factors: the Prussian-dominated German Customs Union of 1834, protective tariffs and uniform Germany-wide laws of trade and exchange, the publicly supported extension of the transportation system (especially railroads), and the important political and economic implications of the founding of the new Reich in 1871. Factors contributing to the excess supply of labor were rapid population growth of 38.7 percent between 1818 and 1845, free trade for handicrafts resulting in the pauperization of masters and journeymen, emancipation of peasants, the declining branch of the Kondratieff cycle, the movement of farm workers from the east into the industrial centers in the west after 1871, long working hours, and the employment of women and children. Wages remained stagnant in this phase. It was in this

---

16 Because of this relationship analysts of the German party system have labeled the political parties agents of economic interest groups. See Ernst Fraenkel, *Deutschland und die westlichen Demokratien*, 3rd rev. ed. (Stuttgart, 1968); and Dieter Grosser, *Vom monarchischen Konstitutionalismus zur parlamentarischen Demokratie* (The Hague, 1970).

period that the first political labor organizations—Stefan Born's Workers Brotherhood, the two Socialist parties of the followers of Marx and Ferdinand Lassalle, and finally the Socialist Workers party, the predecessor of the SPD—were founded. They antedated the founding of German trade unions. In the trade unions at first only skilled workers (e.g., printers and cigar-makers) were organized.[17]

In the second period, from 1887–95 to 1933, industrialization was quickened by World War I and then retarded by the Great Depression during the last years of the Weimar Republic. Between 1887 and 1914, the rate of unemployment never significantly exceeded 2 percent. In addition to increased industrialization, the reasons for the absorption of labor are to be found in shorter working hours and legal limitations upon female and child labor. The real income of the worker grew constantly. It was in this phase of economic development that the organizations of Socialist labor turned toward reformism. The explanation for this phenomenon, as given by Robert Michels before 1914, seems to be valid today after more than a half-century of social research: one of the main reasons for the change in Socialist policy lies with the organizational and numerical growth of the Free Trade Union Federation and the SPD. This process of revising Marxism was also linked with economic factors. The trade unions obtained increasing influence within the labor movement; in the debate on a proposed political strike, the party was forced into a compromise at the Mannheim party congress of 1906 and agreed to the demands of the General-kommission (Executive Committee of the Union Federation) that no strike should be initiated without the consent of the unions. Finally, the ADGB stood out as the main factor in the defeat of the right-wing Kapp Putsch in 1920.

This process of growing union influence started in 1890, after the emergency laws against the Socialists had failed to obtain a

17 A more detailed analysis of this first period would have to answer the following questions. Was there a general oversupply of labor, of unskilled workers as well as skilled workers, or was there a demand for skilled workers in general or in specific industries? If there was a skilled labor scarcity in certain occupations, what did this imply for the unionization of these workers and for the economic and/or political actions employed by these unions? Another question, already pointing ahead to the next period in the labor market and to the next variable, structure of the labor force, is: Which positions in the trade union hierarchy, and also in the political and cultural labor organizations, were taken by skilled and unskilled workers? Did skilled workers dominate the labor movement without regard to the long-term situation in the labor market, or only in times of a general excess labor supply? Which were the organizations most favorable for upward social mobility of unskilled workers? Why?

majority in the Reichstag. The Socialist trade union movement under the leadership of Carl Legien was reorganized and set up a Generalkommission, a relatively centralized executive council of the free trade union federation. The following years saw the amalgamation of craft unions into industry-wide unions. Until 1914, almost two-thirds of all union members were organized in only six big unions. At the same time, the bureaucratization of both the trade union movement and the SPD took place. Collective bargaining became increasingly important. In 1907 900,000 employees were covered by contracts; in 1913, 2,000,000 had such coverage.

The third period, beginning with the founding of the Federal Republic in 1949, is characterized by industry equipped with the most modern machinery as a result of the dismantling of German factories after 1945. Today some industries have entered the phase of automation. This third period shows not only extreme scarcity of labor, but also the employment of about two million foreign workers.[18] Shorter working hours and longer schooling have accentuated the scarcity of labor. It is against this background that the change of the SPD from a workers' to a liberal party must be viewed. After the Socialist euphoria of the first post-war years had waned, economic action became increasingly important for the trade union movement.

It is surprising to see that the ideological orientation of Socialist labor persisted for a long time while the economics of the labor market were working against it and trade unions had gained a relatively strong position at the collective bargaining table. This was only possible because ideology and practical politics were as separate as two worlds from each other. In the realm of declamation, fundamental social change and Socialist revolution were projected into the heaven of the future, and collective bargaining and social legislation were labeled secondary. Thus the Generalkommission remained bound ideologically to the Socialist labor movement after the Mannheim compromise, and as late as 1919 the ADGB declared explicitly that socialism was its main goal. In reality the situation was just the reverse: collective bargaining, the improvement of social, unemployment, and health insurance, and (more for the SPD than for the trade unions) communal policy and election campaigns were the main activities of the movement. Today under conditions of extreme scarcity of labor, the heaven of Kautskyan ideology, which still stretched over the labor move-

18 In the context of this paper, we cannot deal with the complex causes of labor scarcity in the Federal Republic.

ment in the Weimar Republic, has at long last been abandoned.

I will return to the reasons for the staying power of labor's ideology later. At this point I want to call to attention some factors which contributed to the political orientation of the German labor movement. It is a fact of history that the first stable organizations of the German labor movement were political parties, which later often initiated the founding of trade unions. Unions were thus organized after the Socialist party had come into existence and not —as in Great Britain, Sweden, Norway,[19] Australia, or New Zealand—before the Labour party. This weakened the self-confidence of the union movement, which quite often was regarded as an appendix to the political branch of labor. Another point: political decisions and occurrences accelerated the industrialization of Germany (the Customs Union, founding of the Reich, public subsidies for transportation, etc.). Therefore organized labor in Germany came to realize that political and not economic action was needed to solve the problems that industrialization had produced. Bismarck's social legislation, adopted in order to combat the Socialist appeal among labor, strengthened this tendency. Not by way of collective bargaining but by decree of the chancellor, who himself depended on the emperor and not on the Reichstag, had Germany become the country with the most modern social security system of its time.

Founded in a period of extreme excess supplies of labor, the first German trade unions were organized along craft lines. Nevertheless, workers' opposition against the class state was so universal, and the connections between unions and the Social Democratic party so close, that soon unskilled and semi-skilled workers joined the craft unions which after 1890 increasingly amalgamated into industrial unions. Disputes arose on the issue of craft or industrial unionism, but because of the importance of the political sphere they remained a secondary problem and never became, as in the United States, a basis for division. When we relate the first and second variables in German labor history, we have to deal with a historical pattern which can be explained as follows: in the period of excess supply of labor, a radical, universal emancipatory and internationalist labor movement developed, which in the second period— when the excess supply of labor was absorbed—transformed its original concept of fundamental social change into an ideology of

19 In the Scandinavian cases the unions were still in their infancy when the parties were founded. The parties provided for a link among the unions before federations of labor were organized.

party integration into the social life of the nation and became at the same time, in day-to-day politics, more concerned with social insurance schemes, the next elections, or the selection of a council candidate. German labor is presently in a transitional phase in a period of extreme labor scarcity in which, through collective bargaining and legislation, organized labor is integrated into the existing society while part of the national union leadership—sometimes because of the ideological tradition of the Weimar Republic—in resounding phrases proclaims the necessity of fundamental social change without being able to indicate which strategy would lead labor toward this goal.

In turning to the third variable, the structure of the labor force, we enter a field where we have to move cautiously because of methodological problems. While it is possible to find data indicating the change in the occupational structure, it is almost impossible to point out the implications of this change for the policies of organized labor. Looking at the history and current status of organized labor in Germany, one is struck by tendencies too conflicting to derive a theory from empirical experience.

The supposition that industrial unions strengthened the political orientation of a labor movement by organizing unskilled and semi-skilled workers—political power as a substitute and/or addition for rather modest bargaining power—is difficult to prove by the German example. Considering the scarcity of labor, an economic factor which tends against political action of unions, it is surprising to find unionization of the unskilled and semi-skilled in industrial unions after World War II contributing to the persistence of political demands within the DGB, at least in the first post-war decade. Other observations can be made in support of the hypothesis outlined in the papers referred to in the introductory chapter of this volume. Saxony and Berlin, both industrial regions with high proportions of unskilled and semi-skilled workers, always belonged to the most radical districts of the SPD and the free trade unions. Here the Communist party (KPD) was especially strong. The Revolutionary Shop Stewards of Berlin formed one of the most powerful radical forces in the German revolution of 1918–19, demanding the establishment of a revolutionary government on the basis of workers' councils. This organization had its strongholds among the unskilled and semi-skilled workers of the Berlin steel and machine industry. The percentage of unskilled and semi-skilled workers (and of intellectuals) in the KPD was higher than the average in the German labor force, whereas skilled workers were underrepresented.[20]

Before 1914 most of the leaders of the right and center wings of the SPD were skilled workers, as were most of the party leaders after 1918 (August Bebel, Hermann Molkenbuhr, Ebert, Noske, Legien, Wels, Leipart), whereas the leaders of the left wing were usually intellectuals (Rosa Luxemburg, Karl Liebknecht, Franz Mehring, Paul Levi). This seemingly exact correlation is contradicted by the fact that the party and trade union districts of the Ruhr area, with its high percentage of unskilled workers, always belonged to the right wing of the Socialist labor movement. Lest this appear as an inconsequential accidental exception to the rule—insofar as the Ruhr area is predominantly Catholic, whereas Saxony, Berlin, and Hamburg, another stronghold of the KPD, are predominantly Protestant—note that on the fringe of the Ruhr area the knife sharpeners and cutlers of Solingen and Remscheid, probably the most highly skilled workers in Germany, always stood on the extreme left wing of the labor movement. The reason for their radicalism will be found in the local conditions of Solingen and Remscheid.[21] This example shows how difficult it is to separate the "structure of the labor force" variable from other factors, such as religious denomination and local conditions. Yet there is no doubt that this third variable is one of the most important factors determining the pattern of development of a labor movement.[22]

One is even more uncertain when trying to determine which changes of the structure and methods of the German labor movement were brought about by the emergence and growth of white-collar workers. As in the United States today, the number of white-collar employees in the Federal Republic will soon exceed the number of blue-collar workers.[23] Does this imply that the trade

20 See Richard A. Comfort, *Revolutionary Hamburg: Labor Politics in the Early Weimar Republic* (Stanford, 1966). The author gives data for the social structure of the KPD Hamburg. The best history of the KPD in the Weimar Republic is still Ossip K. Flechtheim, *Die KPD in der Weimar Republik,* 2nd ed. (Frankfurt, 1969).

21 For the importance of local radicalism in Remscheid and Solingen, see the memoirs of Wilhelm Dittmann, who before 1914 acted as party secretary in this area. The memoirs will be published by Georg Kotowski and Peter Lösche (The Hague, 1972).

22 The liberal position of the Amalgamated Clothing Workers of America and of the International Ladies Garment Workers Union as compared with other American unions results not only from the Socialist tradition in the needle trades, but also from their dependence on semi-skilled blacks and Puerto Ricans who are organized in these unions today.

23 See Adolf Sturmthal, *White-Collar Trade Unions* (Urbana, Ill., 1966).

union movement, particularly in its attachment to the Social Democratic party, will be weakened and the desire of labor to be fully integrated into society will be strengthened?[24] It is impossible to make
any forecast. Among white-collar employees in Germany one finds a
relatively high percentage of women, a fact which might contribute
to a prevalent prejudice against political involvement of labor. But
it is difficult to organize women; because of this, many white-collar
unions are weak at the bargaining table.[25] Thus they might turn to
political action as a substitute for a low degree of organization. In
the Weimar Republic the AFA-Bund, a white-collar Socialist trade
union, was among the most radical unions and was willing to wage
a general strike against the National Socialists in the spring of 1933.
On the other side of the political spectrum the DHV belonged to
the most conservative forces of organized labor supporting (the
rank and file more than leadership) the NSDAP at the end of the
Weimar Republic.

The white-collar unions in the Federal Republic offer a diversified picture. The German White-Collar Union (DAG) does not
belong to the trade union federation (DGB). It therefore occupies
a weak strategic position, is not at all aggressive at the bargaining
table, but does not turn to political action as a substitute. The ÖTV,
organizing public employees and transportation workers (except
in the railroad industry), bargains militantly, exploits its personal
connections with the SPD in states where the party is in power, and
tries to influence legislation which concerns its members. The GEW,
organizing almost half of the German teachers, has become even
more militant and applies economic and political methods equally:
the union demands the right to strike for all public employees and a
fundamental democratic reform of society. Some of the old universal emancipatory objectives of the German labor movement have
been revived in this union.[26]

This leads us to another consideration. In Germany, white-collar
employees and, of course, professionals have had a better and
longer education than the industrial workers. The school system is
structured almost like a class society: students bound for blue-collar
jobs will attend Volksschule for nine years, future white-collar

24   See Sturmthal, "Economic Development and the Labour Movement," p.
179.
25   There are no exclusive bargaining units in the German labor relations
system. The union bargains with management regardless of how many employees
are unionized.
26   Because no data are available, my observations have to be impressionistic.

workers will attend a school comparable to the American junior high school (and which runs for six years after four years of elementary school), and future professionals have to finish high school as well as college. What is significant in this difference in education patterns for union strategy in organizing blue- or white-collar workers or professionals? Could it be that because of the better education of their members white-collar unions tend to be more politically oriented and to employ the sophisticated ways of political influence and pressure more than blue-collar unions? Some of the survey data taken in recent years suggest that better education corresponds with more political participation, analytical and critical ability, and the demand for social reform. But there are no data informing us of the behavior of trade union members in this respect. Therefore we cannot answer our question except by speculation.

In discussing the structure of the labor force and its implications for organized labor, another factor must be taken into account—the structure of industry. For example, what explains the traditionally conservative position of the building trade unions (and their high regard for collective bargaining) in Germany, the United States, and other countries, compared to the generally more moderate stand at the bargaining table (and more frequent use of political methods) of the metal trade unions? The reason for this difference lies not only with the predominance of skilled workers in the first and of unskilled or semi-skilled workers in the latter industry; it is to be found also in the structure of the respective industries themselves. The building trades are highly decentralized, consist mostly of small companies, and corporate-like organization and behavior prevail. The metal industry is highly centralized—in steel or automobiles a few gigantic companies dominate the field—and the alienation of the conveyor-belt worker in mass production is not a slogan but a dismal reality.[27] In the construction trades paternalism has often survived, whereas in big factories the demands of order and obedience impose military-like behavior on the worker. Furthermore, the organizing efforts of unions in both industries are different: in construction a continuous and diversified organizing campaign is going on, while in a big plant a shorter but more intense battle is likely. Of course, all this has an impact on the

27 Workers' complaints about the high speed of assembly lines and about the dullness of their work, the constant accidents in the factories, and the increasing importance of local issues in collective bargaining are indications of the reality of workers' alienation. Alienation still has the meaning of the Marxian view—the creative potentialities of workers are not realized.

tactics of organized labor. Rank and file unrest over working conditions, wages, or other issues is more easily controlled and absorbed through collective bargaining or simple negotiation in the decentralized industries where small companies prevail. Dissatisfaction in centralized mass production industries tends to turn toward coordinated political action of all workers and their unions in the industry.[28]

In a sense the fourth variable, the migration of ideas and models, seems at first to be irrelevant for German labor history when one excludes the history of the German Democratic Republic.[29] German labor received little impetus from foreign models. However, it served as model for many foreign movements. Until 1914 the Socialist parties of the Second International looked at the Social Democratic party as the organizational incarnation of Marxism. For Hillquit, as well as for Lenin, the German party was the point of orientation. In regard to the Christian labor movement, one could argue that through Pope Leo XIII's encyclical *Rerum Novarum* "foreign" ideas were perceived as having inspired the founding of Christian trade unions. But it should be noted that modern Catholic social teachings were affected in turn by such Germans as Kolping and Ketteler.

After World War I the migration of models became important for the German labor movement in quite a different way, a fact which is often neglected by historians. The success of the Bolsheviks in 1917 and the attempt to export the world revolution to Germany by pressing the Bolshevik type of organization, democratic centralism, on the KPD, had a twofold meaning for the German labor movement. On one hand, the Bolsheviks were successful in using the Third International to reorganize the KPD as a party of the "new type" (democratic centralism) and in submitting the party to Moscow's command against the resistance of the leaders of

28   Regarding the third variable, another development would have to be taken into account: the impact of automation on the structure of the labor force and its implications for organized labor. Since the literature is quite contradictory on the social consequences of automation, and since there are not sufficient data available on automation in Germany, this subject cannot be dealt with in this paper.
29   If one understands the fourth variable to mean the perception of foreign ideas and models in German labor history, this factor has indeed been of relatively little importance. But if one looks at German social democracy as an example for other labor movements, the influence of German socialism before World War I is highly important.

the old Spartacus League. This process has been described as Bol-shevization and Stalinization of German Communism.[30] On the other hand, and of more importance for German labor history, the SPD developed a new facet of its ideology by reacting against what was understood to be the Bolshevik menace. Without taking into account the emotional and unreflective anti-Bolshevism of Socialist and independent Socialist party leaders, the failures of the 1918–19 revolution cannot be analyzed. Fear of Bolshevism was one reason why the Socialist parties did not utilize the democratic potential of a spontaneous workers' council movement, and why they instead sought the support of the imperial bureaucracy and the army high command, leaving the social and economic structure of the country unchanged.[31] The history of the SPD after 1918 cannot be written without this element of anticommunism. In this case one deals not with the perception of foreign ideas or models, but with the funda-mental defense against such influences, an ironic version of the fourth variable.

Finally, after 1945 foreign models became somewhat relevant for the German trade union movement in that the question of whether to organize unions along craft or industrial lines was decided under the influence of CIO representatives who had come with the Ameri-can armed forces to Germany. Of course, there was already a strong German industrial union tradition.

At the end of my discussion in which I applied the hypotheses to German labor history, I want to rate the four variables according to their importance for the development of organized labor. Most important, and providing the clue for the analysis of the political orientation of German labor, was the nonparticipation of the worker in society and in the political system at the time when his organiza-tions were founded. This variable and the "pattern of labor objec-tives" determined the specific German deviation from other patterns of labor history as a political movement, whereas the long-term situation of the labor market and the structure of the labor force are common features in the labor movements of other highly in-dustrialized capitalist nations.

After discussing German labor history, the importance of the

30 See Richard Lowenthal, "The Bolshevisation of the Spartacus League," in *International Communism: St. Anthony's Papers* 9 (1960); Herman Weber, *Die Stalinisierung der KPD* (Frankfurt, 1969). The term "Bolshevisation" was also used by the Communist party of the United States.
31 See Lösche, *Der Bolschewismus.*

scheme as a heuristic and methodological instrument for the analysis of labor history and labor prognosis is obvious. Furthermore, comparative social history of labor movements will be impossible without a systematic model in which variables and criteria are defined.

Hisashi Kawada and Ryuji Komatsu

Post-War Labor Movements in Japan

TRADITIONAL APPROACH AND NEW ORIENTATION OF STUDIES ON THE LABOR MOVEMENT IN JAPAN

BEFORE THE WAR the Japanese labor movement tended to be organized not by workers but by members of the intelligentsia, or proponents of foreign ideologies. Consequently, studies of the movement substantially reflect these external elements, and there has been a strong tendency to focus attention on the political movement *against* the system. This view of the pre-war labor movement corresponds to Perlman's theory of the revolutionary intelligentsia guiding labor.

After World War II, legislation similar to the Wagner Act, which protects labor unions, was established. Some labor unions, the core of which included both white-collar and blue-collar employees, organized according to the enterprise in which they worked. These unions developed rapidly. In spite of this development the study of the labor movement has retained its pre-war characteristic in which it has been classified and discussed in its relationship to proletarian or progressive parties.

Against these trends in scholarship a new approach has developed that reflects the entirely new conditions arising from the economic development after the war, especially after 1955. This view—known as the "industrial relations" approach—considers the labor movement in the light of economic, social, and other basic conditions. But even before this some social scientists drew attention to the fact that the Japanese labor movement is "closed" within the boundary of the enterprise, and that as a result organizations by job or industry beyond the boundaries of the enterprise have come to play a secondary role. In order to explore these conditions, a program of research into the characteristics of the employment relations and the labor market in Japan was developed by Ohkohchi's group at the University of Tokyo. This research has become the center of the study of the Japanese labor movement.

Although this research still has great influence, new analyses have become necessary. Economic growth continues to spiral in Japan. The Japanese economy has been internationalized. A new approach, from a viewpoint of international industrial relations, is now necessary for the study of the Japanese labor movement.

A primary factor in this new approach is that the industrial structure and the relation of demand and supply in the labor market have changed greatly. After 1955 modern industries developed so rapidly that the demand for labor continued to surge upward despite rapid technical change. One result of this growing demand for labor is that the surplus labor force in agricultural areas, previously almost unlimited, has rapidly decreased. The ratio of the number of employees in primary industries to that of all employees decreased from 55 percent just after the war to 19 percent in 1968. However, compared with other industrial countries the Japanese ratio of the numbers of workers in low-productivity industries (small-scale industry or agriculture) is still quite high. Therefore, while in general a labor shortage appears to exist and has tended to become more serious year after year since 1960, and there are many job vacancies, it is rather doubtful whether this should be labeled "full employment."

Nevertheless, in terms of Lewis's theory, from the initial situation where the wage level is determined by subsistence incomes of labor in unlimited supply, Japan has moved into a stage of labor scarcity.

These facts may conform to the hypotheses outlined in the introductory chapter of this volume. Collective bargaining by labor unions now works much more effectively than before, and inevitably the labor movement is influenced by this change.

Labor scarcity may lead to a behavior pattern more similar to that of European union movements. However, it is necessary to analyze the traditional factors that still exert their influence, and the development of new orientations in these areas. In other words, we must face the problem of continuity or discontinuity of traditional factors in Japanese industrial relations.

CHARACTERISTICS OF THE JAPANESE LABOR UNION MOVEMENT

The character of all social movements is determined by economic, social, and cultural conditions. In the case of underdeveloped countries, a technological gap exists between them and advanced countries; if they are to fill this gap, they must either import skills or depend in some other ways on advanced countries, directly or indirectly. During this stage underdeveloped countries import many of the institutional forms of the advanced countries. But the transplanted institutions are changed substantially to fit their new environment. The labor movement in Japan is no exception. This applies especially to three aspects of its institutions and their environment: organizational structure and function, economic structure, and relationship of labor force demand and supply.

Organizational Structure and Function

Japanese labor unions were created by importing various organizational forms and functions developed in advanced countries, including some Socialist countries. One of these imports, the craft union, has not found fertile soil in Japan—it has not been able to control the supply of labor, nor has a consciousness of "job control" been developed. Workers in traditional industries, such as building workers, who were the core of European and American labor movements, have remained outside the unions. The core of the post–World War II labor movement in Japan consisted of workers committed to modern industrial enterprises. This characteristic is closely connected with the facts that for a long time there were few employment opportunities, and that learning new skills is dependent upon employers. It is also based on the development of paternal management and an awareness of social standing going back to the pre-capitalistic era. The basis of labor unions consists of over-committed regular employees in the enterprise. Their organization is entirely different from local unions in Europe and in the United States. The basic unit is not a craft or industrial union tightly linked with unions in other enterprises, but the unity of workers of the same employer.

This grouping of workers in the same enterprise can be consolidated easily and sometimes shows strong group interests, but at the same time it has an inclination to identify with the enterprise more tightly than with other workers. As a result, the industrial union extending beyond the limits of the enterprise tends to be a secondary organization for the union member. When there is competition between enterprises or some conflict which involves the common interests of the enterprise, the enterprise union often deserts the national union.

The progress of industrialization may introduce many changes, such as city planning, urbanization, the conversion from the extended family to the simple family, higher standards of education, or bringing the economy nearer to full employment. These changes release the individual from the restrictions of the community within the enterprise and allow him to determine his own destiny more independently. Possibilities of changing employers increase, as do opportunities of employment. Moreover, the political movement toward socialism loses its appeal because it is based on the ideology of class consciousness and the claim for political rights, as well as freedom from political and economic dependency.

The basic character of industrial unions has not changed at all, though future developments in the progress of industrialization may lead to some changes. Basically, the control of the enterprise units by the national unions continues to be very weak, and the latter function only when they are supported by the enterprise organization. The same applies to union finances; in many ways the big enterprise unions have the greater power. The development of a highly industrialized society means that the conditions necessary for the strengthening of industrial unions are gradually realized.

Economic Structure and Labor Unions

A characteristic factor of Japanese economic development is that the basic part of the double structure, agriculture and small and medium-size industries of low productivity, is larger, relative to the modern sector, than in other advanced countries. In an economy with unlimited supplies of labor, the existence of a sector with low productivity and pre-modern characteristics prevents workers from strengthening their organizations and keeps the labor movement in an unstable condition. Yet during the poverty stage it has a potential of forming an alliance between poor tenant farmers and factory workers; it also provides a strong basis for an anti-establishment political movement.

After the war, as a result of agricultural reform, owner farmers became the main source of agricultural production. Tenant farmers changed into owner farmers, and many marginal farmers with little farmland became multiple jobholders in manufacturing and other industries.

The urban labor force share of small and medium-size enterprises is now much larger in Japan than in many other advanced countries. Partly because there are few craft unions, the degree of union organization is very low in this sector of the economy. While the unionization rate is 75 percent in large industries, it is only a few percent in firms with fewer than thirty employees.

By contrast, at one time before the war the labor movement was confined to small and medium-size enterprises. The unions were organized outside the plants and closely connected with a class-conscious party. Employment had little stability, so it was difficult to establish stable organizations—in contrast to the West, where the craft or general union outside the enterprise was often the monopolistic supplier of labor.

But today in the large firms more than half of all workers are regular employees, committed to their work. Their jobs are secure until retirement; there is little labor turnover. The employment guarantee for the permanent workers is effectuated by increase or decrease of the number of temporary workers or of the employees of subcontractors.

The large enterprises, spearheads of economic development, grew during the post-war era; as a result, the permanent workers' unions in the large industries expanded. These workers have been able to enjoy the fruits of technological change, in the form of improvements in wages and other working conditions as well as welfare plans and other fringe benefits.

There have been attempts to organize the workers of small and medium-size industries, and especially of subcontractors of large enterprises, but except in a few cases they have not obtained good results. The national industrial union or national center insists on establishing uniform labor standards. But it does not succeed in this demand because the union leadership has no statutory control over the enterprise union.

As a result, enterprise unions enhance their position within the labor movement and strengthen their power. As long as economic growth continues and the big enterprises increase their profits and output, the enterprise unions will continue to expect growing wage increases out of the rising enterprise profits. Under these circumstances enterprise unions tend to come nearer to business unionism, aiming at economic advantages within the limits of the given social system. This mechanism of enterprise unions with large industry as its core is the main factor in the change of the course of the labor movement from traditional, anti-establishment class struggle to a reform movement within the limits of the establishment.

Relationship of Labor Force Demand and Supply

This evolution of the characteristics of the Japanese labor movement cannot be ascribed directly to the change from unlimited labor supply to a limited labor supply economy. The labor market factors have influenced the long-run development of the Japanese labor movement only through the enterprise union, an institution peculiar to Japan. Unlimited labor supply was an important factor in this form of union organization, but it was not the only factor.

Thus when conditions change, as is the case in the present labor shortage, it cannot be assumed that this alone will destroy the enterprise union. On the contrary, as long as the Japanese economy continues to develop, employment increases, and the labor market becomes even tighter. These stresses enhance the position of the enterprise union within the labor union movement and in society, especially in large enterprises. They are in a better position than small enterprises in hiring workers during a labor shortage. As a result, the large enterprise unions have grown in size and influence.

Accordingly, if economic growth continues, the differences between large and small industries will grow in terms of their ability to hire workers under the pressure of a general labor shortage. Faced with increased labor costs and comparatively higher costs of production, industries with slowly rising or stagnant productivity will have to raise their prices, which, in turn, will increase the general price level. General price increases will continue until they hamper Japanese competitiveness on the world market and the balance of payments shows a deficit. Then the low-productivity sector will shrink, and economies of scale will be attained through competition, not only in manufacturing but also in other fields. These effects of the stresses of the labor market have become readily apparent since 1965; they are expected to become even stronger in the 1970's.

Such a change in the structure of the Japanese economy can be clearly seen in the relationship between agriculture and other activities, and it will extend to other sectors from now on. Consequently, the position of the enterprise union in large establishments will be enhanced. Similar stresses on the labor market strongly influenced the development and change of the labor movement in the 1960's.

Government and public workers or the workers in small enterprises and their unions, lacking the advantages of the workers in large enterprises, naturally show entirely different characteristics from those of the workers in large enterprises. Engaging in political action remains their main weapon. But since the role of industrial unions in the larger private enterprises has become more important, the movement as a whole shows increased emphasis on economic action.

MAIN PERIODS IN THE POST-WAR LABOR MOVEMENT

In two periods since the end of World War II, the occupation period immediately after the war and the period after the conclusion of the peace treaty, political factors were the most important. Post-war unionism was greatly influenced by the occupation policy. In terms of the economic environment, the post-war period can be divided into three subperiods: 1945–55, when GNP recovered to the pre-war level; 1955–60, when a major change took place in labor supply and demand relationships; and 1960–70.

In terms of the development of the union movement itself, it is reasonable to suggest that the first period of development was 1945 through 1950, when left-wing and radical Sanbetsu (National Congress of Industrial Unions) led the movement. Then Sohyo was formed; in the process of reorganization of the labor movement, Zenro (Japanese Trade Union Congress), advocating economically oriented trade unionism, split from it. Sohyo itself changed its policy from "People's struggle" to "Japanese way of trade unionism" around 1960, when there was a change in its leadership. The years from 1950 through 1960 may thus be considered the second period of development.

After 1960, during the chronic labor shortage resulting from rapid economic growth, labor unions concentrated on improving working conditions and lessened their emphasis on the political struggles which had carried over from the previous period. In spite of several economic slowdowns, unions have been successful in their economic struggles. As a result the economic orientation of the labor movement has been greatly enhanced, and there has been a movement toward the unification of the labor unions with a strong economic orientation, regardless of their national-level affiliation. This movement has been led by the big enterprise unions; public employee unions are outside the movement.

FROM POLITICAL CONSCIOUSNESS
TO ECONOMIC CONSCIOUSNESS

During the Occupation (Period of Revival)

Even before Japan entered into hostilities with the West, the organizations of labor had been destroyed and the labor movement had ceased to exist. During the last stage of the war, manufacturing itself became impossible because of the shortage of material, funds, and labor.

Right after the defeat, manufacturing was still highly limited in scope and the workers were in distress. These circumstances compelled the workers to try to protect their livelihoods. Many factory workers and white-collar employees were drawn into the labor movement; some had trade union experience before the war, while some were newcomers to the movement.

During this period there was no definite, steady direction to the movement, though it developed strongly and covered a wide area. This was a prologue to the stabilization of the post-war movement after 1950; preparations were made for the developments of the future. With the defeat in the war as a turning point, the activities of Japanese labor underwent a great change which workers in most other countries had never experienced. Following the trend of democratization, a Labor Union Act was proclaimed (in December, 1945), followed by the proclamation of the new Japanese constitution (in November, 1946). As a result, the workers' rights to organize, bargain, and strike were admitted legally for the first time in Japan. Moreover, right after the war management lost its self-confidence and was in disarray, while labor found it difficult to earn its livelihood and had to endure poverty.

But the policies of the Occupation authorities, the government, and the labor movement were not consistent throughout this period. There was a considerable difference between the period before the attempted "2–1" strike, scheduled for February 1, 1947, and the years that followed.

Both government and Occupation forces endeavored to assist and improve the labor movement as an offset to the policies of militarism and hostility to democracy before and during the war. But after the 2–1 strike they tended to suppress the labor movement and to strengthen the influences of capital. Examples of this new policy were MacArthur's note (July, 1948), the Red Purge, and the restrictions on political actions of public officials. Especially in relation to the international developments leading to the outbreak of the Korean war, the position of Japan became more important as the base of anti-Communist activity. This tendency of suppression and roll-back was an expression of Japan's new role in this activity.

Still, major unit unions and national unions were organized throughout the whole period, and two national union confederations of these unions were formed: Sanbetsu (All Japan Congress of Industrial Unions—organized in August, 1946; 1.63 million members) and Sodomei (Japanese Confederation of Labor—organized in August, 1946; 850,000 members). The unit unions were organized on the basis of the vertical or closed labor market, i.e., individual enterprise. The most important characteristic of those unions was the way they adjusted to the fact that both blue-collar and white-collar workers suffered from post-war confusion and poverty. In response to this the unions adopted the form of enterprise organizations, composed of all workers in an enterprise for the purpose of dealing with their employer. Many middle-management officials were even drawn into the movement, like Kaoru Ohta, who later became the chairman of Sohyo (General Council of Trade Unions of Japan).

In the first half of this revival period the radical mood of the movement, shown in the production control or anti-government struggles, was noticeable (see Table 1). It reached its climax in a strike for wage increases and other demands by some unions of government and public officials, followed by the so-called 2–1 strike.[1] After the 2–1 strike failed due to lack of wide support among the workers, the unions engaged in self-criticism. They admitted that they had attached too much importance to the strike and that they had been severely divided into several factions. Also, the so-called democratization leagues developed within the labor unions. The result was a strengthening of the movement after 1950.

However, for the time being, while Mindo (Unions' Affiliated League for Democratization) arose, all radical movements did not disappear completely. But on the whole Sanbetsu retreated rapidly because of the defeats of some of its main member unions (National Railway Workers' Union, All Communication Workers' Union, Toshiba Workers' Union, etc.). Instead Mindo became the main

1 The prices of the products of the main industries, as well as the wages of government and other public workers, were controlled at the time. Since this policy made the rise in prices and wages dependent on the administration, the strike inevitably became a political one.

Table 1A.   Unions with Strike Experiences (by Size of Union)
(Fall, 1947)

Size of enterprise	1 Number of unions surveyed	2 Unions with strike experience	3 Col. 2 as % of Col. 1
Fewer than 50 employees	4	1	25.0
50–99	17	5	29.4
100–199	34	12	35.3
200–499	76	42	55.3
500–999	56	25	44.6
1,000–4,999	94	41	43.6
More than 5,000	32	23	70.2
Unknown	8	2	—
	321 total	151 total	47.0 average

Table 1B.   Unions with Strike Experience by National Affiliation
(Fall, 1947)

According to affiliation	Number of unions surveyed	Unions with strike experience	Col. 2 as % of Col. 1
Sanbetsu (National Congress of Industrial Unions)	129	89	69.0
Sodomei (General Federation of Japan Trade Unions)	93	20	21.5
Others	99	42	42.4
	321 total	151 total	47.0 average

SOURCE: Tokyo University, Shakai-Kagaku Kenkyu-jo (Social Science Research Institute), *Sego Rodo-Kumiai No Jittai* (*The Postwar Situation of the Labor Unions*). (Tokyo: Nihon Hyoronsha, 1950), pp. 313, 315.

center of all national and unit unions. These movements continued into the period after 1950, and the post-war labor movement gradually stabilized.

As mentioned above, the workers were concerned with both living or economics and politics, and the labor movement alternately put its emphasis on economics and politics. As a result, the number of labor unions and unionists underwent great changes (see Table 2). From the fact that there were radical strikes and political struggles under the confused and fluid circumstances of the time, one may infer that Japanese industrial relations had not yet reached maturity and that the labor movement itself was still in confusion.

Nevertheless, the workers gradually progressed toward acting on the basis of collective agreements and other common rules, which in turn were promoted by the enactment of the new constitution and

Table 2. Number of Labor Unions and Unionists

	Number of labor unions	Number of unionists	Estimated rate of unionization
December, 1945	509	380,677	3.2%
June, 1946	12,006	3,679,971	41.5
June, 1947	23,323	5,692,179	45.3
June, 1948	33,926	6,677,427	53.0
June, 1949	34,688	6,655,483	55.8
June, 1950	29,144	5,773,908	46.2
June, 1951	27,644	5,686,774	42.6
June, 1952	27,851	5,719,560	40.3
June, 1953	30,129	5,842,678	40.4
June, 1954	31,456	5,986,168	37.6
June, 1955	32,012	6,185,348	37.8

SOURCE: Ministry of Labor, Dictionary of Labor, based on *Rodo-Kumiai Kihon-chosa* (*Labor Union Basic Survey*), published annually. There are other sources giving different data, e.g., Mikio Sumiya, *Nihon Rodoundo-shi* (*History of Japanese Labor Movement*) (Tokyo: Yushindo, 1966).

the Trade Union Law. However, this trend developed not only because the workers' rights were legally secured, but also because the workers had tried to find the road to progress for themselves, and the attitude of management had changed gradually as the new era unfolded.

During the second half of this period, management, especially in big enterprises, began to recover self-confidence and established well-planned principles and policies. Industrial rationalization and the formation of the Japan Federation of Employers' Associations in April, 1948, were main elements in shaping management policies. Also employers, especially those in big enterprises, abandoned their former suppressive policies and started to offer some benefits to workers by means of the reestablishment of the length-of-service system and the lifetime employment system, as well as the organization and expansion of enterprise welfare institutions. This trend toward offering greater benefits to the workers progressed as time went on.

Period of Settlement: 1950–60

During the second period, when Sohyo was formed (1950) and the economy expanded rapidly, the post-war labor movement reached a stage of continuity.

The early 1950's witnessed the organization of Sohyo in July, 1950. Under the chaotic conditions following the defeat, for a while Sanbetsu took a leading part in the Japanese labor movement.

But later it was disorganized by the rise of democratization leagues within it, in opposition to its radical strikes. At the same time, inside Sodomei (General Federation of Japan Trade Unions) there was an apparent split between the left and right wings. As a result, in July, 1950, Mindo, the left wing of Sodomei, and some independent unions abandoned Sanbetsu and Domei and jointly organized Sohyo (General Council of Trade Unions of Japan).

Sohyo did not develop smoothly. It contained several different currents, though all of them maintained harmony to the point of electing Takeo Mutoh the first chairman and denying control or even influence to the Communist party. Yet internal factionalism soon came to the fore.

In response to greater hostility by employers and to the prosperity caused by the outbreak of the Korean war in June, 1950, the confrontation of the left and right wings within Sohyo became sharp. Some important political problems (the peace treaty, rearmament, revision of labor legislation, etc.) further sharpened this cleavage.

It manifested itself as early as the second congress of Sohyo in March, 1951. The left wing (consisting of the Japan Teachers' Union, National Railway Workers' Union, All Communication Workers' Union, etc.) and the right wing (represented by the All-Japan Seamen's Union, Japan Federation of Textile Workers' Unions, etc.) came into sharp conflict. The first group supported the so-called Four Principles for Peace (conclusion of an overall peace treaty, observance of strict neutrality, opposition to the establishment of U.S. military bases in Japan, and opposition to rearmament), while the latter supported conclusion of a separate peace treaty and armaments for self-defense. The debate ended in a victory for the first group, and Minoru Takano of the left wing was elected secretary-general. This was the beginning of lasting control of Sohyo by the left wing and the leadership of the government and public workers' unions. Later on, this caused the withdrawal of the right-wing unions, such as the All-Japan Seamen's Union and the Japan Federation of Textile Workers' Union, and the formation of Zenro. Once established, the leading role of the government and public workers' unions became a characteristic of the Japanese labor movement for a long time.

By adopting the four principles for peace, Sohyo changed its character from a moderate economic stance to one that attached great importance to political struggles. Sohyo accordingly engaged in such movements as the campaigns against a peace treaty, against a security treaty between Japan and the United States, against the establishment in Japan of U.S. military bases, and against a worsening of labor legislation; it organized strikes to defend education until about 1953. Needless to say, Sohyo, which had orginally started under the slogan of "anti-left wing of Sanbetsu," did not devote itself exclusively to political struggles but carried out some realistic economic movements, such as the continuation of wage struggles and preparing a "draft of general principles concerning wages," which it had originally started under the slogan of "anti-left wing of Sanbetsu." Still, its political ambition was quite strong.

The strategy of the movement under the leadership of Takano was to advance the movement from strikes in a given industry to movements including the whole area and the family members of the striking workers. In other words, it was a strategy aimed at the establishment of a nationwide resistance movement.

Thanks to the procurement boom of the Korean war, many enterprises expanded and their managements became more and more progressive. In these circumstances the trend toward political struggles and the economic orientation of the movement were bound to come into conflict.

Even inside Sohyo criticism rapidly appeared. The All-Japan Seamen's Union and the Japan Federation of Textile Workers' Union that had already opposed the Takano leadership after the second congress sharpened their criticism after 1953. They pointed out that Sohyo's strategy ignored reality and put too much emphasis on political issues. In 1954 these two organizations seceded from Sohyo and, together with Sodomei, organized Zenro (Japanese Trade Union Congress, with a membership of 700,000).

At about the same time, especially after 1953, modernization and mechanization progressed; this caused discharges of personnel, and the number of lost strikes increased. As a result other unions, besides the two mentioned above, opposed the Takano leadership. Finally Takano was replaced by Kaoru Ohta and Akira Iwai in 1955. This change was characterized, first, by resistance to "rationalization" measures and to the progress of the movement for higher productivity, and second, by the introduction of the "spring offensive" aimed mainly at wage increases.

Of course, the Japanese labor movement still engaged in political campaigns, as shown in the struggles against the introduction of the teachers' efficiency rating system, the revision of the Police Duties Law, and the conclusion of a U.S.-Japan Security Treaty. But it is characteristic for this period that the struggle for economic or industrial objectives, such as demands for wage increases or a minimum wage system, came to the fore.

The core of the Japanese labor movement now was Sohyo, though Zenro extended its influence late in this period. As early as the years of Takano's leadership, the United Struggle Committee for the Spring Wage Offensive (formerly the United Struggle Committee of the Five National Unions) was organized by Kaoru Ohta and other Sohyo leaders; thus the movement for all-industry wage campaigns started. Later this became the main task of the movement and evolved into unified industrial struggles, aimed mainly at wage increases under the leadership of Ohta-Iwai. These campaigns were called "Shunto," the spring labor offensive.

In 1955 the output of the mining and manufacturing industry was twice as high as in pre-war days. Enterprise unions could not overcome the boundaries of enterprises by their own efforts or those of all unions in a given area, because firms extended their markets and developed into monopolies. The spring offensive was designed to meet this situation, and Shunto is the method which has been used ever since. In the economic conditions after 1955 and given the high rate of economic growth in the 1960's, the spring offensive, supported by increased demand for labor, has produced good results in terms of wage increases (see Table 3).

Table 3.   Monthly Wage Increases Obtained during Spring Offensive (Average)

	1960	1961	1962	1963	1964
Demanded amount	2,561¥	4,105¥	5,000¥	4,815¥	—
Amount of agreement	1,691	3,009	2,515	2,237	3,305
Rate of wage increases	8.2%	14.2%	10.7%	9.1%	12.4%

The spring offensive implies that every spring each unit union in every industry starts bargaining for the improvement of working conditions and wages and tries to obtain the advantages of unified industrial movements in order to overcome the enterprise-wide character of Japanese unionism. Spring is the beginning of a new business year. The spring offensive is thus a form of simultaneous collective bargaining between labor and management. Different from the traditional political struggles with ideological connotation, it has the character of an economic struggle, with wage increases as the main point. Agreement is usually reached in a short time.

The number of unions and unionists who take part in the spring offensive has continued to increase with time (see Table 4). This has made the offensive more effective. Especially after the third

Table 4.   Number of Unionists Taking Part in Shunto (Spring Strikes)

Year	Union members in the private sector (000)	Union members in the public sector (000)	Other[a] (000)	Total (000)
1957	990	880		1,870
1958	1,234	805		2,039
1959	1,501	895		2,396
1960	1,705	904	374	2,609
1961	1,977	887	928	3,792
1962	2,400	887	527	3,814
1963	2,713	898	1,367	4,978

[a] Union members whose union is not under the control of the United Struggle Committee for the Spring Wage Offensive.

SOURCE: Ministry of Labor, *Shiryo Rodo-undo-shi* (*Documentary History of the Labor Movement*), published annually.

period, its effects have become remarkable in view of the labor shortage in the Japanese economy; they have proved the effectiveness of collective bargaining more clearly than before. Emphasis on collective bargaining and its proven effectiveness were the result of mutual trust and consultation that had gradually grown between labor and management throughout the post-war days. This is a characteristic feature of the latter part of the second period and the third period.

Still, until 1960 the spring offensive was not always the center of the labor movement, nor was it always fully effective. The violent strike by the National Railway Workers' Union (1957), the struggles against the teachers' efficiency rating system (1958) and against the U.S.-Japan Security Treaty (1960), were so sensational that they gave the impression that those movements were the essence of the labor movement at that time. Yet the importance of economic struggles and the effectiveness of collective bargaining were undeniably confirmed, and the basis for the later movement in which main emphasis was placed on economic struggles was established by this confirmation.

The labor movement during these years developed steadily, supported by the gradual growth of influence of the spring offensive, accompanied by criticism of Takano. One of the results was the expression "the Japanese way of trade unionism" by Rodosha Doshikai, the Workers' Association of which Sohyo was the main member. It called for economic demands to be put first. But the fact that such a tendency was expressed while strikes against the U.S.-Japan Security Treaty or the Miike coal miners' strike continued—fierce conflicts in which many workers participated—shows the limits of business unionism under Japanese conditions. In other words, present and former political conflicts would not be forgotten by the movement.

It is characteristic of the labor situation in Japan that it could not establish a definite direction for itself. There was a tendency toward emphasis on economic struggles by way of the spring offensive, but there were also many signs pointing to political struggles because of the traditional characteristics of the Japanese labor movement. Political campaigns for the objectives mentioned above, or strikes aiming at the overthrow of a cabinet, were now combined with economic struggles. This continued strong political consciousness may have had some connection with the periodical inactivity of the Japanese labor movement or with the stagnant rate of union organization after 1955. The change of the industrial structure led to a corresponding change in the structure of the labor force and that of the labor movement. It was shown in the decline of coal-mining industries symbolized in the Mitsui-Miike strikes, and in the growth of iron and steel manufacturing, motor, and petroleum industries with a corresponding growth of influence of the unions in these industries. Later in the 1960's this tendency became even more pronounced.

At the end of this period the defeat of the Mitsui-Miike strikes and the end of the struggles against the Japan-U.S. Security Treaty represented a turning point in the evolution of the Japanese labor movement. It entered a period of reflection.

Continuity and Change: 1961-Present

The third period has been a time of severe trials for the unions, in the midst of further "rationalization" of industry. Severe problems arose in the beginning of this third period, such as a tendency toward internal conflicts within the leadership of the movement, a trend toward internationalization expressed in the establishment of the Japan Council of the International Metalworkers' Federation (IMF-JC) in 1964, efforts to reorganize the union movement, continued split of the labor movement into two federations (Sohyo and Domei), together with a move of some unions toward a Federation of Independent Unions or Domei away from Sohyo, inactivity of the Socialist movement (mainly of the Japan Socialist party and the Democratic Socialist party), an increase in the number of members indifferent to labor unions, and the radical anti-establishment feeling of young workers. Of these, the stagnation of Sohyo in terms of its membership (see Table 5), increases in the number

Table 5. Evolution of Union Membership, 1960–68

Year	Total	Sohyo	Domei	Shin-sanbetsu	Churit-suroren	Other
1960	7,661,568 (100.0)	3,745,096 (48.9)	924,076 (12.1)	46,063 (0.6)	—	3,080,867 (40.2)
1961	8,359,876 (100.0)	3,968,123 (47.5)	1,107,867 (13.3)	42,847 (0.5)	—	3,257,336 (39.0)
1962	8,971,156 (100.0)	4,122,099 (45.9)	1,202,596 (13.4)	56,779 (0.6)	831,476 (9.3)	2,780,665 (31.0)
1963	9,357,179 (100.0)	4,191,683 (44.8)	1,348,268 (14.4)	49,450 (0.5)	895,475 (9.6)	2,954,539 (31.6)
1964	9,799,653 (100.0)	4,206,546 (42.9)	1,466,278 (15.0)	58,360 (0.6)	935,614 (9.5)	3,213,352 (32.8)
1965	10,146,872 (100.0)	4,249,703 (41.9)	1,659,063 (16.4)	60,521 (0.6)	983,572 (9.7)	3,300,206 (32.6)
1966	10,403,742 (100.0)	4,247,493 (40.8)	1,715,800 (16.5)	65,876 (0.6)	1,020,751 (9.8)	3,471,589 (33.4)
1967	10,566,436 (100.0)	4,208,097 (39.8)	1,775,210 (16.8)	69,839 (0.7)	1,037,908 (9.8)	3,587,963 (34.0)
1968	10,862,864 (100.0)	4,214,317 (38.8)	1,848,226 (17.0)	71,280 (0.7)	1,269,769 (11.7)	3,523,296 (32.4)
Rise on fall compared to the previous year	296,428 (2.8)	6,220 (0.1)	73,016 (4.1)	1,441 (2.1)	231,861 (22.3)	−64,667 −(1.8)

NOTES: The number of union members of the major national centers (including "Other") does not add up to Total because some unit unions are affiliated with two or more national centers.

The figures of Domei for 1960 and 1961 are those of Zenro.

SOURCE: Ministry of Labor, *Rodokumiai Kohon-chosa Hokoku* (*Labor Union Basic Survey*), 1968.

of workers indifferent to the labor movement, and the stagnation of the labor movement as a whole resulted from rapid economic growth, employers' aggressiveness, and developments in personnel administration—but also from employment stability and wage increases due to labor shortage. A movement toward the reorganization of the entire labor movement, which can be seen in the formation of IMF-JC and Minrokon (which is composed of the presidents of the major private enterprise unions), as well as proposals for the unification of the labor movement, were the result of changes in the economic and employment structure. Leaders of key private enterprise unions were able to develop a movement of their own against Sohyo, whose major supporters have been public employees.

In the spring offensive of 1961 the unions succeeded in obtaining large wage increases against the background of general price increases. But soon business conditions deteriorated in reaction to excessive economic growth in the previous period, and the recession became more serious in 1964 and 1965. "Rationalization" of enterprises advanced strongly under the slogan of "defense of enterprises" propagated by the Japan Federation of Employers' Associations. In order to overcome the recession they chose to expand rather than contract business and lay off workers. Employment thus grew, and the excess supply of labor decreased consistently during and after the slow-down. Because of this favorable supply-demand relation of labor, wage increases and the improvement of working conditions have been realized over a wide range since 1960, in spite of the recession.

Demand for young workers increased especially rapidly, due to the characteristic nature of Japan's employment system. This tendency was enhanced by increased efficiency of operations caused by mechanization and automation.

These factors have been basic to the progressive concentration of the labor force in large enterprises, the change of casual workers in some industries (the construction industry, dock work, etc.) into permanent workers (navvy, coolies, carpenters, handymen, etc.), and the realization of large amounts of wage increases every year in spite of management opposition.

Furthermore, the problems of wage differentials or other differences in working conditions, which characterized the dual structure of large enterprises and medium and small shops in Japan, has changed greatly, particularly as far as young workers are concerned. The wage increases can also be viewed as the result of the activities not only of Domei, but also of Sohyo, and the emphasis on the spring offensive and the increased efficiency of collective bargaining strategy by way of pattern bargaining and the setting up of pace-makers.

Under these circumstances a noticeable tendency in this latest period has been high regard for the results of the Shunto movement led by Sohyo, and decreased interest of rank and file in the radical union movements. The labor movement has become fluid. This may have some connection with the fact that the benefits of economic growth have accrued not only to the employees in large enterprises by way of improved welfare facilities and higher employment as before, but also to other workers, because of the generalization of wage increases. Another factor may be the inability of union leadership to deal effectively with various problems caused by economic growth and technological change. When technological changes are introduced in the plant, the union often fails to discuss the problem with the engineers and technicians concerned; technological changes are carried out by the company's initiative. Also, union leadership fails to hear the voice of the rank and file and simply issues strike orders on its own.

Such tendencies are apparent in the fact that the rate of increase of membership is higher in the moderate JCL than in Sohyo, whose main interest is in political struggles (cf. Table 5), and in expression of indifference toward the labor movement, especially among young workers, demonstrated in many investigations. Moreover, continued from the latter half of the second period, the split of the labor movement in Sohyo and Domei has been aggravated. The continued advance of Domei and Churitsuroren (Federation of Independent Unions) into private industry and increases in the number of Sohyo-affiliated unions favoring a policy close to that of Domei prove this point.

It thus becomes clear that the labor movement would not have been able to attract general laborers in a period of high economic growth and technical improvement if it had continued to embark on traditional political strikes or ordered strikes of managing staff without making a correct analysis of economic development, market conditions, or the state of mind of the workers beforehand. Consequently, in the 1960's the leaders began to speak of a deadlock of the labor movement and its tendency to grow bureaucratic. New movements aiming at the unification of the union leadership and rank and file, to organize Minrokon, or to unify the labor front grew little by little.

In any case, if economic and technological improvements continue through the 1970's, changes in the structures of the economy and the labor force will become inevitable. As already estimated or projected by various governmental councils, the economic return to workers in terms of wages, social welfare, and social investments will continue to increase. Accordingly, the economic character of the labor movement will also be strengthened.

Thus a new situation will arise in which the attitude and policies of the labor movement inherited after the war will have to be basically reexamined, and the two big camps, Sohyo and JCL, will have to be readjusted. From this viewpoint we can safely say that the labor movements that have operated during the last twenty-five years have come to an important turning point.

The Japanese labor movement in the years since World War II has faced many trials and made many errors. The form of union organization with the enterprise as the basic unit has not changed, although the utilization of collective bargaining has been extended and its effectiveness has been confirmed. Together with the constant increase in the number of unionists and the gradual realization of the improvement of conditions of employment, the character of the labor movement has gradually changed from a political to an economic one. In addition to these changes there is the unavoidable fact that economic development and its fruits can be shared more and more by workers, through welfare institutions within the enterprises, steady employment (decrease of the rate of unemployment), wage increases, and the extension of social welfare and social development.

However, Japanese labor unions have not yet become completely stable. In fact, their basic structure is still fragile and does not meet the stress of long strikes or provide the staying power necessary to implement long-term policies, as compared with conditions in foreign countries.[2]

Accordingly, although it appears certain that the emphasis on the economic aspects of the movement will be stronger in the future than that on political action, the Japanese labor scene will be still fluid in many ways—for example, the balance of power between unions, tendency of rank and file members, the direction in which union leadership should move, industrial relations, etc.

It is also important to recognize that while the labor movement as a whole tends to become a part of the establishment, the anti-establishment has penetrated into organized labor through some groups of young workers. This implies the possibility that as the labor movement becomes more a part of the establishment, the more anomalous become various contradictions in the midst of general prosperity: that therefore the stronger will become critics of the establishment.

The 1970's will be another crucial decade for Japanese labor, deserving our full attention.

CONCLUSION

As analyzed in the previous sections, the labor movement in the post–World War II period has greatly changed from its pre-war counterpart, mostly due to the enactment of labor laws. After the

2 For instance, the number of workers who take part in a strike is larger than in foreign countries, but time lost because of strikes is less, and the position of the union leaders is more uncertain compared with other countries.

public recognition of the "three labor rights," workers, especially those of big enterprises, rapidly formed labor unions. Those labor unions have come to improve employment conditions, using collective bargaining as their chief weapon; this is in sharp contrast to the pre-war situation, where unions were forced to rely upon "street struggles."

The post-war Japanese economy has been successful in attaining a rapid rate of growth in spite of its total destruction as a result of the war. This rapid economic expansion has generally provided the labor movement with favorable conditions for its development, although it has not been an entirely unmixed blessing. As a result, under the spur of rapid post-war economic growth the labor movement developed quickly at some times, while at others it suffered from setbacks or stagnation. In spite of such fluctuations the Japanese workers have expanded their rights and increased and secured their social power. Today it is difficult to discuss the development of the national economy without referring to the labor movement; it is one of the basic factors.

The so-called Japanese characteristics of the labor movement may be summarized as follows:

Organization:
(i)   Predominance of the occupationally mixed form of enterprise (plant or multi-plant) unions
(ii)   Existence of national unions and national centers for the purpose of covering the weaknesses of enterprise unions

Function:
(i)   Collective bargaining, collective agreements, and joint labor-management conferences at the enterprise level
(ii)   Political and legislative activities (primarily by national unions, national centers, and public employee unions)

Nature of the Movement:
(i)   An exclusive movement of the "regular" workers of big enterprises
(ii)   Political orientation
(iii)   Tendency for internal splits and disintegration
(iv)   Transformation from the political orientation to the economic orientation (under the slogan of "Japanese way of trade unionism") as a long-run trend

Among these characteristics, those at the enterprise level reflect the nature of what is called "vertical hierarchical society," while at the national level political orientation is the basic characteristic of the movement.

The fact that those two characteristics have continued to coexist indicates that although economic orientation has been set as the main goal of the movement under the slogan of the "Japanese way of trade unionism," the labor movement has not been transformed into the Western type of trade unionism. Even if the Japanese labor movement has been differentiated from the social reform movement due to its increasing degree of economic orientation, it is still different from Western counterparts that have developed on the foundation of craft unionism.

The Japanese labor movement has an inner logic which makes it extremely difficult to completely wipe out its political nature. Thus economic orientation and political orientation have continued to coexist with enterprise-level activities and national level activities.

POLITICAL RADICALISM IN THE LABOR MOVEMENT

A primary characteristic of the Japanese labor movement is that political radicalism, which sometimes exhibited strong anti-capitalist orientation, always existed during any of the post-war periods. It can be seen in the following forms of the movement: frequent occurrence of fierce political strikes which challenge the basic social system; labor-management relationships, which involve an extreme confrontation between the parties, at a certain stage of many disputes; the fact that workers and their organizations have continued to have political problems as a goal of their movement, together with the intra-industry problems; and the fact that the labor movement has had a close relationship with Socialist parties or that it has become their major source of support—many union leaders have become party members or party representatives in national and local politics and unions, and their members have supported the party financially.

The factors which have contributed to shape the political nature of the Japanese labor movement can be seen in the paternalistic social system, the processes of economic development, and economic, historical, and political processes of the labor market. More specifically, the following are important factors:

(a) The existence of a remnant of traditional paternalism
(b) The organizational form of the labor union due to the backwardness in the development in the labor market
(c) Poor working conditions, resulting from the fact that workers' interests have tended to be sacrificed in exchange for rapid economic growth in the allocation of the fruits of economic growth

(d) Association of the labor movement with the Socialist parties due to the sense of oppression on the part of the workers.

THE LONG-RUN TREND TO THE POST-WAR LABOR MOVEMENT

These characteristics have been apparent in both right-wing and left-wing unions in every period; however, as a long-run trend of the labor movement in the entire post-war period, we can observe the gradual transformation of its focus from political to economic orientation. In other words, the labor movement has come to play a function independent from the influence of the Socialist parties. This long-run trend is caused partially by the nature of the labor movement within the Japanese environment and partially by the increasing tightness of the labor market due to the post-war economic growth. Those points may be summarized as follows.

(a) Whenever a union takes a radical course, the mild right-wing faction and the middle-of-the-road faction rise and promote an internal split of the union. By this mechanism union radicalism of the left-wing faction has been checked. For example, the Sanbetsu (All-Japan Congress of Industrial Labor Organizations) has been disorganized by the internal split initiated by Mindo (Democratization League), which later became Sohyo and Sodomei. When Sohyo itself became radicalized later, opposing forces within it took over the leadership; moreover, Zenro split from Sohyo to become Domei, which is a rival organization of Sohyo. This affects the national, industry, and enterprise organizations.

(b) Collective bargaining has become institutionalized as a major function of the labor movement, and it has attracted growing interest on the part of workers.

(c) Causes of the labor disputes have shifted from the political to the economic sphere. The tendency has continued at an increasing speed. Disputes over political causes, which had increased around 1960, can no longer attract the attention of the workers.

(d) As a result of the continuous criticism against the close tie of the union with a particular party, the degree of party control of the union has decreased.

Thus a rise in the economic orientation is the long-run trend of the labor movement in post-war Japan. What are the causes for it? First of all, economic growth. But economic growth does not directly affect the labor movement; it affects the demand and supply situation on the labor market, which in turn influences employment opportunities, wages, and working conditions. Changes in those can be directly perceived by the workers.

Japan's economic growth has been so rapid that it has created a time lag in terms of the adjustment in employment conditions and social welfare; this lag has a potential to direct the workers toward radicalism. Yet, as the fruits of economic growth gradually came to be distributed among workers as improvements in wages and fringe benefits in the enterprises and increases in social security and social welfare at the national level, the labor movement has become more concerned with economic and industrial problems. This tendency of economic orientation has become apparent since 1965. This can be illustrated for each of the post-war periods as follows: economic growth shown in terms of increases in national product promoted the expansion of fringe benefits and welfare facilities at the enterprise level, especially of big enterprises in the first period (or the reconstruction period); the expansion and stability of employment in the second (or stabilizing) period; and increases in wages and improvement in social investment and welfare in the third period. Naturally, such developments have affected the workers, and this in turn has influenced the orientation of the labor movement.

The characteristics of supply-demand relationships on the labor market and their connection with economic growth in each period may be summarized as follows. In the first period the expansion of welfare facilities, primarily by the big enterprises, was partially caused by union pressure. But more important, it was initiated by the big enterprises as a means to retain a work force of good quality.

In the second period and thereafter, the pressure of labor shortage, due to economic reconstruction and growth, became increasingly severe and extended to the medium and small enterprises. The expansion of employment in the second period is best illustrated by the decrease in the rate of unemployment observed in the records of unemployment insurance. This tendency has generally continued to exist until now as a result of sustained and rapid economic growth.

In spite of the pressure of labor shortage, the demand for labor was at first selective; as the degree of labor shortage intensified, it has become less selective. A characteristic of the second period is that, as a result of the change in the industrial structure due to industrialization, an increasing proportion of the new school graduates were employed by big and medium enterprises in the secondary and tertiary industries, while the ratio of those employed by primary industry decreased. High school graduates rather than junior high school graduates were in demand by the big enterprises in the third period, and in addition to new school graduates an increasing number of workers moved from agriculture and small enterprises to the big enterprises.

As a result of these changes in the labor market, labor shortage, especially a shortage of young workers, has become a general phenomenon. Since the second period, and especially in the third period, wage increases, particularly increases in the starting wages of the young workers, have been achieved every year. In addition, expansion and improvement of enterprise welfare facilities, as well as increases in social welfare such as social security, housing, environmental conditions, pollution, and transportation, have come to attract increasing attention. This tendency toward wage increases and improvement in social welfare will continue to grow stronger.

Japan's post-war economic growth has created a labor force of good quality capable of adjusting itself to change; however, it has also created a long-run tendency of labor shortage, which is a favorable condition for the workers. The effects of economic growth upon the workers as well as the latters' expectation of further benefits from economic growth have created and enhanced a psychology which favors the capitalistic system among the rank of workers. As the economy expands an increasing number of workers have come to participate in the economic activities which emphasize improvements in employment conditions by means of collective bargaining. The annual increases in the number of union members participating in the so-called Shunto movement illustrate this tendency.

For the 1970's we may predict the following: the moderate group, mostly composed of the "regular workers" of the big enterprises, will dissent from traditional radicalism, and the labor movement will split into many factions; in respect to its political orientation, the labor movement will clarify the functional differences of the Socialist movement and the labor movement and will strengthen its economic orientation.

NOTE—THE RELATIONSHIP TO LEWIS-STURMTHAL MODEL

The above-mentioned characteristics of the labor movement in post-war Japan vividly show us the processes through which economic growth absorbs the originally unlimited labor supply, and how changes in labor supply affect the nature of the labor movement. Now to summarize these processes.

When the Japanese economy entered into the stage of high economic growth, there was an abundant supply of labor. In addition, there was disguised unemployment. Therefore the labor supply was almost unlimited. In the face of the abundant labor force, demand for young workers or junior high school graduates, who had the high adaptability required by technological change, rapidly increased. Those workers were hired primarily by the big and medium enterprises; as a result the small enterprises, which had heavily relied upon those workers, came to have difficulties recruiting them. As the speed of growth increased, and as a growing proportion of junior high school graduates came to enter high school, companies began to hire high school graduates as manual workers. The mobility of workers among industries and from small to big and medium enterprises also increased. The pressure of general labor shortages is expected to continue, and in the long run workers will move from the low productivity sector to the high productivity sector or to the sector where consumers' demand greatly increases.

The impact of economic growth upon the labor market has resulted in an increase in employment in the faster-growing big and medium enterprises. Since the bulk of union membership is composed of the workers of the big and medium enterprises, increases in employment in those enterprises automatically enhance union membership. Furthermore the competition for manpower on the part of employers has created a situation favorable for the young workers as well as for the workers in the big enterprises.

In this situation unions, especially those of the big enterprises, have emphasized economic activities using collective bargaining as the major weapon. The development of Shunto, which is carried out and expanded every year, well illustrates this point. The effectiveness of the labor movement in this respect is largely due to the post-war labor legislation, but, more important, it results from the increase in union membership as well as the labor shortage, which started among the young workers and later became a general phenomenon.

Those changes will accelerate and institutionalize the economic orientation of the Japanese labor movement and free the labor movement from its intimate connection with the political movement, although the unions might not go so far as to completely sever their relationship with the Socialist movement.

Koji Taira

Labor Markets, Unions, and Employers in Inter-war Japan

THIS BOOK is mainly concerned with the conditions under which a reasonably permanent collective bargaining system can be established and is in fact likely to come into being. In Japan, this "reasonably permanent collective bargaining system" had not come into being until a "democratic social revolution" was ushered into Japan under the aegis of the Allied Occupation Forces after World War II, as discussed by Kawada and Komatsu in the previous chapter of this book. Yet there were at least two waves of pre-war Japanese labor movement. The first was perhaps only a ripple, a short-lived movement for a period between the Sino-Japanese War of 1894–95 and the Russo-Japanese War of 1904–5. The second wave was more substantial in length and in extent of workers, employers, general public, and government involved. It started shortly before World War I, peaked in the early 1930's, and declined to a total demise at the beginning of World War II. Thus there was a vigorous labor movement during the inter-war period of Japan, but no "reasonably permanent collective bargaining system" came into being as a product of that movement. This suggests that certain prerequisites for that system explored in the introduction to this volume were not fulfilled in inter-war Japan. This chapter explores

This paper is an outgrowth of certain sections of the author's *Economic Development and the Labor Market in Japan* (New York: Columbia University Press, 1970). However, I take a fresh look at Japan's inter-war labor market and offer new materials and observations. I am grateful to Adolf Sturmthal and James Scoville for comments on an earlier draft of this paper.

the economic, social and political aspects of these aborted pre-requisites in the specific setting of inter-war Japan, with special emphasis on what all workers, either individually or through or-ganized efforts, are always interested in: wages and working con-ditions.

Japan's inter-war period (1920–40) is full of interesting eco-nomic and institutional events posing a worthy challenge for co-herent explanation. Among these are certain interrelated groups of factors which should be systematically explained from the stand-point of labor economics. These are: (1) general economic con-ditions (aggregate demand, money supply, and price level), (2) labor market events (wages, employment, and labor turnover), (3) organized institutional factors (trade unions and employer as-sociations), and (4) public policy. This chapter focuses on the labor market events and attempts to interpret them in relation to changes in general economic conditions and organized institutional factors.

For the purposes of this paper, labor market may be defined as a socio-economic mechanism that accommodates and reconciles em-ployers' and workers' objectives as they are individually and inde-pendently formulated, expressed, and pursued. This is another way of saying that the labor market clears demand for and supply of labor, with special emphasis on *independent* decision-making strate-gies by *individual* participants. When some workers or employers join a group and act *collectively* in the manner and scale that would not have been possible individually, the functioning of the labor market can be expected to be modified by that organized institu-tional factor to varying degrees. In inter-war Japan, such institu-tional factors were present, and this paper attempts to evaluate their impact on the functioning of the labor market. The chapter consists of three sections respectively devoted to the labor market events of inter-war Japan, trade unions, and employer associations. A brief note is added on the kinds of public policy relevant to the labor market analysis.

THE LABOR MARKET

The labor market determines wages and employment, subject to the pressures of forces external to this market, such as changes in the aggregate demand, institutional factors, and public policy.[1]

1   It is conventional to formulate the functioning of the labor market by two simultaneous equations, which may be written as follows:

Three meanings of the term "wages" need our attention. These are money wages, real wages, and relative wages. Wages may be rates or earnings. Throughout this chapter, wages refer to daily wage rates. Chart I compares consumer prices, money wage rates, manufacturing output, and factory employment for the period 1910–38. Chart II presents indices of real wage rates and of labor productivity in manufacturing, together with the time series of unionization rates and of workers on strike. The dimension of time is extended back to 1910 for perspective.

There was sharp inflation during World War I. (Although the index of wholesale prices of manufacturing products is not shown on Chart I for fear of cluttering the chart too much, it fluctuated more violently than the consumer price index shown on the chart.[2]) During the 1920's prices decreased on the whole, while money wage rates continued to increase at least up to 1928. Prices fell precipitously between 1929 and 1931. Although money wages also fell, they fell more slowly than prices. Consequently, real wages kept going up and peaked at the trough of prices and money wages in 1931. Thereafter wages did not keep pace with prices, and real wages decreased.

Wages and prices, 1920–31

Sticky money wages during a period of falling prices implies that employers either do not want to cut money wages or do not have to resort to it because of alternative ways of maintaining their profits. Suppose, for example, that employers desire to maintain profits as a given sum of money while the prices of their products are falling. What are the conditions that enable them to do so while holding money wages constant? In this case, the employers are caught in a price-wage squeeze. If one assumes, for further heuristic convenience, that profits are proportional to the net proceeds of labor cost, an answer to the question may be this: hold money wages and employment constant and increase output at a rate equal

---

Demand for labor: $N_d = f(w, Y, Z, A)$
Supply of labor: $N_s = g(w, Y, Z, A)$
The two equations determine w (wages) and N (employment $= N_d = N_s$). But this determination cannot be effected unless the values of Y (aggregate demand), Z (institutional factors), and A (public policy) are given.

2 Kazushi Ohkawa et al., *Prices: Estimates of Long-Term Economic Statistics of Japan Since 1868,* vol. 8, pp. 192–193. (Cited as ELTES hereafter.) Also available in this volume are data on daily earnings. These show slightly greater flexibility, both upward and downward, than wage rates, although observations on the basis of rates apply equally to the analysis of trends and variations in earnings.

Chart I.   Consumer Prices, Money Wage Rates, Manufacturing Output, and Factory Employment

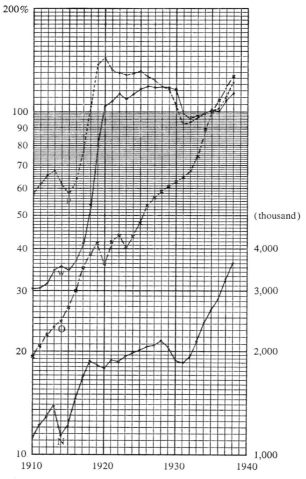

p = index of consumer prices (1934–36 = 100). Source: Kazushi Ohkawa et al., eds., *Estimates of Long-Term Economic Statistics of Japan Since 1868*, vol. 8, *Prices* (Tokyo: Toyo keizai shinposha, 1967), pp. 135–36.

w = index of money wage rates in manufacturing (1934–36 = 100). Source: *ibid.*, p. 243.

O = index of manufacturing output (1935 = 100). Source: Yuichi Shionoya, "Patterns of Industrial Development," in *Economic Growth*, ed. Lawrence Klein and Kazushi Ohkawa (Homewood, Ill.: Richard D. Irwin, 1968), pp. 100–109.

N = Factory employment in thousands (scale on the right in Chart I) in plants employing five or more workers. Sources: For 1910–20, Kazushi Ohkawa, ed., *Nihon keizai no seichōritsu* (*The Rate of Growth of the Japanese Economy*) (Tokyo: Iwanami, 1956), p. 83; for 1920–38, *Kōjō* (later *Kōgyō*) *tōkeihyō* (annual publication by the Ministry of Commerce).

Chart II. Unionization Rate, Striking Workers, Real Wage Rate, and Labor Productivity in Manufacturing

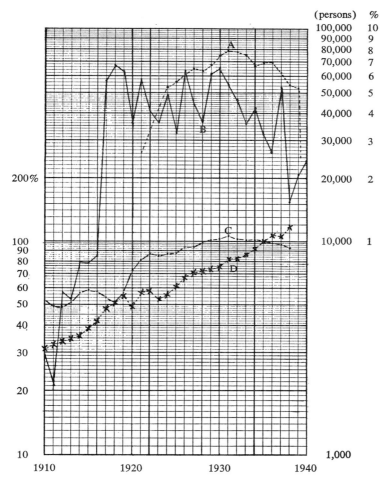

A = unionization rate of all paid workers. The scale in percentages is on the right.
  Source: *Nihon rōdō undō shiryō* (*Historical Materials on Japanese Labor Movement*),
  vol. 10, ed. Commission on Historical Materials on Japanese Labor Movement
  (Tokyo, 1959), p. 424. Lines before 1924 and after 1939 are only indicative of
  general trends.
B = number of workers on strike. The scale in persons is on the right. Source: *Nihon
  rōdō undō shiryō*, vol. 10, pp. 440–41.
C = index of real wage rates: w/p from Chart I. The scale is on the left.
D = index of labor productivity in manufacturing: O from Chart I divided by an index
  of manufacturing employment. Source: for manufacturing employment, Kazushi
  Ohkawa et al., *The Growth Rate of the Japanese Economy Since 1878* (Tokyo:
  Kinokuniya, 1957), pp. 245–46.

to the rate at which prices decrease.[3] This simple solution seems to have obtained during the price deflation of 1920 to 1931 in the manufacturing sector of Japan. A precipitous fall in prices took place between 1920 and 1921, and between 1929 and 1931. Between 1921 and 1929 the wholesale prices of manufacturing products decreased by 20 percent, while output increased by 45 percent. For the entire period covering the whole downswing from peak to trough between 1920 and 1931, prices decreased by 59 percent. During the same period output increased by 79 percent. But this figure owes much to the unusual dip in output that occurred between 1919 and 1920. When the output figure for 1919 (an all-time high before 1920) or that for 1921 (which returned to the 1919 level) is used as the base, the increase in output up to 1931 was 55 percent. On the whole, therefore, one may suppose that during the 1920's, despite the persistent fall in prices, there were objective conditions that at least kept employers from being hurt by the price-wage squeeze implied by the deflation and sticky money wages. The difference between output increases and price decreases during a good part of the 1920's even allowed some room for adding to employment. In fact, factory employment increased by 13 percent between 1921 and 1928. The increase in the labor cost due to this increase in employment coupled with sticky money wages should have been adequately covered by the increase in the proceeds brought about by output expansion.[4]

---

3   The profit (π) in this case can be stated: $\pi = k \; (pO - wN)$ where k is a constant fraction, p = product price, O = output, w = wage rate, and N = employment. The maximization process yields the following condition:

$$p \cdot \triangle O = -O \cdot \triangle p$$

or

$$\frac{\triangle O}{O} = - \frac{\triangle p}{p}$$

which means that the output increases at the same rate as the rate of decrease in the price.

4   There are many identification problems involved in relationships among output, prices, wages, and employment. Here output and prices are regarded as exogenous to the labor market on which attention is focused. However, one may wonder what incentives spurred manufacturers to produce and supply more goods when prices were persistently going down during the 1920's. Did the Japanese producers reason that, when prices were falling, the only way to maintain or improve their proceeds was to produce and sell more, only to end up with further decreases in prices? This kind of producer behavior is not unknown in economic analysis; in fact, it is the well-known behavior of producers under pure competition. Although one may frown upon it, the inference is that Japanese producers during the 1920's may well have been operating under conditions like pure com-

The above exposition of employers' choices for the objective of maintaining profits in the face of price deflation points up three equally likely strategies. One possibility that did not obtain in the 1920's until 1929 was to cut employment while maintaining money wages and output.[5] Another possibility was to cut money wages while maintaining output and employment.[6] This course of action was impossible to entertain because of the stickiness of money wages. The third possibility was mentioned in the preceding paragraph; i.e., expand output while maintaining money wages and employment. The availability of multiple courses of action for employers raises the question why employers in inter-war Japan preferred, or were compelled into, one course of action against others. Employers allowed money wages to be sticky downward and, to compound the difficulty, maintained or even increased employment. This choice should have been the most difficult of all choices open to them, for it required employers to undertake additional investment and reorganize (or "rationalize," to use the popular term of the period) productive activities in their plants so that more output could result from each worker kept on the payroll. Given the combination of the on-going negative price incentive and of the technical difficulties involved in rationalization and capital formation, one wonders what made employers during the 1920's embark upon this particular course of action. Eventually employer capability to adhere to this course of action ran up against its limits. With the onslaught of the Great Depression, it was no longer possible to maintain employment and money wages in the face of sharply falling prices. Attempts were made (with some success) to cut money wages, but they were not effective or drastic enough to match falling prices. Real wages rose further,

---

petition. Another analytical snarl is to what extent the price decreases during the 1920's were due to increases in the supply of goods and to what extent they were due to other factors, like money supply and fiscal policy. Fiscal policy was avowedly deflationary, and the keynote in it throughout the 1920's was to return to gold at the rate that prevailed before World War I. Money supply, too, decreased somewhat during the 1920's. For further light on inter-war fiscal and monetary policies, see Hugh Patrick, *Japanese Government Macro-Policy: Failure in the 1920's, Success (of a Sort) in the 1930's,* Yale University Economic Growth Center Discussion Paper no. 50 (1968).

5 In the framework of maximization under note 4, this would be

$$O \cdot \Delta p = w \cdot \Delta N$$

where the change in the proceeds is equal, while O and w remain constant, to the change in the wage bill.

6 This would be $O \cdot \Delta p = N \cdot \Delta w$ where O and N remain constant, again requiring the change in proceeds to be equal to the change in the wage bill.

and employers resorted to reduction of employment or went bankrupt.

Not only was there a multiplicity of choices open to employers, but these choices may also have been ranked by degree of difficulty in achievement. As far as product prices were concerned, employers as producers and suppliers of products were at the mercy of forces beyond their control: fiscal and monetary policies and competitive product markets. Product prices were the most difficult for individual employers to influence; cuts in money wages were next in the scale of difficulty confronting employers. Consequently, from individual employers' points of view, prices, money wages, and real wages had to be reckoned with as data determined by markets and the system as a whole. Cutting employment was not easily resorted to, but it was easier to accomplish than cutting money wages. (One may be reminded in this connection that the notion of lifetime employment is a myth as a primary characteristic of employment relations in Japan.) What was more fully under the control of employers was how to improve the utilization of workers they already had. Whatever happened to prices and wages, the long-run strategy along the line of least resistance was to keep trying to improve labor productivity. Indeed, the movements of prices and the transition of socio-economic events during the 1920's gave a danger signal for the stability and viability of the Japanese economy. Yet labor productivity in the manufacturing sector increased at a healthy rate abreast of Japan's historical trends.

Wages and prices, 1931–39

Both wholesale and consumer prices bottomed out in 1931 and turned upward. Money wages fell, although not as steeply as prices, between 1929 and 1931 and also took another dip in 1931–32 before they turned upward. During the remainder of the 1930's money wage rates lagged behind prices. Thus real wage rates tended to fall. During the 1930's manufacturing employment increased at an unprecedented rate. It looked as though the supplies of labor to the manufacturing sector were "unlimited" at falling real wage rates. However, this should not be considered as a phenomenon falling under the Lewis-Fei-Ranis model of economic development with surplus labor, because it was largely cyclical in nature. In this connection it is useful to distinguish factory employment from manufacturing employment as a whole. It is factory employment that experienced the most unusual expansion during the 1930's. Conventionally, "factory" is defined as a manufacturing plant that is large enough to employ five or more paid workers. The number of paid workers in factories was below half of the total manufacturing employment during much of the inter-war period. Only as recently as 1938 did factory employment begin to rise above 50 percent of total manufacturing employment. (Of course, paid workers employed in the manufacturing sector were more numerous than factory employment at any time, because smaller subfactory plants also had some paid workers. Paid workers in manufacturing were about 60 percent of total manufacturing employment in 1930, when factory employment defined in this paragraph was slightly above 40 percent of the same total.)

Two interrelated dichotomies in the structure of employment may be noted. One is the dichotomy of factory employment and nonfactory manufacturing employment. The other is the dichotomy of manufacturing employment (together with employment in other nonagricultural sectors) and agricultural employment. In this kind of economy, factory workers do not have to originate solely in agriculture; they may well be drawn from the manufacturing sector itself or from other nonagricultural sectors. Similarly, workers leaving agriculture may not consider factories as the sole employers. They have a greater probability of finding jobs at the subfactory level of manufacturing activities or in the tertiary sector. They may also employ themselves in a variety of pursuits in manufacturing, trade, and services. In any case, since factory employment was small in inter-war Japan, it was obviously impossible for factories alone to absorb all the workers leaving agriculture. At the same time, there was no reason for factory managers to prefer workers fresh from agriculture to workers from other sectors and with experiences other than agriculture. One should therefore not take too literally the popular models of dualism, which tend to reason about the labor allocative process within the framework of the agriculture-industry dichotomy only.

Between 1931 and 1939 factory employment more than doubled while real wage rates tended to fall. This relationship between wages and employment was brought about by unusual socioeconomic circumstances during the inter-war period. In 1931, real wages were at an all-time high; there had been an accumulation of unemployed and underemployed workers, due to the contraction of factory employment during 1928 to 1931 and due to natural increases in the labor force. The precipitous fall in factory employment between 1928 and 1931 was on the order of 13 percent of the 1928 level. Factory employment returned to the 1928 level in 1933. But during the period 1928–33, increases in the labor force accumulated, and a portion of them should have become a ready labor reserve for factory employment. How long it took factories to absorb this reserve may be seen by comparing the annual level of factory employment with its long-term trend value. Trend-adjusted factory employment consistently decreased between 1918 and 1932. Factory employment was on the trend line in 1926 and, having fallen to its below-trend trough in 1932, returned to the trend line in 1937.[7] (The accumulation of the labor reserve started before the absolute level of factory employment began to turn downward in 1928.) The first two years of the 1931–37 period were necessary for absorbing the unemployed, and the next five years were necessary for absorbing the labor reserve that had been accumulating since 1926. Thus one may well suppose that a good part of the 1930's was indeed a period of infinitely elastic labor supplies to factories.

The industrial expansion of the 1930's has been called Japan's second Industrial Revolution. It was led by a revolutionary development of metal-working, machinery, and chemical industries. The share of these industries in factory employment was 27 percent in 1930, when that of textiles was 52 percent. Metals, machinery, and chemicals were employing 53 percent of factory labor by 1940, while textiles' share had fallen to 28 percent. The legacy of the textile-led Industrial Revolution of Japan came to an end during the 1930's. One would have thought that the so-called heavy and chemical industries should have suffered from the growth-stunting effect of skill shortage and, in attempting to relieve themselves from this constraint, should have raised wages both absolutely and relative to all other industries. The fact was quite to the contrary. These industries, the champions of the modern sector, apparently not only suffered from very little skill shortage but also enjoyed unlimited supplies of labor. Wages in metal and machinery industries fell relative to textiles and other light industries after 1935. Before this, as expected, wages in these industries were rising relative to other industries. The wage differential between metal-machinery and textiles reached its maximum in 1936. The widening of the wage differential up to 1936 was in part a lagged response, seen in many other wage differentials, to the depressed labor market conditions during the late 1920's and early 1930's.[8] It is hardly plausible to interpret the rise in metals-machinery wages relative to wages

---

7   Taira, *Economic Development,* p. 38.
8   *Ibid.,* pp. 66–69.

in other industries between 1931 and 1936 as something induced by relative shortage of skills and labor to metal and machinery industries.

Within heavy industries it was larger firms that enjoyed more than an average share in the most "unlimited supplies" of labor to these industries, despite the decrease in wages offered by them relative to wages in other, smaller firms during the latter half of the 1930's. There was no mystery about this situation, for wages had risen in these firms relative to others up to around 1932. Yet the superiority of large firms over others in wages and working conditions in the 1930's was something new in Japanese industrial history. Prior to 1920, and to some extent prior to 1925, large firms were not particularly attractive relative to small firms or workshops. It was widely believed that workers would show up to apply for jobs in large firms as a last resort after losing jobs in small firms or workshops and failing to find jobs with similar employers. The acute labor shortage during World War I and the rising tides of labor disputes induced large employers to undertake different labor policies. Wages and working conditions began to improve perceptibly in large firms after 1920.[9] By 1930 the superiority of large firms in the net advantage of employment conditions was no longer in question. On the strength of superior conditions of employment, large firms during the 1930's were able to hire as many workers as they wanted at the standards of quality and skill they prescribed without necessarily raising wages relative to other firms and industries.

Whatever wage differentials one may turn to, they behaved in the same way as the inter-industry and inter-firm wage differentials mentioned above. Among the major divisions of the economy (such as agriculture, mining, manufacturing, construction, transportation, gas, and electricity) for which inter-war wage data are available, wages rose in high-wage divisions up to 1933–35 and then decreased relative to low-wage divisions. Real wages in agriculture and mining even decreased absolutely during the depressed

9   Data on wage differentials between large and small firms (or establishments) in the form of time series are particularly scarce. Wage differentials of this kind for isolated years such as 1909, 1914, and 1932 are reviewed in *ibid.*, Ch. 7. Some of the much-needed time series of wage differentials by size of firm are presented in Konosuke Odata, "A History of Money Wages in the Northern Kyushu Industrial Area, 1898–1939," *Hitotsubashi Journal of Economics* 8 (February, 1968): 71–100; and Ryoshin Minami, "Further Considerations on the Turning Point in the Japanese Economy (I)," *ibid.*, 10 (February, 1970): 45–47, 53.

years agound 1930. Wage differentials by length of service, age, and sex also widened during the 1920's and early 1930's and narrowed after 1935. The skilled workers' wages increased relative to the unskilled workers' up to 1932 and then turned downward. The wage differentials among geographical areas such as prefectures and cities likewise widened and narrowed.[10]

The behavior of wage differentials indicates that money wages in inter-war Japan tended to be stickier downward and upward in industry than in agriculture, in heavy than in light industries, in large than in small firms, for skilled than for unskilled trades, for male than for female workers, and in high-wage than in low-wage areas. Furthermore, it has been ascertained time and time again that patterns of wage stickiness were associated with degrees of employment flexibility; i.e., employment rose and fell by greater proportions where wages were relatively sticky than where they were relatively flexible. Thus, during the downswing phase of the business cycle as in the 1920's and early 1930's, when downward stickiness of money wages generally came into play, employment increased less rapidly and at a later stage decreased faster where money wages were stable than where they were not. During the upswing in the rest of the 1930's employment increased faster where money wages were sticky upward than where they were not.

The different degrees of employment flexibility were also related to labor turnover rates. For example, labor turnover was rapid in textile industries where women and girls were predominant. Frequent refillings of vacancies enabled employers to revise wage rates downward frequently, at least for newly hired workers. Since wage costs went down quickly in this way through adjustments in wage rates, the need for cost reduction through reducing employment was not acute in these industries. By contrast, workers in heavy industries were mostly skilled adult males with family responsibilities and tended to stay longer on their jobs than textile workers. Therefore, employers' opportunities to revise wage rates downward with relative ease were limited in these industries, where attrition without new hires, dismissals for cause (legitimate or contrived), or quits induced by discharge allowances, not to mention occasional mass layoffs at the risk of labor disputes, were relied upon as means of cutting labor costs. Thus wage flexibility was inversely associated with employment flexibility by industry. There were different degrees of ease with which employers were able to cut

10   Taira, *Economic Development,* Ch. 1.

cost. For example, paying lower wages to newly hired workers was easier than cutting wages for workers already employed, while reducing employment through a variety of means was easier than cutting wages for all workers. It may be supposed that the different degrees of freedom or convenience in employer choice of labor strategy were associated with different degrees of acceptability of various measures to workers.

We have so far explored the possibility of explaining labor market events in terms of individual preferences and strategies of employers and workers. However, these preferences and strategies are not random. They tend to be predictably structured. Eventually one may have to admit that individual behavior is culturally conditioned and that there is societal consensus about what one may or may not do. Insofar as the labor market is concerned, there are intermediate factors that intervene between individual choice and cultural consensus. These are organized institutional factors, of which there are two groups of utmost interest here: trade unions on the supply side, and employer associations on the demand side. This and following sections explore how such organized institutional factors may have influenced the labor market events of inter-war Japan.

INSTITUTIONAL FACTORS: THE LABOR MOVEMENT

In inter-war Japan the extent of trade unionism as measured by the proportion of wage earners organized reached its peak in 1931, as shown in Chart II. During the same historical period, real wage rates (money wage rates deflated by the wholesale price index or consumer price index) likewise reached their peak in 1931. Therefore a nearly perfect positive fit obtained between union strength and real wages. Does this suggest that trade unions had a role to play in the rise and fall of real wages in inter-war Japan? Or was the relationship between wages and unions largely spurious, merely accompanying like a shadow changing economic conditions and market forces?

In general, the trade union may be regarded as an indicator of workers' efforts to promote what is desirable to them and to resist or remove what is not in their interest. However, desires, aspirations, and grievances of workers are multi-dimensional. For analytical convenience one may imagine that at any moment a given trade union has an "objective function" whose elements reflect workers' various desires, aspirations, and grievances, ordered according to degrees of urgency. Because of exigencies of strategy or for a number of other considerations, the ordering of priorities in the union's objective function changes or fluctuates from time to time; this creates difficulties in analysis. The union may be interested in obtaining higher wages and greater job security for its members, or it may work as a part of a broader labor movement for enhancing the welfare of the working class as a whole. Sometimes the union's survival and growth as an organization may take precedence over the short-run welfare of its individual members. At other times concerns with the visible improvements of labor conditions for individual members may push the union into an action that risks its organizational viability. The labor movement as a whole may be more concerned about workers' personal dignity, education, political rights, class solidarity, and other broader aspects of man and society. These goals or objectives, either at the individual union level or at the level of the labor movement, may be short-run or long-run, and they may be complements sometimes and substitutes at other times. In sum, the emphasis of the union or of the labor movement is so volatile most of the time that it is difficult to assign stable weights to its various objectives in order to derive a clear-cut pattern of impact on wages and employment.[11]

The above paragraph is a warning against any simple attempt to correlate wages or employment with quantifiable aspects of trade unionism with the intention of proving or disproving hypotheses about "union impact" on wages or employment. This impact is likely to be only a small portion of total emotional, ideological, and political feedback that develops between the labor movement and general society, especially when the labor movement arises for the first time in the history of a nation and makes a serious bid for recognition as a lawful institution representing workers' demands. In the first place, it may be utterly incomprehensible to the public, employers, and even workers in such a society that some workers should assume and openly say that they have demands to make on society and employers. Thus many events involving the labor movement are often newsworthy and become known to

11 The attempt to relate trade unions to the labor market in the manner employed in this section is in the tradition of Clark Kerr, "Wage Relationships: The Comparative Impact of Market and Power Forces," in *The Theory of Wage Determination*, ed. John T. Dunlop (New York: Macmillan, 1957), Ch. 12. For an alternative approach to the analysis of interrelations between labor markets and trade unions, see S. B. Levine, "Labor Markets and Collective Bargaining in Japan," in *The State and Economic Enterprise in Japan*, ed. W. W. Lockwood (Princeton, N.J.: Princeton University Press, 1965), Ch. 14.

workers, employers, and the public well beyond the immediate industrial relations context of the events. In other words, the labor movement generally generates "externalities" through nonmarket channels of information, in addition to whatever direct influences it may exert on the functioning of the market to which it is immediately related. One may even suppose that the externalities of major events like prolonged strikes, bitter disputes, large-scale industrial accidents, etc., far outweigh their impact on their immediate labor market settings—firms, workers, and localities involved or implicated in them. In the labor literature, these externalities are commonly called "spillovers." The extent of any event's spillover effect depends upon the event's capability to shock the general public, the degree of importance that societal consensus attributes to it, or the lessons that society draws from it. This section will argue that the downward stickiness of money wage rates in the face of falling prices during the 1920's was due largely to the spillover effect of industrial disputes and trade union activities.

The labor movement had its modest start in Japan soon after the Sino-Japanese War (1894–95), but this early attempt quickly came to an end, partly because of suppression by the government and partly because of the lack of experience on the part of workers and their leaders.[12] Bunji Suzuki, a young intellectual, graduated from the Imperial University of Tokyo in 1912 and, inspired by his Christian ideals, gathered several workers around him and called the group Yuaikai (Friendly Society), which marked the revival of trade unionism in post-Meiji Japan. (The celebrated Meiji Era, 1868–1912, came to a close with the death of the Emperor Meiji in 1912.) Operating within the social and political climate intensely hostile to any kind of labor movement, Suzuki's Friendly Society, to avoid public misgivings, professed to aim at the moral and cultural uplifting of workers. But as a group friendly to workers the Friendly Society from the outset could not avoid involving itself in helping workers obtain a favorable settlement of industrial disputes. The Friendly Society expanded rapidly, from the initial 15 in 1912 to 1,295 in June, 1913, to over 7,000 by July, 1915, and eventually to 30,000 in 1920. Unions not affiliated with the Friendly Society also sprang up in many parts of Japan during World War I. The Friendly Society itself underwent an organizational transformation. In 1919 it shed its camouflage and proclaimed itself to be a labor federation determined to become the

12   Iwao F. Ayusawa, *A History of Labor in Modern Japan* (Honolulu: East-West Center Press, 1966), pp. 69–75.

Japanese counterpart of the AFL. At this time "Friendly Society" was retained as a subtitle of the organization. It was eliminated entirely in 1921, when the formal title adopted was Nihon rōdō sōdōmei (Japan Federation of Labor, to be cited as JFL.)[13]

The membership of all trade unions including the JFL at the end of World War I stood at about 100,000 workers, which exceeded 2 percent of nonagricultural wage earners at the time. It signified a remarkable rate of union growth, having risen from zero only eight years earlier. A great spurt occurred in 1924, adding more than 100,000 workers in one year to the 1923 membership of 125,-000. In reference to all nonagricultural wage earners, the rate of unionization in 1924 amounted to 5.3 percent.[14] It took unions five more years to take on a further 100,000, and seven years in addition to make another gain of 100,000. In 1936 trade union membership was at its inter-war peak with 420,600 workers. After that, Japan's increasing involvement in armed conflicts with China and the deepening political crisis at home created a social climate unfavorable to the labor movement, which increasingly had to contend with a negative image, however mistaken, as an unpatriotic, selfish movement. Right-wing worker groupings not worthy of treatment as trade unions spread throughout Japan and, with the help and encouragement of the government and employer organizations, eventually drowned out the bona fide labor movement. In 1941 less than 1,000 workers remained in unions. By 1945 trade unions had disappeared entirely. In terms of rates of unionization, organized labor peaked in 1931 with 7.9 percent of wage earners organized. (See Chart II.)

The movements of real wages and unionization rates on Chart II suggest an almost perfect correlation. However, since the unionization rate was a modest 8 percent at its peak in 1931, one may wonder how such a low rate of unionization could have affected the course of real wages so substantially as implied by Chart II. It is in this connection that the notion of spillover effect becomes important. The rise and progress of unionization, however modest, is an indicator of workers' aspirations and demands. Although the general rate of unionization never exceeded 8 percent, the ground swell of workers' aspirations and demands should have been many

13 Stephen S. Large, "The Japanese Labor Movement, 1912–1919: Suzuki Bunji and the Yuaikai," *Journal of Asian Studies* 29 (May, 1970): 559–79.
14 For a useful compendium of labor data, see *Nihon rōdō undō shiryō* (*Historical Data on the Japanese Labor Movement*), vol. 10. (Cited as NRUS hereafter.) The data on the rate of unionization are on p. 424.

times this rate. The common sentiments shared by the working population should have had their effect on the processes of wage determination in many firms. The 1920's were also characterized by a number of socio-cultural and institutional changes, popularly summed up under the rubric "Taisho Democracy," connoting the individualistic social climate, upward shifts in materialistic preferences for better living, demands for political rights, international pressures like those from the ILO on Japanese social policy, etc., which characterized the reign of Emperor Taisho, 1912–26.

Chart II suggests that the sharpest rise in real wage rates took place between 1918 and 1922. This was a lagging response to the prosperity brought about by World War I. History indicates that the accelerated increases in real wages after 1918 took place in association with social disturbances and industrial disputes. In 1918 there arose shocking consumer uprisings called "rice riots" in a number of urban centers to "liberate" rice (to use the language of the 1970's) from the speculative hoards of merchants. Industrial disputes had also reached serious proportions by this time. "In 1914, there were fifty strikes involving 7,904 workers. In 1915, there were sixty-four strikes involving 7,852 persons. In 1916, strikes numbered 108, involving 8,413 workers. In 1917, the number shot up to 398, involving 57,309 workers."[15] Workers' dissatisfaction mounted. In 1918 there were 417 strikes in which 66,457 men were involved. This was the largest number of workers on strike for the entire inter-war period.[16] In 1919 industrial disputes continued at a high level. The statistics became more refined, too. The number of disputes with or without strikes in 1919 was 2,388, involving 335,225 workers. Of these, 497 were strikes, with 63,-137 workers participating.[17] It seems therefore that the combination of growing unionism, social explosions, and accelerated industrial disputes finally set the floor to falling real wages and pushed them upward.

The wave of industrial disputes receded after 1919 to the trough of 1923 with 68,814 workers involved in 647 cases, of which strikes were 270 cases with 36,259 workers participating. It is difficult to detect periods or cycles of industrial disputes in the sawtooth movements of the time series (see Chart II). The first cycle, as mentioned above, seems clear enough. The second cycle peaked in 1930 with 191,805 workers involved (of whom 64,933

15 Large, "The Japanese Labor Movement," pp. 565–66.
16 *Ibid.*, p. 570.
17 *NRUS*, pp. 440–41.

workers were on strike), and receded to a low in 1936 with 92,724 workers involved in disputes (of whom only 26,772 were on strike). This cycle seems to be reasonably well correlated with the movement of real wages, with the lag of a year or two. Then the pattern is breached abruptly. There was a remarkable flare-up of disputes in 1937, involving 213,622 workers. There was another, less marked surge in disputes in 1939 with 128,294 workers involved, followed by a sudden drop in 1940 to 55,003 workers. The number of workers involved in disputes then steadily decreased to 16,694 in 1944.[18]

One major difference between the first dispute cycle (1914–24) and later cycles (1925–36, followed by irregular movements) is that the average number of workers per case was considerably larger during the first cycle. This indicates that the larger firms were involved in disputes during 1914–24. The firms or establishments struck during and after World War I included many of the well-known concerns in the private sector and several military arsenals. That larger firms were the targets of labor offensive during these years had an irreversible impact on the trend of employers' labor policies. It may be recalled, however, that by 1932 wage differentials by size of firm had widened considerably, indicating the superiority of larger over smaller firms in employment conditions. While this owed much to the worsening economic conditions of depression which hit smaller firms with greater severity, it reflected in large part the fruit of the efforts on the part of larger employers to improve wages and working conditions in response to their earlier disputes with workers.

The latter half of the 1920's was again a period of trade union militancy and political polarization in Japan. In 1925, the ideological strife within the JFL reached an irreparable pitch, and a left-wing faction broke away to form a militant labor congress (Hyōgikai). In 1928 this movement was forced to dissolve by the government, which branded it as Communist and applied the terms of a new Public Peace Maintenance Law (passed in 1925) to it. During the whole inter-war period the Japanese government failed to recognize trade unions as lawful organizations, although sporadic attempts were made during the 1920's to enact some kind of trade union law to accord legal recognition to carefully defined types of unions. During earlier years after World War I the government

18   *NRUS*, p. 440. For a further analysis of dispute statistics, see Taira, *Economic Development*, pp. 148–51.

even hand-picked labor representatives to the annual conferences of the International Labor Organization. In 1924, after the JFL dramatically exposed the scandal in the arena of the ILO conference, the Japanese government conceded to trade unions the right to elect their representatives to the ILO. At the same time the government schemed unabashedly to turn the tide in its favor by bringing into being a sizeable right-wing union of workers employed in naval installations. By this time the government had moved to a position in which it was ready to acquiesce with moderate, at worst libertarian, trade unions, while resolving ever more to suppress radical ideas and movements. On one hand, the government repealed the detested Article 17 of the Public Peace Policing Law of 1900, which had been used to harass the labor movement time and again. Furthermore, universal manhood suffrage, which the labor movement had been demanding for some years, was promulgated in 1925. On the other hand, a new law intended for "thought control" (the aforementioned Public Peace Maintenance Law) was simultaneously enacted to suppress the spread of revolutionary ideas or movements. But at the first general election after the universal manhood suffrage, the parties of "have-nots"—that is, of workers and peasants—elected eight representatives of their own to the House of Commons. Conservative leaders were alarmed, and reactions to this modest expansion of civil liberties were not far in the offing. The military was already preparing its dynamite to blow up Manchuria.

Until the Manchurian Incident of 1931 began to push Japan in the direction of jingoistic reaction, the labor and proletarian movements in Japan had achieved substantial progress in advancing the interests of workers, peasants, and the poor.[19] Considering the grossly inhospitable climate in which trade unions had to operate, the rate of unionization attained during the 1920's, however modest, was a significant achievement. The same resolve and efforts under more agreeable conditions should have resulted in a far higher rate of unionization than that attained during the 1920's. Paradoxical though it may seem, the extent and intensity of union impact on employers, government, and society at large during this period should be gauged by the enormity of counter-measures that the political and business elites of Japan were able to contrive to suppress or demoralize the labor movement. With less than 10 per-

19 Ayusawa, *A History of Labor in Modern Japan,* Ch. 4. For the relief of the poor in particular, see Koji Taira, "Public Assistance in Japan: Development and Trends," *Journal of Asian Studies* 27 (November, 1967): 95–109.

cent of wage earners organized, the "macro-social" impact of inter-war unionism was more dramatic than that of post-war unionism with 40 percent of workers organized.[20]

At the micro-economic level, it is plausible to assume that effective unionization is likely to arise among adult, male, or skilled workers more readily than among young, women, or unskilled workers. Japan's factory labor force comprised almost as many women and children as men during the 1920's. Therefore, although the overall rate of unionization of factory labor in 1928 was less than 5 percent, the rate of unionization of male workers in Japanese factories exceeded 10 percent. This was a respectable rate of unionization, and it was rising. In 1932 nearly 20 percent of male factory workers were organized in unions. Not only did the propensity to unionize differ between male and female workers, but it also varied among industries reflecting sex and skill differences. For all workers of both sexes, the metal and machinery industries had 28 percent of their workers organized, while textiles in which women and girls predominated had less than 2 percent of their workers organized.[21] Interestingly enough, the male-female and inter-industry wage differentials widened during the 1920's. Unionization started from scratch at the beginning of World War I. It proceeded most rapidly among male skilled workers in the metal and machinery industries. At the same time, real wages increased most rapidly in these industries.

Outside the manufacturing sector, public utilities like gas and electricity had attained an exceptionally high rate of organization by 1932, rising to more than 80 percent of workers in these industries. Unions in transportation and communication also became substantial, growing to the peak of 33 percent in 1936. Miners were poorly organized—contrary to their counterparts in foreign countries, who were among the highly organized workers. In Japan their peak of unionization was only 3.6 percent in 1931. Day laborers' rate of unionization recorded its interwar high in 1933 at a meager 2.9 percent. Public utilities were traditionally high-wage industries and kept up with metals and machinery in the rising trend of real wages during the 1920's and early 1930's. Miners and day laborers who were largely unorganized understandably suffered from stagnant, or even decreasing, real wages during the same period. The almost totally unorganized, and perhaps disor-

20　For post-war trade unionism, see S. B. Levine, *Industrial Relations in Postwar Japan* (Urbana, Ill.: University of Illinois Press, 1958).
21　Taira, *Economic Development*, p. 145.

ganized, agricultural day laborers suffered from significant decreases in their real wages during the same period. The rate of unionization universally returned to zero by 1945, by which time all kinds of wage differentials became almost extinct. It may therefore be said that during the 1920's and early 1930's real wages rose more rapidly (or, to say the same thing differently, money wages tended to be more sticky downward) in industries where unionization spread relatively fast than in industries lagging in unionization. In the late 1930's and early 1940's the disappearance of unions in formerly organized industries was associated with the disappearance of wage differentials over other industries.

It is obvious that unions welcome higher wages and press for them wherever possible, while resisting cuts in wages to the best of their ability. This type of union behavior was highly correlated with movements of wages and wage differentials in inter-war Japan. But the first section of this chapter showed that these wage phenomena could be explained reasonably well by the logic of the labor market, if appropriate concessions were made to elements of imperfections in the real world, without recourse to trade unions as an explanatory factor. Furthermore, the characteristics of wages and wage differentials during the inter-war period were fundamentally the same as what happened even before 1920 in Japan. What differences, then, did the presence of unionism during the inter-war period make in relation to the behavior of wages and wage differentials?

One interpretation may be hazarded: trade unions perhaps accentuated the imperfections of the labor market and amplified the fluctuations of wages and wage differentials beyond what one would have expected from the working of the labor market alone. Thus the usual inertia of the labor market would have made money wages sticky downward in any case, but in inter-war Japan trade unions may have had the effect of making money wages unusually sticky in the face of sustained price decreases over a long period. However, whatever grips unions had on wages loosened after 1931, and the labor market functioned with one less imperfection. Real wages, which had risen to a level too high to clear the market, did not rise any more, and wage differentials which were too wide to be sustained on grounds of allocative efficiency began to diminish in due course. Observing that real wages in Japan fell during the 1930's, W. Arthur Lewis offers an interesting explanation which may serve as an adequate summary for this section: "The explanation of this lies in the mobility of labour. . . . That so large a transfer of labour should occur without wages rising is most unusual; only the weakness of the trade union movement made it possible. The net result was that profits increased enormously as a proportion of the national income, and large voluntary entrepreneurial savings offset the government's expenditure and prevented inflation."[22]

One important indicator of the weakness of trade unionism in inter-war Japan was the inability of unions to establish collective bargaining with employers as the dominant wage-setting arrangement. In March, 1936, there were 121 collective agreements covering a bare third of the trade union membership. One half of these agreements had been concluded during the three-year period 1932–35. Four-fifths of workers covered by collective agreements were seamen and other workers related to the marine transport industry. Even this modest development was destroyed completely after 1938.[23] If unions had influenced wages in inter-war Japan, this influence had largely been exhausted *before* collective bargaining began to be practiced to a limited extent in the 1930's. The stage of collective bargaining in inter-war Japan thus coincided with the declining phase of real wages and of union power. In inter-war Japan, therefore, the emergence of collective bargaining was an indication of the weakening of unions' capacity to threaten or frighten employers. That this should have been so may be seen more clearly when the rise of employer militancy through employer associations in inter-war Japan is examined.

INSTITUTIONAL FACTORS: EMPLOYER ASSOCIATIONS

In a country like Japan where harmony in interpersonal relations is a prized value and anything short of perfect harmony is considered delinquent, it was natural that the eruption of industrial disputes during World War I caused great consternation on the part of the Japanese employers. In December, 1919, business and political leaders organized a foundation with the capital of no less than six million yen ($Y = 50\phi$; then equivalent to $3 million), called "Harmonization Society" (Kyōchō-kai), in order to identify the causes of unrest and to seek methods of dealing with the problem. The Harmonization Society was motivated by a defensive reaction of the Japanese elite through the logic of noblesse oblige.

22 W. Arthur Lewis, *Economic Survey 1919–1939* (New York: Harper Torchbooks, 1969), p. 120.
23 Taira, *Economic Development,* pp. 147–48.

It was headed by Iyesato Tokugawa, a man of the highest prestige, only next to that of the Emperor, and a direct descendant of the principal family of the Shogunate House of Tokugawa. The pipeline of information was even directly extended to the Imperial Household with the effect of wrapping the Harmonization Society in an awe-inspiring aura emanating from the divine Emperor. With this formidable array of personages from the upper reaches of Japanese society, the executive of the Harmonization Society declared that employers and workers should recognize the need for mutual restraint and concessions in the spirit of partnership in efforts to ensure social peace and general welfare. The declared principles that guided the activities of the Harmonization Society were progressive for Japan of the 1920's, where even a lip service to any kind of egalitarianism was dangerously subversive rhetoric.

Many employers were uneasy about the idea of equality implied in the declaration of purpose of the Harmonization Society, while workers were dissatisfied with the emphasis on harmony. Some of the powerful employer associations withheld full cooperation with the Harmonization Society, while Suzuki's JFL rejected an invitation to join the Harmonization Society. By 1920 the Japanese socio-economic system and many enterprises had become too complex to be managed by traditional, intuitive methods without the help of analysis and planning. One of the operational concepts for management that the Harmonization Society promoted was "rationalization," which required the knowledge and practice of modern organizational techniques supplanting or supplementing traditional methods. During the 1920's the Harmonization Society accomplished a great deal in research and counsel for employers. During the late 1930's it promoted a patriotic movement which demoralized and finally crushed trade unions; i.e., Sampō (a short for Sangyō Hōkoku Undō, Movement in Service of the Country through Industry).[24]

The Harmonization Society was one of the many quick responses that Japanese employers made to the social upheavals confronting them. Even before World War I, Japanese employers showed a high propensity to organize themselves for diverse objectives ranging from the promotion of friendship among themselves to price

24 Employer organizations have so far attracted very little attention. Yoshio Morita almost singlehandedly fills a large part of this void in social research. See his *Nihon keieisha dantai hattenshi* (*A History of Employer Organizations in Japan*) (Tokyo: Nikkan rōdō tsushinsha, 1958). On the Harmonization Society, see pp. 57–59, 257–74.

fixing or wage fixing. When Japan joined the ILO, there was already an array of employer organizations to serve as an elective base for the nomination of the employer representative to the ILO. Those designated by the government for the purpose were Chambers of Commerce in six urban centers, Japan Industrial Club (organized in 1917), Osaka Industrial Association, Japan Mining Society, Greater Japan Federation of Cotton Textile Manufacturers, Federation of Associations of Cotton Fabric Exporters, Federation of Associations of Silk Exporters, Federation of Associations of Match Manufacturers, Federation of Paper Manufacturers, Society of Shipbuilders, Japan Electric Society, Imperial Railroads Association, Federation of Sugar Manufacturers, and Conference of Mine Operations.[25] Although this list by no means exhausts the then extant employer organizations, one at least senses from it the flavor of the employer propensity to organize for the purpose of promoting employer interests in response to the challenge of common interest. With the rise of the labor movement and labor legislation, these employer organizations expanded their activities to meet new needs, such as research into labor conditions, counseling for rational management, resistance to governmental encroachments on managerial prerogatives, collusion and propaganda against organized labor, voluntary discipline among employers for setting and raising the standards of industrial safety and sanitation, inter-employer facilities for employee training and welfare, etc.[26] Of these employer organizations, those in textiles were of the longest standing in Japanese history and always active in regulating employer competition for labor and in fixing labor standards by consultation or collusion. Although it is debatable whether their attempts to interfere with the labor market processes were really successful, it is significant that the employer side of the labor market was as highly organized, as indicated by these associations, when the supply side was little affected by trade unions.[27]

Employer associations multiplied during the 1920's. They also became increasingly militant in opposition to the government's labor policy. They stalled revisions of the Factory Law intended to strengthen protective measures for workers. They effectively opposed government attempts to accord legal recognition to trade

25   This owes to Morita's earlier work, *Wagakuni no shihonka dantai* (*Employer Organizations in Japan*) (Tokyo: Toyo keizai, 1926), p. 197. The titles of the organizations mentioned in text are my translations.

26   *Ibid.*, pp. 78–104.

27   See also a discussion of this question in Taira, *Economic Development*, pp. 111–16.

unions. A bill for this purpose was drafted by the Ministry of Agriculture and Commerce as early as 1920. It was revised, debunked, and revived many times during the 1920's. Nothing came out of all this, and the government finally gave up the idea forever in 1930. Constant vigilance against legalization of trade unions and final victory by causing the government to abandon the attempt united employers enormously and resulted in the 1931 inauguration of a powerful anti-labor arm of employer organizations, National Federation of Industrial Associations (Zensanren in short, NFIA hereinafter).[28] In effect, NFIA was the counterpart on the employer side of the JFL. But unlike the increasingly battered JFL, NFIA was full of vigor throughout the 1930's and outmaneuvered organized labor, while promoting enlightened labor policy as the best way to get rid of unions and safeguard employer interests. The pendulum of relative power began to swing to the employer side in 1931, curiously coinciding with the topping off of the unionization rate among workers and the Manchurian Incident. If the rising tide of unionism and social unrest during and after World War I was in part responsible for higher real wages as previously mentioned, the restraint on real wages after 1931 may, by the same logic, be attributed in part to the rise of unified employer opposition to unionism. During the inter-war period employers were increasingly aware that public policy and crude opposition to workers' demands could not alone work in their favor. The tactical advantage that employers were determined to maintain was not to oppose any improvement in labor conditions as such, but to institute improvements only insofar as individual employers considered them necessary from their respective points of view, and to keep alive in the public mind the image of upright, charitable, understanding employers. Therefore employers opposed almost anything that was forced upon them, whether it was done by trade unions, by spontaneous riots, or by public policy, although once the pressure was off their necks they "voluntarily" implemented measures which they had rejected. After all, peace at workplaces and healthy morale among workers were necessary conditions for employers' sustained profits. Unions, riots, and public policy at least suggested that there was something wrong about the conditions of the workplace and the terms of employment. Even within the strict logic of profit-oriented enterprise, it was desirable to remedy these deficiencies before one hoped for a steady

28   Morita, *Nihon keieisha dantai hattenshi*, pp. 186ff.

flow of work. When they came to their senses after initial shocks and frettings, employers began to experiment with different techniques of work force management. In particular, larger firms that were the targets of labor offensive during the first wave of industrial disputes during and immediately after World War I were forced by events to think afresh about the problems of management and to institute innovations in the hope of forestalling future difficulties with employees.

Whenever new problems arise in Japan, those who are facing them usually turn their eyes to other countries for possible lessons. So it was with industrial relations problems. Bunji Suzuki was the pacesetter in international borrowing of institutional technology. His JFL was intentionally modeled after the AFL. Now it was the turn of employers. In 1921 twenty-four top executives of leading firms organized a study team and toured in the United States and Europe for six months, talking and listening to their counterparts in many large firms for their experience and advice. They returned to Japan with bags full of notes, which subsequently produced a series of innovations in work force management. Employers' labor strategy thus emerged: oppose any outside interference with business, but undertake maximum feasible improvements in the structure of work and reward, fringe benefits to employees, and services to the general community.[29] In this learning process the National Association of Manufacturers (NAM) of the United States attracted considerable attention. The seemingly solid front that American employers showed against labor through NAM evoked a great envy among Japanese employers.[30] The aforementioned NFIA was one way to approach the NAM model in the Japanese setting. Japanese employers also cleared their minds as to what kinds of unionism they would tolerate and what types of communication with employees they would welcome. Industrial or national unions were rejected; craft unions were regarded as tolerable; company unions were welcome. Collective bargaining was distasteful; works councils were acceptable.[31] In other words, the Japanese-style management commonly called "paternalism" emerged in a

29   *Ibid.,* pp. 73–93.
30   *Ibid.,* pp. 145–47.
31   On plant sociology having to do with the new type of labor policy in Japanese firms, see Levine, "Labor Markets and Collective Bargaining in Japan." On the question of works councils, see George O. Totten, "Collective Bargaining and Works Councils as Innovations in Industrial Relations in Japan during the 1920's," in *Aspects of Social Change in Modern Japan,* ed. R. P. Dore (Princeton: Princeton University Press, 1967), Ch. 7.

number of large firms. Paternalism as a response to the inter-war labor movement was the Japanese counterpart of the "American Plan" which also had the effect of demoralizing the AFL during the 1920's.

To be effective, the paternalistic practices had to be initiated and implemented by individual firms according to their own designs and calculations. By differentiating in a complex fashion its own work force management from the practices of all other firms, each firm hoped to balkanize the labor market and to tie the well-being of employees closely to the success of the firm. With proper inducements for employee commitment to the firm, paternalism had the effect of winning employees away from trade unions or converting the organizations into harmless company unions. By the early 1930's many large firms had on the whole succeeded in restructuring labor-management relations in all their aspects, ranging from recruitment to retirement of employees, and reduced or eliminated the need for trade unions as protectors of workers' interests. Thus individual firms out-unioned unions, while employer associations were making substantial political gains. Once large firms' remarkable superiority in wages and working conditions became an established fact in the 1930's, these firms effortlessly attracted job applicants in numbers far exceeding their needs and were able to raise hiring standards to skim off the cream of the labor force without any more improvements in wages or working conditions. As these firms expanded in output and employment without raising wages, the situation looked surprisingly like economic development with "unlimited supplies of labor."[32]

PUBLIC POLICY

A few words may be added in relation to the role of government in securing minimum tolerable standards of safety, sanitation, and worker protection at places of work. The Mining Law of 1905 and the Factory Law of 1911 stipulated such standards for miners and factory workers. A workers' health insurance law was enacted in 1923. The passage of this law in the national legislature had an element of comedy. Employers who were required to contribute half of the premium would have objected to it, but ever since 1920

---

32   For a discussion of how the 1930's fit into the Lewis-Fei-Ranis model, see Minami, "Further Considerations on the Turning Point in the Japanese Economy (I) and (II)," *Hitotsubashi Journal of Economics* 10 (February, 1970), and 11 (June, 1970).

they had been too preoccupied with the problem of a trade union bill to pay attention to a seemingly innocuous matter like health insurance, in which the prestige of employers was not involved. This seems to suggest that, in opposing trade unions, employers were acting on principle rather than on the basis of costs. In 1923 there were laws to define the minimum age for factory workers and seamen. In 1926 the Factory Law and related legal provisions were revised to upgrade worker protection and expand workmen's compensation. In 1931 the Law to Aid Injured Workers was passed to cover those wage earners like day laborers not covered by existing laws. In 1936 the Law for Funding Retirement Allowances and Payments was enacted, requiring factories and mines to pay allowances to retiring or dismissed workers. Thus there was substantial progress in social provisions for workers during the inter-war period. One may suppose, however, that these basic or minimum standards only weighed down on relatively small and inefficient employers with a force of discipline, and that larger and more efficient employers were instituting better benefits for their employees on their own initiative.[33]

CONCLUSION

In search of coherent explanations about the interactions of economic and institutional factors impinging upon the labor market, this paper has attempted to interpret the movements of the wage level and relative wages in inter-war Japan in relation to changes in general economic conditions, individual market strategies, and institutional factors. Institutional factors discussed in this paper are trade unions on the supply side of the labor market and employer associations on the demand side. General economic conditions were deflationary during the 1920's and, after the depression of 1929–31, inflationary in the 1930's. The wage level and relative wages changed in response to the changes in general economic conditions in the fashion that was to be expected from the nature of the labor market and from the tendencies of market forces observed in Japan before World War I. However, the amplitudes of fluctuations in the wage level and relative wages in inter-war Japan were unusually large, much larger than would be expected from other labor market experiences. These magnified amplitudes may very well have been due to the ebb and flow of such institutional fac-

33   For a further analysis of public policy, see Taira, *Economic Development,* pp. 133–42.

tors as trade unions and employer associations. Trade unions as extensive and militant as they were in inter-war Japan were new phenomena in Japan's modern history, while employer associations, if not specific to the period examined, were greatly extended and strengthened as organizations to counter the labor movement. The by-products of this paper are descriptions of some cultural and socio-psychological aspects of workers' and employers' organized efforts to safeguard and promote their interests. Both trade unions and employer associations, though called into being by Japan's internal socio-economic dynamics, were heavily in debt to the experiences of Western countries from which they borrowed techniques of interest-group organization. In a sense, both workers and employers during the 1920's fought each other in an imitative process of learning based on borrowed ideologies and tactics. When international crises confronted Japan with the rock-bottom issue of national honor and survival, the borrowed ideological coating of labor-management conflicts melted away. Solidly united after 1939, both workers and employers went down the path of destruction under the onslaught of World War II. In 1945 Japan had to start over from scratch.

Carlos E. Sánchez and Aldo A. Arnaudo

The Economic Power of Argentine Manufacturing Labor Unions

INSTITUTIONAL FRAMEWORK

The Labor Movement in Argentina

INCIPIENT FORMS of trade unionism existed since 1860, but it was only in the last years of the nineteenth century that labor organizations appeared in Argentina, with the most important ones in Buenos Aires. The massive immigration from Europe during the 1870–1914 period and the development of commercial and industrial activities stimulated the growth of union activity.

From 1930 onward the Argentine labor market experienced two radical changes. First, European immigration practically halted, and migration from the countryside began. Second, policies initiated during the Great Depression protected and stimulated the process of industrialization.

By that time Argentine unionism, molded by the immigrants' political ideas, was not an all-inclusive working-class organization but a limited one, including only craftsmen, mostly in Buenos Aires. A large part of the working class remained outside the unions, the thousands of migrants from the countryside were not impressed by the leadership's political ideas, and unionism had not been extended to the smaller cities.

This type of labor organization soon became obsolete. It was not

The authors wish to thank their colleagues Carlos A. Givogri and Fernando Ferrero as well as the editors of this volume for helpful suggestions and criticism.

suited to the new dynamics of the Argentine economy: rapid industrialization, mass production, the appearance of large quantities of unskilled and semi-skilled workers and of new types of skilled workers. Moreover, it was ill prepared for the political change which occurred in 1943 when Peron came to power. The unions, in short, had neither political nor economic power.[1]

The influx of thousands of new common laborers and the fractionalization and lack of representativeness of the existing trade unions put enormous pressure on the supply side of the labor market. Weakness was obviously the main characteristic of the labor movement during the late 1930's and early 1940's. Under these circumstances the attainment of a higher labor standard necessarily depended on the political support the movement could get.[2] This was not a matter of unfettered choice for the Argentine labor movement.

From 1943 onward Juan D. Peron promoted the consolidation and centralization of the labor movement. As secretary of labor (1943–46) and president of Argentina (1946–55) he sought to convert the trade unions into a politically powerful machine supporting his government, and he was very successful in doing so. As a result the labor movement became one of the country's most powerful pressure groups, not only on economic but also on social and political matters.

Under his direction unions were organized as an all-inclusive and geographically widespread labor movement subject to government dictation. The government promoted and supported higher labor standards by enacting labor and social legislation to the advantage of the workers. In Peron's words: "The government needs organized unions and a large confederation of workers, as powerful as possible, because this is the support that it will have in the future in order to achieve the great destiny of this country. . . . A large confederation of workers is the best guarantee for the gov-

---

1 We are not saying that the pre-Peron, European-type labor organizations and their members had no participation in the new type of labor movement started after 1943 and described below. On the contrary, it has been argued that they actually had intensive participation. See J. Portantiero and M. Murmis, *El movimiento obrero en los orígenes del Perónismo* (Buenos Aires: Centro de Investigaciones Sociales del Instituto Torcuato di Tella, 1969). The analysis of this point is not relevant for the purpose of the present paper. See Roberto Carri, *Sindicatos y poder en la Argentina* (Buenos Aires: Editorial Sudestada, 1967), Chs. 1, 2; Mario Abella Blasco, *Historia del sindicalismo* (Buenos Aires: APL, 1967), Ch. 2; and Robert J. Alexander, *Labor Relations in Argentina, Brazil and Chile* (New York: McGraw-Hill, 1962), Pt. 2.

2 Portantiero and Murmis, *El movimiento obrero*, p. 124.

ernment which has no power but the power of the labor force."[3]

The political change brought about by the overthrow of Peron in September, 1955, led to the break up of the union-government alliance. The labor movement was no longer part of the political machine of the government; it was on its own. Interpretation, defense, and achievement of labor aims became the exclusive responsibility of the unions. They were politically well equipped for such a task, however. There was a greatly expanded, disciplined, and politicized organization. At the same time, workers realized their presence as a powerful group and the importance of collective bargaining as an element to be incorporated into the arsenal of unions' weapons.

However, the lack of strong government support returned the workers to a situation similar to that prevailing during the pre-Peron years, except for their long and fruitful political experience. Action was therefore undertaken in order to gain political ground for their demands.[4] There was an explicit or implicit agreement between labor unions and Arturo Frondizi, one of the candidates in the 1957 presidential election. The highly organized labor movement backed Frondizi with the power of its numbers, and he won the election. Shortly after his term began, the new administration enacted the Ley de Asociaciones Profesionales under which the labor movement is organized.

But Argentine unions did not fight their most important battles after 1958 in the political field. In addition to actions seeking political support for demands common to the whole labor force, individual economic action was undertaken by each union. With its own interest in mind and with its leaders subject to control from its rank and file, each union tried to obtain higher standards and to satisfy the expectations of its members as well as possible.

Although collective bargaining was already well established before and during the Peron administration, it was only under his regime, and especially after the enactment of the Law 14.250 regulating collective bargaining in 1953, that it became the exclusive procedure for setting the wage rate and conditions of work.

After Peron and until 1958 collective bargaining played a limited role. During the 1955–58 period wage rates were set by law. There

3   J. Perón, *Doctrina peronista: Perón expone su doctrina,* Sub-secretaría de Informaciones de la Presidencia de la Nación, Buenos Aires, p. 286.

4   Adolf Sturmthal, "Economic Development and the Labor Movement," in Arthur M. Ross, ed., *Industrial Relations and Economic Development* (London: Macmillan, 1966), p. 168.

was an across-the-board 10 percent increase in February, 1956, and one of 60 percent in May, 1958. It was only at the end of 1958 that collective bargaining once again gained real importance; this situation lasted until 1967, when the government began an anti-inflationary policy which included the interruption of collective negotiations.

The importance of collective bargaining as a means of express-ing the aims and power of individual unions reached its peak dur-ing 1959–66, the period under study. Wages and general condi-tions of work were freely set by agreements between workers' and employers' organizations.

The Legal Framework

Government regulations of union organization were first enacted in 1945, abrogated by the revolutionary government in 1956, and reinstated in 1958. Both the 1945 and the 1958 versions con-tained similar provisions. They were intended to build a centralized labor movement with practically no room for the existence of more than one union representing wage earners in each industrial branch.

Law 14.455, enacted in 1958, defines a union or "professional association" as the group organized for the defense of the work-ers' professional interests. Two types of associations are allowed: groups of persons working in the same industry or economic ac-tivity, and groups formed by workers of the same profession even though they may work in different industries or activities. How-ever, unions of the second category are practically nonexistent in Argentina.

According to the provisions of the law, workers are entitled to organize unions freely, but not all unions have the right to bargain with the employer. For that to be possible a certification of "trade-union representativeness" (personeria gremial) is required. This is granted by the government to the most important union (mainly in terms of its membership) in each activity, which can then rep-resent the workers before the government and bargain with the em-ployers' organizations. Nevertheless, in a few cases, mainly for po-litical reasons, trade union representativeness has been granted to more than one union.

Workers also have the right to join a union or not. However, the terms of the labor contract agreed on by the representative union and the employer are compulsory for all workers in the activity, whether union members or not.

Local unions (the so-called associations of first degree) may join in federations and confederations. Trade union representativeness is also required in this case, which explains the existence of only one confederation (Confederacion General del Trabajo, or CGT) legally entitled to represent the workers.

The general practice is that the different local unions of the same and related activities join together in a national federation. This national federation bargains with the employers' organizations.

The system of collective bargaining was established by Law 14.250, enacted in 1953. This law substituted national collective bargaining for local negotiations and made compulsory the terms of the labor contract for all the workers and firms in the activity (industry or sector). For example, the federation of unions in the chemical industry bargains with the chemical employers' organization at the national level, and the terms of the agreement are compulsory for all of the workers and firms in the chemical industry throughout the country. In this way wages and working conditions are centrally determined. Regional wage differentials are sometimes included in the collective agreement, and wage rates in the different regions of the country are expressed as proportions of the basic wage rate.

The Inflationary Process

To complete the picture of the context in which labor unions operated, it should be said that the Argentine economy experienced strong inflation throughout the period under study.[5] This circumstance conditions the whole process of wage adjustment since, independent of any other consideration, the increase of prices alone requires an increase in money wages if real wages are to be maintained. Such an assertion does not involve a position on the cost-push vs. demand-pull debate. During a period of inflation economic forces operate, with or without the mediation of unions, driving wage rates upward.

At the point of contract expiration each party, union and management, will consider the observed and expected rate of inflation as an indicator of paramount importance in the policy to follow at the bargaining table. Given the fact that contracts are negotiated at discrete intervals, the union faces the problem of getting in each contract a money wage rate high enough to maintain or even to improve its position in relative and real terms.

5   The average rate of inflation for this period, expressed by both the rate of increase of consumers' prices (cost of living) and wholesale prices, was around 24 percent per year.

THE RELATIVE POWER OF UNIONS

Measurement of the Relative Power of Unions from the Supply Side

Unions and Labor Supply. For most models of wage determination under trade unions, the existence of noncompetitive conditions in the labor market is assumed. Otherwise, given a labor supply independent of union influence, the level of wages would be the exclusive result of the action of competitive market forces: changes in wages would be accounted for by changes in market demand and supply of labor. Further, a situation where competitive conditions prevail on the supply side and employers' organizations have monopsony power may also arise; this case of monopsony would yield lower wages than those of a competitive market.

If competitive conditions prevail (at least on the supply side) in the various industries, relative wage standing would not be an adequate measure of union strength. However, if unions can affect the conditions of labor supply, the results obtained, i.e., relative wage changes, might be an indication of strength differentials among unions, given certain conditions still to be discussed.

Therefore, are the relative gains (losses) in wages observed for any union the result of its power or of market forces? This question is difficult to answer, since the true demand and supply functions and their shifts are unknown. We only have data on observed wage-employment pairs, which may or may not correspond to equilibrium points. For example, a union with decreasing employment and increasing wages could be a strong union, provided a leftward shift in supply is due to union pressure. Or, alternatively, increases in both wage and employment might not be an indication of union's strength if the observed wage-employment pair represents only an upward shift of demand.

The problem can be partially solved under the fairly realistic assumption of a relatively stable aggregate labor supply function, not necessarily inelastic. This assumption is based on the relatively high degree of labor immobility in the Argentine labor market. Given this assumption, the demand for labor—a derived demand—will shift as a result of changes in the product market.[6] Three cases might be considered:

6   A similar argument is presented by Robert Ozanne, "Impact of Unions on Wage Levels and Income Distribution," *Quarterly Journal of Economics* (May, 1959). He argues that the lack of correlation between the movements in wages and employment in an industry is empirical evidence of union power that affects

(a) Movements in the same direction of relative wage and employment. They will indicate weakness on the union side if the observed data correspond to competitive equilibrium points. Over a seven-year period (1959–66), it seems reasonable to assume that movements in employment and relative wages will parallel movements in the unobserved underlying equilibrium solutions, even if data for any year do not necessarily reflect an equilibrium.

(b) Movements in opposite directions of relative wage and employment.
   (1) When employment falls and wages increase, unless some other factor can be identified on the supply side, it demonstrates a presumptive case of union bargaining strength.
   (2) If the wage rate happens to be falling despite increasing employment, a noncompetitive situation arises where all or most of the power is on the buyer's side.

(c) Cases of constant wages or employment can be easily assimilated to the corresponding situations discussed above.

We can draw from the above argument the following rules of thumb: unions falling in case (b-1) can be safely assumed powerful enough to impose supply restrictions; those in (b-2) are too weak to control increases in labor supply. Unions coming under heading (a) can be tentatively assumed weak in the sense that the wage level is only dictated by the market demand for labor.

Once the unions falling in each of these categories have been identified, the unions' relative strengths can be ranked and a fur-

---

the outcome of market forces. He assumes a constant true labor supply function and shifts in the demand function. So if demand moves (Figure A) from D_0 to D_1 and employment does not increase from N_0 to N_1 but the wage level does (from W_0 to W_1), this is due to union pressure shifting the labor supply from SS to S'S.

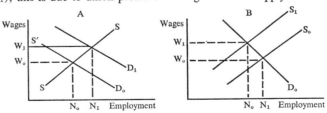

Lowell E. Gallaway, "Impact of Unions on Wage Levels and Income Distribution: Comment," *Quarterly Journal of Economics* 74, no. 2 (May, 1960), commenting on this question, gives an alternative interpretation of lack of correlation. He assumes the changes in employment reflect primarily movements along the labor demand function (Figure B). However, if wages are rising and employment is not increasing, that explanation is not applicable.

ther measure based on the movements of relative wages can be devised.

Union Strength in the Argentine Manufacturing Sector, 1959–66

For our empirical study of the economic power of the Argentine trade unions, the manufacturing sector is divided into twenty different industries, each with its corresponding industrial union. The number of "unions of first degree" (plant unions) included in each industrial union varies considerably. The figures presented in Table 1 give an idea of the number as well as the relative importance of each group in terms of the number of workers represented at the bargaining table.

Table 1. Number of Unions and Workers in the Manufacturing Sector

Industrial activities[a]	Number of local unions ("associations of first degree") (1)	Number of workers[b] (000) (2)
Rubber (RB)	2	15
Metal (ML)	2	250
Chemical (CH)	18	55
Automobile (AT)	6	150
Paper (PP)	6	20
Food (FD)	86	107
Footwear (FT)	1	40
Clothing (CL)	8	70
Printing (PR)	12	35
Wood (WD)	8	120
Tobacco (TB)	2	5
Textile—Wood and Cotton (TXW and TXC)	2	194
Glass (GL)	2	17
Concrete Tile (CNT)	13	20
Leather (LT)	4	14
Wine (WN)	5	42
Ceramics (CR)	5	10
Meat (MT)	24	50
Milk (MK)	1	20

SOURCES (1) Ministerio de Trabajo y Seguridad Social, *Censo Nacional de Asociaciones Professionales* (Buenos Aires, 1965). The number of unions included amounts to 96 percent of the manufacturing unions reported in this source. The omitted 4 percent are formed by unclassified unions. The figures correspond to 1964.

(2) Ministerio de Trabajo y Seguridad Social, *Convenios Colectivos de Trabajo* (Buenos Aires, 1962). 1961 figures.

[a] The abbreviated notation is used in the following tables.

[b] Number of workers covered by the labor contract, not the membership.

The wage data used in the analysis are a measure of the per hour wage rate, excluding seniority supplements, for unskilled workers as specified by the labor contracts. This rate excludes any kind of fringe benefits and adjustments for conditions of work. The last two types of benefits, important as they may be, are difficult to measure and the corresponding data are not always available. Furthermore, as has often been noted, there is usually a high positive association between wages and nonwage benefits.

The choice of the unskilled wage rate is dictated not merely by the availability of information. The figures presented in the statistical sources only distinguish between skilled (oficiales) and unskilled (peones) workers. Since the proportion of unskilled workers within total employment is much larger than the proportion of skilled workers, and the Argentine unions are typically all-inclusive organizations, it is more representative to analyze wage rates earned by the former. In addition, the differences between both rates are not only small but showed a decreasing trend during 1959–66.[7]

Industrial Activity	1959	1966
RB	10.4	11.1
ML	16.1	22.3
CH	23.9	13.7
AT	27.8	29.7
PP	13.1	10.7
FD	3.0	5.6
FT	37.6	16.1
CL	40.0	25.1
PR	36.0	27.4
WD	15.0	13.2
TB	12.0	13.3
TXC	13.5	13.5
TXW	3.5	3.5
GL	11.4	9.5
CNT	16.0	17.5
LT	10.3	6.7
WN	6.0	2.3
CR	13.6	10.0
MT	24.6	19.0
MK	2.7	1.3

7   The percentage differences between a skilled worker's and an unskilled worker's wage rates in 1959 and 1966 in the different activities were:
These narrow (and narrowing) wage differentials between skilled and unskilled workers are the result of minimum wage policies and other factors—strong egalitarian sentiments prevailing in unions' policies, wages centrally determined, and rapid inflation. See Richard Perlman, "Forces Widening Occupational Wage Differentials," *Review of Economics and Statistics* (May, 1958). The deterioration of the skilled labor wage standing makes cheaper the use of this type of labor relative to the unskilled, thus favoring a more intensive use of the former. See John E. Maher, "The Wage Pattern in the United States, 1946–1957," *Industrial and Labor Relations Review* 15, no. 1 (October, 1961).

We now proceed to apply a crude test to determine whether unions in the various industries have been successful in affecting the conditions of labor supply. As a second step, two further measures of power will be considered successively to test the ranking of unions obtained.[8]

Unions and Labor Supply. A simple procedure, dictated by the availability of information, might be used to test the ability of unions to affect labor supply. This is the comparison of the difference between the average of the annual rate of change in employment in each industry and the average annual rate of change in total employment (which indicates whether a given industry gained or lost employment in relative terms), and the average annual rate of change in the corresponding relative wage. The comparison covers the 1959–63 period, since no information on employment by industry is available for 1964–66.

Unfortunately, data on employment by industry were more aggregated than those on wages, and only thirteen industrial activities could have been identified: Food, Wine, Meat, and Milk are aggregated in the Food and Beverages industry; Textile-Wool and Textile-Cotton in Textile; Leather and Footwear in Leather; and Glass, Concrete Tile, and Ceramics in Stone, Clay, and Glass Products.

According to the figures of Table 2 a group of unions formed by Metal, Automobile, Chemical, Paper, Leather, Rubber, and Stone, Clay, and Glass apparently was able to impose restrictions on labor supply. They could obtain wage gains despite falling levels of employment, although it must be pointed out that Leather and Rubber had small wage gains and small employment decreases. Printing and Tobacco could not obtain wage gains even though relative employment grew. The rest of the unions had falling wages and employment, so they did not have enough power to offset falling demand by restrictions on the supply side.

Relative Wages. The reference point for the analysis is the wage structure of the manufacturing sector in March, 1954. The relative position of each union at that date was the result of the wage rates established by the "official" labor contracts characteristic of the

8 The sources of the labor statistics other than those already mentioned are: Ministerio de Trabajo y Seguridad Social, *Boletín de investigaciones sociales* (Buenos Aires, 1964–66) and the same organization's unpublished data about wage rates; Ministerio de Economía y Trabajo, *Informe económico* (Buenos Aires, 1967–69), for wages; Ministerio de Trabajo y Seguridad Social, *Conflictos del trabajo* (Buenos Aires, 1961, 1965, 1967, 1969); and the same organization's unpublished data about the occurrence of strikes.

Table 2.   Tentative Classification of Unions According to
Relative Wages and Employment. 1959–63

Industrial activities	Relative wages	Relative employment
Powerful group		
ML	.2	−4.4
CH	41.5	−2.3
AT	2.2	−1.2
PP	3.9	− .6
GL-CNT-CR	1.9	−5.0
LT-FT	.6	− .3
RB	.1	− .8
Weak group		
TB	− .9	.3
PR	− .9	2.2
WD	− .2	−9.1
CL	−1.0	−2.2
TX	−2.6	−3.8
FD-WN-MT-MK	−1.8	−4.2

Peronist period. A different situation prevailed from 1959 onward when the standards written into the collective bargaining contracts were the result of a free bargaining process.[9]

Therefore, if we contrast the evolution of the wage structure during 1959–66 with that observed in March, 1954, and the comparison indicates that a substantial change has occurred, we can take such a change as an effect in part of the power differentials among unions in demanding a higher wage income.[10]

According to the available information, no important changes took place during the administered wage policy period, at least from 1950 to 1958, as an analysis of the wage structure at several points in time (for example, 1950, 1954, and 1958) shows. Therefore, most of the variation occurring between 1950 and 1966 was the result of the free collective bargaining conditions prevailing from 1959 onward.

Let us take the ratio RW_i (1966/1950) as a measure of the change in relative wages from 1950 to 1966. The change in variance from 1950 to 1966 is equal to the sum of the changes in variance of the subperiods 1950–54, 1954–58, and 1958–66.

9   See the first section. The period April, 1954–December, 1958 records two wage increases officially established. Both were across-the-board increments and therefore did not affect the wage structure. If any union influence was exerted regarding the amount of the increments and the date they were provided, this was expressed as a collective political action by the whole labor movement.

10   There might well be a number of factors producing changes on the demand side which could lead to the same result. In spite of the scarcity of data, these demand aspects are considered in the third section.

$$\triangle\text{Var RW}_i \ (1966/1950) = \triangle\text{Var RW}_i \ (1954/1950)$$
$$+ \triangle\text{Var RW}_i \ (1958/1954) + \triangle\text{Var RW}_i \ (1966/1958)$$

The values obtained show that 60 percent of the change took place from 1958 to 1966, 10 percent from 1954 to 1958, and 30 percent from 1950 to 1954.

The wage structure at the base date (Table 3) shows that the

Table 3. Classification of Unions According to Their Relative Wage

Rank	1954	1959	1960	1961	1962	1963	1964	1965	1966
1	MT	WN	CH	CH	CH	CH	CH	CH	CH
2	TXW	LT	LT	LT	LT	GL	AT	AT	AT
3	PP	ML	TB	AT	AT	PP	ML	ML	PP
4	CH	TB	AT	PR	PP	AT	PP	PP	ML
5	TB	PR	ML	TB	GL	MK	GL	MK	LT
6	CNT	MK	PR	ML	PR	LT	MK	GL	MK
7	WN	MT	WD	GL	MK	ML	LT	LT	TXW
8	TXC	AT	FD	WD	TB	TB	TB	WD	WD
9	RB	CNT	RB	WN	WD	RB	CR	TXW	GL
10	ML	GL	GL	PP	ML	CR	WD	CR	CNT
11	WD	TXW	MT	RB	WN	WN	RB	RB	TXC
12	MK	FD	PP	TXW	TXW	WD	WN	TB	CR
13	AT	RB	CR	FD	CNT	FD	TXW	FD	RB
14	FT	TXC	WN	MK	RB	CNT	FD	PR	TB
15	FD	PP	MK	TXC	CR	PR	PR	TXC	FD
16	GL	WD	CNT	CNT	FD	TXW	TXC	WN	CL
17	CR	FT	TXW	CR	TXC	TXC	MT	CL	WN
18	PR	CR	TXC	MT	MT	CL	CNT	CNT	PR
19	LT	CL	FT	FT	CL	MT	CL	MT	MT
20	CL	CH	CL	CL	FT	FT	FT	FT	FT

unions enjoying the highest relative wages were those of the Meat, Textile-Wool, Paper, Chemical, and Tobacco industrial activities. At the bottom of the ranking we find unions in the following activities: Glass, Ceramics, Printing, Leather, and Clothing.

From the end of 1958 onward, after collective bargaining had resumed, individual action of unions produced substantial changes in the structure of relative wages. Some unions climbed to the top or, being already high at the beginning, remained at those levels. Others dropped from the highest positions to the lowest places or, being already low at the beginning, remained at the bottom. Finally, a third group moved around the intermediate positions that they had in 1954.

In the first group we find Chemical, fourth in 1954, ranked first from 1960 to 1966; Automobile, thirteenth in 1954, appeared among the five first placed from 1960 onward and remained at the second place from 1964 to 1966; Paper, already among the high-wage unions in 1954, dropped to the fifteenth place in 1959 and shortly after recovered its previous level; Metal, tenth in 1954, rose to the third place in 1959, moved down from 1960 to 1962 and rose again from 1963 onward; Leather, Milk, and Glass, nineteenth, sixteenth, and twelfth respectively in 1954, gradually improved their relative standing to occupy higher positions after 1962.

To the second group belongs Meat, first in 1954 and among the last since 1960; Wine, seventh in 1954, gradually moved down occupying the seventeenth place in 1966. Finally, Clothing, Printing, and Footwear did not modify substantially the relatively disadvantageous standing they had in 1954.

Textiles-Wool and Tobacco dropped from the second and fifth places at the base date to intermediate during 1959–66; these and the remaining unions are included in the third group.

In 1966 the unions with the highest relative wages were Chemical, Automobile, Paper, Metal, and Leather. Milk was sixth, and Glass, sixth or fifth in the preceding years, was ninth in 1966. The group with the lowest relative wages included Clothing, Wine, Printing, Meat, and Footwear.

In general, unions classified as powerful by the previous test rise in the wage structure or maintain a high position. Weak unions remain near the bottom, in some cases, or experience a rapid fall in standing.

Coincident with the violent shift of the wage structure when collective bargaining resumed in 1959 and unions begun to act independently, relative wage dispersion also experienced a tremendous increase. The immediate consequence of free collective bargaining was therefore the introduction of a great deal of variability in the relative distance among the different money wage rates. Once the adjustment period after 1959 was over and unions gained experience and knowledge of their power, becoming more acquainted with the process of free collective bargaining, the initial relative wage dispersion decreased. However, there seems to be a long-run tendency toward an increase. This is shown by the coefficients of variation presented in Table 4. A similar conclusion is obtained when considering another measure of the relative dispersion, the interquartile range divided by the median.

The values of the average wage and the second quartile or median (Table 4) indicate that the wage distribution was skewed to right in 1954 and during the 1964–66 period, skewed to left in

Table 4. Measures of Location of Money Wage Rates and Dispersion of Relative Wages

	Measures of location			Measures of dispersion	
Year	Mean	Median	$\dfrac{\text{Mean}}{\text{Median}} \times 100$	Coefficient of variation	$\dfrac{\text{Interquartile range}}{\text{Median}}$
1954	4.84	4.77	101.5	.0541	.0907
1959	16.87	17.36	97.2	.1204	.1139
1960	21.48	21.53	99.8	.1097	.1701
1961	26.50	26.85	98.7	.0991	.1382
1962	33.10	33.24	99.6	.0805	.0793
1963	40.37	40.67	99.3	.0922	.1211
1964	52.24	51.52	101.4	.0970	.1502
1965	69.30	67.40	102.8	.1093	.1200
1966	94.47	92.55	102.1	.1226	.1223

1959 and 1961, and symmetrical in 1960, 1962, and 1963.[11]

What has been said so far indicates that in 1959 a group of wages fell well behind the average wage (distribution skewed to left). During 1960–63 wages tended to be more concentrated around the mean, but since 1964 a group of unions pushed their wages to a very high relative level (distribution skewed to the right), which is again reflected in a larger dispersion.

For instance, Chemical and Paper ranked among the top groups in 1954 and dropped to the fifteenth and twentieth places, respectively, in 1959. The same unions—jointly with Automobile and Metal and in a lesser degree with Milk, Leather, and Glass—rapidly advanced from 1962 onward because they earned wages larger

11 We have drawn the frequency distribution of the money wages in three typical years in order to make this clearer. The distribution is skewed to the left in 1959, almost symmetrical in 1962, and skewed to the right in 1965. See T. Yamane, *Statistics: An Introductory Analysis*, 2nd ed. (New York: Harper and Row, 1967), p. 55.

Distribution of Unions According to Money Wages

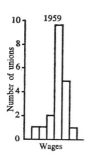
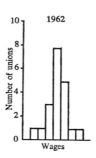
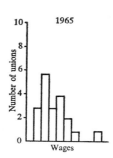

than the value of the third quartile. The average wage of this group grew at a higher rate than the average wage of the unions below the first quartile. The unions which occupied the unfavorable positions were Footwear, Meat, Printing, Wine, and Clothing.

Strike Activity: Some Conflicting Evidence. The strike activity relevant for this study is that originating in disagreements with the employer with regard to wage standards in the collective bargaining process. A record of the actions of Argentine manufacturing unions undertaken in the form of work stoppages for this reason is shown in Table 5.

Table 5. Strike Activity in the Manufacturing Sector, 1959–66

Union(s)	Number of strikes	Average duration (days)	Total strike days	Man-years worked per strike day[a]
Powerful	*24*	*19*	*454*	*10,414*
ML	3	15	45	44,444
CH	5	1	5	88,000
AT	1	21	21	57,143
PP	11	8	88	1,818
RB	1	3	3	40,000
GL	0	0		
CNT	1	236	236	1,593
CR	0	0		
LT	0	0	56	9,143
FT	2	28		
Weak	*15*	*11*	*161*	*26,981*
TB	1	1	1	40,000
PR	1	2	2	140,000
WD	1	1	1	960,000
CL	0	0	0	—
TX	5	19	95	16,337
FD	2	10		
WN	0	0		
MT	1	34	62	28,258
MK	4	2		

[a] Calculated from 1961 employment (Table 1 above) times eight years, divided by number of strike days.

The data of Table 5 tend to support our earlier conclusions. With only slightly more workers covered (591,000 to 543,000), the powerful unions undertook strike action more frequently and for shorter average duration, if the single very long strike in Cement Tile is excluded. In general, the summary figures shown in column 4 reveal a higher strike involvement for most powerful unions than for their weaker counterparts. For the groups as a whole, the powerful unions are found to have struck two and a half times as often as the weak unions. This appears to have helped them maintain or increase wages in the face of declining labor demand.

SOME QUALIFICATIONS TO THE ANALYSIS OF UNION STRENGTH

We assumed above that union activity was the dominant element affecting wages during the period under study. Nevertheless, there might be other factors explaining the evolution of the wage structure, such as differing rates of growth in demand and varying rates of technological change in the various sectors of the economy. These factors cannot be entirely incorporated into the analysis because of the lack of adequate information in some cases and the inconclusive empirical evidence found in others. These neglected, though relevant, factors are some of the many aspects of the Argentine labor market that deserve further study.

As an example of a factor not explicitly considered, let us take technological change. Katz[12] found a dramatic surge of technological progress in the main manufacturing sectors of Argentina over the 1954–61 period. A number of reasons produced a strong association between technological progress, productivity growth, and the degree of business concentration. Katz concludes that those industries in which productivity went up more than average tended to increase their wage rates more than average and, conversely, lower than average increases in productivity tended to be associated with lower than average increases in wage rates.

What does this mean for a supply-oriented analysis of relative union strength? Since a higher than average increase in productivity was observed in industries such as Automobile and Chemical, does this mean that our inclusion of the two corresponding unions in the powerful group is wrong?

To answer this question we might follow Katz again. He gives two interpretations of the process of wage change, the first supply oriented (union's strength), and the second demand oriented (employer's permissiveness). The former argues that some industries incorporated new techniques of production which needed skilled labor to be operated, but these skills were in short supply. The

12   J. Katz, *Production Functions, Foreign Capital and Growth in the Argentine Manufacturing Sector, 1946–61* (Buenos Aires: Centro de Investigaciones Económicas del Instituto Torcuato di Tella, 1968).

latter points out that when collective bargaining resumed after Peron, industries with larger increases in labor productivity "offered greater scope for wage increases" than the others.[13]

Therefore, Katz's first interpretation relates to the union's power, while the second relates to the industry's permissiveness. Given the high association between productivity and wages, it would be difficult to isolate each one. The task becomes much more difficult when the present availability of information is considered. In view of the fact that the 1959–66 period is characterized by an excess supply of unskilled labor in the urban manufacturing sector, a clearly available solution to eliminate the influence of demand conditions is to work with the wage rate earned by unskilled workers (as we did) instead of an average wage rate (as Katz did).[14]

Lack of data on changes on the demand side does not permit an explicit consideration of the factors associated with it. However, we might attempt to check the reliability of our conclusions on union strength by application of the neoclassical analysis of bilateral monopoly.

Accordingly, we must determine the weakness or permissiveness of the industries. The following elements, as stated by Marshall, affect the elasticity of the demand curve for labor and, therefore, the degree of permissiveness: the higher (lower) the elasticity, the lower (higher) the permissiveness. For the demand for labor to be inelastic, the labor factor must be essential in the production of the final product, the demand for the product must be inelastic, labor cost must be a small fraction of total cost, and the supply of the other factors of production must be inelastic.[15]

Since no information is available on the elasticity of the demand for the product, we take the evolution of gross profit margins as a proxy. This is based on the assumption that high margins are associated with low elasticities of demand. We computed the percentage differences between the value of the gross profit margin in each of the years 1959–65 and that of 1958,[16] and followed a reasoning

13   *Ibid.,* pp. 123–24.

14   Katz's first argument is hard to maintain in a generally loose labor market where skill differentials are narrow and rapidly diminishing.

15   Milton Friedman, "Some Comments on the Significance of Unions for Economic Policy," in David McCord Wright, ed., *Impact of the Union* (New York: Kelley and Millman, 1951), follows this argument with a different approach. He argues that unions have potential power only if the demand curve for labor is inelastic. Since this potential power can be exercised or not, we think it is more convenient to speak of weakness or permissiveness of the employer.

16   The profit data are the gross profit margins computed in Aldo A. Arnaudo et al., *Márgenes de beneficio en el sector manufacturero Argentino,* Serie Material

and measure similar to those developed in the case of wages. Figures are more aggregated than those on wages, so only twelve industrial groups are identified.[17]

The fraction of the total cost accounted for by labor costs can be computed at a higher level of aggregation than that of wages; again, only twelve industrial groups can be identified.[18] The range of variation of this fraction, extending from 6 to 26 percent, was divided in quartiles. It is assumed the values belonging to the first quartile (6 to 12 percent) denote a more permissive situation than those denoted by the values of the second and third quartiles (13 to 19 percent), while the values of the fourth quartile (20 to 26 percent) correspond to the nonpermissive situation.

There is no information on the supply elasticity of the cooperating factors, so this fourth condition cannot be considered here.

Under the assumption that in the short run all the industries adjust the factor proportion by modifying only the quantity of labor, we can use the elasticity of substitution between capital and labor as another element which influences the elasticity of the demand for labor. If this assumption is correct, two industries having equal or similar elasticity of substitution also have a demand for labor of the same or similar elasticity. Thus, if the former is low, the latter is also low in both industries. This elasticity of substitution was estimated for 1954–61[19] in twelve industrial sectors. The range of variation, which goes from .30 to .64, was also divided in quartiles. The closer to zero the value of the elasticity, the more permissive the industry, and conversely. Therefore, the group in the first quartile (the corresponding values are .30, .32, and .33) defines permissive industries; by the same token, the group included in the fourth quartile (the values are .60, .61, and .64) is composed of nonpermissive industries. By exclusion, those in the second and third quartiles fall in the intermediate situation.

---

de Trabajo no. 1, Instituto de Economía y Finanzas (Córdoba, 1966), for 1959–65.

17 There is no information on the wine industry, so we used the inclusive group of Beverages (where it is the principal item) as a substitute. Food, Milk, Meat, and Ceramics, Concrete Tile, and Glass are aggregated in groups. No information on the wood industry is available.

18 The source of data is Banco Central de la República Argentina, *Transacciones inter-sectoriales de la economía Argentina* (Buenos Aires, 1964). Food, Wine, Milk, Meat, and Ceramics, Concrete Tile, Glass, Paper, and Printing are aggregated in groups.

19 The source of data is J. Katz, *Production Functions*, p. 60. The aggregation is equal to that of note 18 above, except Paper and Printing, now included in two different groups. Information on the wood industry is not provided.

Table 6 presents the classification of industrial activities according to the three criteria for employers' permissiveness and crosses it with the classification of unions. The cases of coincidence of classification (i.e., located in the main diagonal) might disprove our conclusions on union strength since the high (low) wage position might be due to a high (low) permissiveness of the industry; on the contrary, the much more numerous off-diagonal cases support our ranking of unions according to strength because the employers' situation is likely to be irrelevant.

The identification of the diagonal cases depends to some extent on the weight given to each criterion when they do not coincide. Although there are a few discrepancies, it seems adequate to consider the profit margin as the more relevant variable because it probably has a much greater influence in the short term; besides, it might include the effect of the remaining variables.

Finally, short-run changes in production affect profits rather than wages, so attention should be paid to cyclical movements. This was done by selecting those industries in which profits and production were correlated (value of r larger than .5) and estimating the production elasticity of profit margins. Production did not seem greatly to affect profit margins within the range of variation observed in the years under consideration. Incidentally, wider varia-

Table 6.   Cross-Classification of Unions and Industrial Activities According to Strength and Permissiveness[a]

Industrial activities		Unions	
		Powerful	Weak
Permissive	Profits	CH	TB (FD) (MK) (WN) (MT)
	Incidence of labor cost	RB	TB (FD) (MK) (WN) (MT)
	Elasticity of substitution	CH	PR CL
Intermediate	Profits	(CNT) (CR) (GL) (FT)	TX CL
	Incidence of labor cost	CH (LT) ML PP (CNT) (CR) (GL)	CL PR
	Elasticity of substitution	AT PP RB (CNT) (CR) (GL)	TX (MK) (FD) (MT)
Nonpermissive	Profits	ML RB AT PP (LT)	PR
	Incidence of labor cost	AT	TX WD
	Elasticity of substitution	ML (LT)	TB

[a] Symbols in parentheses indicate use of separate industry permissiveness data for cases while union strength was initially analyzed in combination with other industries.

tions in production were found in the industries where margins do not seem to depend on them. Thus the conclusions do not need qualifications for this reason, nor do profit margins need to be adjusted accordingly.

CONCLUDING REMARKS

The Argentine labor movement, characterized by the existence of large quantities of unskilled urban workers organized in unions representing all grades of labor, initially needed political assistance in order to achieve its demands.

Political support was given by the Peronist government for the first time in the 1940's. It was later lost when Peron was overthrown in 1955. During the 1955–58 period the Ley de Asociaciones Profesionales was abrogated, the government did not support labor demands, unions could not command any political assistance, and labor standards were very low. However, political activity was very intensive during these years,[20] in an effort to maintain union power.

It was precisely by political means that labor unions regained power in 1958; the new administration granted a 60 percent across-the-board wage increase in May and shortly after enacted Law 14.445 (similar to the Peronist law). This law is the instrument that gives legal power to unions. Under its provisions unions constitute a strong monopoly, which is something crucial for a numerically large labor movement organized on an all-inclusive basis.

After this basic political goal was met, unions could improve their bargaining power. During 1959–66 they exerted it in the labor market with various degrees of success.[21]

Some unions were able to achieve high relative standards while others were less fortunate, as seen in Table 2.

The structure of wages as well as the type of economic weapon used by manufacturing unions in the process of collective bargaining were consequences of their relative strength. Powerful unions could stop work with a higher probability of success than could weak and intermediate unions, and this expected successful out-

20 Carri, *Sindicatos y poder,* p. 77.
21 We are not saying that political action was absent during this period. What we want to stress is that unions had economic power throughout these years. In 1957 and 1958 only 25 percent of work stoppages can be related to strictly economic goals; conversely, in 1959 and the following years this figure was around 70 percent. See Ministerio de Trabajo y Seguridad Social, *Conflictos del trabajo.*

come required short work stoppages. Consequently, unions included in the former group went on strike more frequently than those included in the other groups, and the typical duration of their strikes was shorter than that of the rest.

These conclusions are not modified by the analysis of the third section. In the powerful group only one union, Chemical, developed its activity in a generally permissive environment. In the weak group, the low level of power attached to Printing could have been at least partially the result of the unfavorable situation the industry suffered during the period. The lack of suitable information unfortunately precludes our drawing more precise conclusions regarding the influence of economic conditions on the unions' positions. This point, however, deserves further discussion, which goes beyond the scope of this paper.

James G. Scoville

Pre-Industrial Industrial Relations: The Case of Afghanistan

A GENEROUS ESTIMATE would put employment in Afghanistan's modern industrial sector at about 30,000, or perhaps two-thirds of 1 percent of the labor force as usually defined. By way of contrast, civil service employment (excluding education and health) has been placed at 60,000.[1] We are therefore talking about a very modest fraction of economic life in one of the poorest, least industrialized nations on earth. Due to the shakiness of numbers like those above, and to their total absence since 1967, one cannot even be certain that this modest fraction has changed perceptibly in the last few years. Nevertheless, the Afghan situation permits the formulation of a number of propositions about the lot and role of labor at the very outset of economic development.

I shall examine the applicability of W. A. Lewis's model of economic growth[2] to movements of industrial wages and the differential between the modern (capitalistic) sector and the subsistence

My visits to Afghanistan in 1967 and 1970 were sponsored by the United States Agency for International Development. Views expressed are not necessarily those of the U.S. government or any agency thereof. Helpful assistance from several sources must be acknowledged. Deputy Minister of Mines and Industries Abdul Quddus Majeed provided indispensable letters of introduction to the government plants and some of the older private enterprises. The Miner Associates team and Sarwar Bayat, secretary of the Investment Advisory Committee, provided assurance of my good intentions to most of the new private enterprises.

1 Department of Statistics, Ministry of Planning, Kabul, *Survey of Progress 1969,* September, 1969, p. 37.

2 W. A. Lewis, "Economic Development with Unlimited Supplies of Labour," *Manchester School,* May, 1954, and subsequent writings.

economy. Adolf Sturmthal's speculations about nascent labor movements (elsewhere in this volume) can also be compared with recent patterns of industrial unrest.

This essay focuses on the course of events between two surveys which I conducted.[3] To give a picture of the situation in 1967, it is easiest to quote at length the major conclusions from the first survey.

1. Total remuneration generally consists of a number of components. For day labourers in industry (as in agriculture) it is usually made up of a cash wage only. Manual workers above this level, as well as nonmanual employees, receive additional forms of compensation. The most frequent are: subsidised flour or payments based on the price of flour ("co-operatives"), free lunch, medical coverage, an annual bonus, and (least frequently) free housing. Such fringe benefits are more prevalent for clerical and administrative employees than for manual workers.

2. The levels of annual total remuneration for various occupations have been estimated as follows:

   Unskilled year-round labourers .... 9,000 afghanis[4]
   Mechanics .... 23,000 afghanis
   Electricians and carpenters .... 24,000 afghanis
   Power-loom weavers .... 18,000 afghanis
   Clerks (starting rate) .... 23,000 afghanis
   Clerks (after six years) .... 28,000 afghanis

   Furthermore, the rate for common labourers generally lies between 25 and 30 afghanis a day. These occupational differentials appear to correspond approximately to those in other developing countries.

3. The pattern of regional differentials in Afghanistan is the reverse of what is generally found: in this country the value of total remuneration tends to be lower in the big cities and higher in the smallest industrial towns. However, this pattern is probably quite appropriate to the Afghan situation.

4. Finally, the interdependence of the various elements in the remuneration structure must be emphasised. For virtually all

---

3   A lengthy volume on this subject is also available: Horst Büscher, *Die Industriearbeiter in Afghanistan* (Meisenheim am Glan: Anton Hain, 1969). The section on standard of living (pp. 166ff.) is of particular interest. Unfortunately, Büscher's work is marred by a number of errors (with respect to the importance of government wage scales, the size of fringe benefits, and regional wage differences, among others), which raise questions about its accuracy in areas beyond the present field of inquiry.

4   The free-market rate for the afghani (af, for short) was about 75 to the dollar in 1967 and 85 in 1970.

clerical and administrative employees, as well as three-fifths of production workers, the government pay scales are used to determine the level of industrial wages and salaries, although fringe benefits in industry exceed those in government service. Hence a change in government wage and salary schedules will be reflected in a general shift in the level of industrial remuneration.[5]

In the three years since those conclusions were reached, there have been a number of changes in the country's economic environment. Each of these might be expected to have some impact on the structure and levels of blue- and white-collar earnings in industry. The Foreign and Domestic Private Investment Law (FDPIL)[6] was approved in 1967, and fifty new enterprises with about 3,500 workers are apparently in operation. This would represent a significant expansion of the private sector from the situation three years ago. Has this expansion affected the tendency then noted for private plants to give better compensation for the same work than do the government enterprises? Perhaps more important, have these new enterprises moved away from reliance on the government wage scales as the basic building block for the wage and benefit schemes in industry?

A second item of recent history might also have had effects on the structure of compensation. It was estimated in 1967 that 21 percent of the permanent production and maintenance workers, and 26 percent of the white-collar staff, received either the right to buy wheat flour at a subsidized price or a monthly payment based directly on the market price of flour.[7] It would be interesting to know whether these arrangements survived the extraordinary fluctuation in the flour price which occurred in 1967 and 1968, and which appeared to be headed for a repeat performance in the late summer of 1970.

A third new factor on the Afghan scene is hard to appraise but might have had some effect on blue-collar wages. In the last few years a number of instances of labor unrest have occurred, some of them involving protracted strikes or violence toward management. In several cases part of the "settlement" (if we may use the term

5   James G. Scoville, "Remuneration in Afghan Industry," *International Labour Review* (April, 1969): 399–400.
6   This law revised procedures for granting investment permits and encourages private investment through exemptions from income taxes and import duties. The 19,000 new jobs heralded by the *New York Times* (November 2, 1969) are mostly future prospects.
7   *Ibid.*, p. 386.

in a society where collective bargaining is vaguely understood, if at all) was a promise of wage increases.

Finally, a number of sources[8] profess concern about a shortage of jobs for high school and university graduates and point to a growing problem of unemployment in this area. If so, there may be tendencies toward a narrowing of the white collar–blue collar differential, or a reduction of the often large regional differentials in the compensation of clerical and administrative workers.

OFFICIAL EARNINGS INFORMATION

Since the most recent available official data on industrial incomes apply to the Afghan year 1346 (1967–68), their relevance to our topic may not be immediately obvious. However, as they apply to the same year as the earlier AID-sponsored study, any contrasts may be informative, particularly with respect to the quality of my data. Moreover, a brief discussion of them should be a useful reminder that availability is not the sole criterion by which data should be judged.

The 1969 issue of the *Survey of Progress* presents on its last page, with no discussion, figures for the "average annual salary of industrial workers." It is unknown whether these numbers accurately include the numerous and important components of compensation other than salary. It is also unclear whether they pertain only to permanent, full-time workers, or include persons who work three to four months per year in raisin cleaning, sugar-beet processing, cotton ginning and the like. For what they are worth, the figures, by industry, are given below.

As these numbers apply to industries, they are not easily compared with the occupational data of the 1967 report, summarized above. But where comparisons are possible they are suggestive of deficiencies in the official numbers, while reinforcing our conclusion about the level of common labor rates. In certain industries skills and capital intensity are quite low, and the wage structure is correspondingly simple. Examples would be mining and briquetting—the mines visited in 1967 paid people either a daily wage or a piece rate, with no other fringe payments involved. Thus it is reassuring to find that the averages given in Table 1 for briquetting and two kinds of mining are not far from the 1967 estimate of

8   For example, the *Survey of Progress* and the *Education Report*. See also Harvey H. Smith et al., *Area Handbook for Afghanistan* (Washington: U.S. Government Printing Office, 1969), pp. 294–95.

Table 1. Average Annual Salary of Industrial Workers, 1346 (1967–68)—Official Statistics

	Afghanis
Coal mining	10,693
Mining of nonmetallic minerals	7,787
Food production processing	(a)
Textile and cotton cleaning	13,188
Mobile manufacturing and carpentry	17,609
Printing and publications	15,842
Briquetting	9,584
Building construction materials	14,575
Car repairing, transport equipment, and metal works	16,094
Generation of electricity	13,529
Other industries	10,756
Industrywise [*sic*] average annual salary	13,335

(a) Blank—figure for 1345 was 7,351.

9,000 afghanis for year-round unskilled labor. The figure for food production processing is also low, but this industry works half the year at best.

To the extent that they are comparable, the other industry figures appeal to reveal a consistent bias toward underestimation. The 1967 occupational estimate of 18,000 afs as the average compensation for weavers is more than one-third above the official textile and cotton cleaning average.[9] The earlier estimates for mechanics (23,000), electricians, and carpenters (24,000) are also 30 to 50 percent above averages for those industries which they presumably dominate (mobile manufacturing, car repairing). These sizable differences are no doubt due to omission of important parts of the compensation package which are found in industries more advanced than mining and briquetting.

SURVEY COVERAGE, 1970

During July and August, 1970, visits were made to twenty-five enterprises; thirteen of these were repeats from the 1967 survey. Of the twelve companies new to the survey, only one had been in existence in 1967; the rest are new creations under the Private Investment Law.

The approximate coverage of this survey is shown in Table 2.

9 By way of contrast, in one large textile plant visited in 1970, power loom weavers earn *less* than the average for all production workers. Considering salaries alone, the whole blue-collar work force averaged 977 afs per month, while weavers averaged 885 on twenty-year-old looms and 926 on newer looms.

Table 2. Approximate Employment in Afghanistan, and Survey Coverage by Industry

Industry	1346 (1967–68) employment	FDPIL employment	Approximate 1349 (1970–71) employment	Number surveyed	Percentage surveyed
Coal mining	1,582	0	1,582	0	0
Mining of nonmetallic minerals	469	0	469	0	0
Food production processing	5,230	650	5,880	1,602	27
Textile and cotton cleaning	12,271	2,460	14,731	14,731	68
Mobile manufacturing and carpentry	616	0	616	0	0
Printing and publications	1,092	40	1,132	0	0
Briquetting	89	0	89	0	0
Building construction materials	1,761	20	1,781	1,065	60
Car repairing, transport equipments, and metal works	1,592	110	1,702	1,400	82
Generation of electricity	1,044	0	1,044	0	0
Other industries	579	200	779	368	47
Totals	26,325	3,480	29,805	14,499	49

SOURCES: Column 1: *Survey of Progress*, August, 1968, p. 42.
Column 2: "List of Factories Open as of June 30, 1970," prepared by H. N. Sallee, Thomas Miner Associates, Kabul.

The overall survey percentage shown in that table (49%) is almost certainly an underestimate, since a number of the larger companies revisited have experienced substantial declines in employment since 1967–68. These cannot be allowed for in column 1, because more recent figures do not exist. A rough estimate of industrial employment in 1970 has been made by adding new employment under the Private Investment Law to the unadjusted totals for 1967.

THE STRUCTURE AND FIXING OF COMPENSATION IN INDUSTRY

To read most studies of industry in the less developed countries is to get the impression that wages are the sole, or at least overwhelmingly dominant, source of workers' compensation. The Afghan case suggests that great care must be taken to be certain that this is true.[10] Nonwage elements may be exceedingly important

10   In five textile plants in 1967 compensation other than wage or piece rates for weavers ranged from 4% to 47%, with the average share about one-third. Scoville, "Remuneration in Afghan Industry," p. 387.

when we turn to assessment of skill differentials or the difference between incomes in industry and in traditional or agricultural employment. Tables 3 and 4 show the number of plants surveyed and the approximate percentage of white-collar and permanent blue-collar workers covered by various components of compensation. The right-hand portion of each table shows the comparable situation in 1967.

Table 3. Compensation of White-Collar Workers, 1967 and 1970, by Component

	1970		1967	
Item	Number of plants	Percentage of white-collar employment	Number of plants	Percentage of white-collar employment
Cooperatives	10[1]	76	6	96
Flour	2	22	3	26
Vegetable oil	1	7	1	17
Cash	8	55	2	53
Food	17	81	6	93
Free lunch	5	21	n.a.	n.a.
Food allowance	12	60	n.a.	n.a.
Housing	7	72	5	92
Annual bonus	18[2]	96	8	100
Medical provisions	9	76	8	100
Employee only	1	1	5	27
Employee and family (free)	6	66⎫		
Employee and family (subsidized)	2	9⎭	3	73

1 One company provides two cooperatives, flour and vegetable oil.
2 One additional plant does not give an automatic bonus.

The percentage of white-collar workers covered by various compensation factors has been estimated for both years on the assumption that white-collar employment is the same proportion of total employment in all plants. Eight plants were covered in 1967; 22 in 1970.

As can be seen from these two tables, the system of compensation continues to be the sum of a wide variety of fringe benefits added to the basic wage or salary.[11] The meaning of most of these categories should be obvious to the reader, as they are largely self-explanatory. It should be emphasized that the annual bonus (usually one month's pay just before the independence holidays) is generally automatic, paid without reference to the year's performance

11 Piece rates are relatively rare. They are utilized frequently in textiles but seldom elsewhere. Administrative complexity and inequity of shifting the burden of raw material supply irregularities to workers are reasons most often cited against them.

Table 4. Compensation of Permanent Blue-Collar Workers, 1967 and 1970, by Component

Item	1970 Number of plants	1970 Percentage of employment	1967 Number of plants	1967 Percentage of employment
Cooperatives	8[1]	71	8	79
Flour	4	50	4	21
Vegetable oil	1	7	1	14
Cash	4	22	3	44
Food	17	81	9	74
Free lunch	8	61	n.a.	n.a.
Food allowance	9	20	n.a.	n.a.
Free housing	4	34	3	32
Annual bonus	17[2]	87	9	76
Medical provisions	11	79	10	80
Worker only	3	4	8	63
Worker and family (free)	6	66 ⎫		
Worker and family (subsidized)	2	9 ⎭	2	17

[1] One company pays two cooperatives, flour and vegetable oil.

[2] Three additional companies have provisions for bonus, but they have not been paid due to lack of profit.

The number of plants covered was 15 in 1967; 25 in 1970.

by either the company or the worker. The only item requiring extensive explanation is "cooperatives." This component of compensation takes its name from the German (a legacy of that nation's early influence in Afghanistan) but bears no relationship to "consumers' cooperatives" or the like. In government service the employee's cooperative takes the form of a right to purchase certain amounts of flour and vegetable oil at subsidized prices from government warehouses. In industry the commodity allotment is usually hypothetical: the worker is paid a sum in cash equal to the "allotment" times the difference between the bazaar price and some fixed subsidized price. The major changes in the structure of compensation over the three-year period have been a substantial increase in the degree of medical coverage for blue-collar workers and their families, a general reduction in the importance of noncash compensation for white-collar workers, and increased importance of cooperatives based on the price of flour for blue-collar workers.

The probable causes of these trends are quite varied. Demands for increased medical protection were prominent in the agitation of 1968; they appear to have had some results. Part of the apparent reduction in the importance of fringes for white-collar workers is due to a change in the sample: most of the small private plants pay only salary to their small clerical staffs. But the trend toward stable cash payments in place of variable payments or provision of goods also appears in the responses of the seven white-collar employers who repeat in the 1970 list. Of these, three had gone from provision of cheap flour or oil to cash allowances (based on family size in two cases); two companies which had no cooperatives introduced family allowances in cash; and one company now gives cash instead of a free meal. Finally, the trend toward cash commutation of parts of the wage bill is evident even among the blue-collar workers whose flour-based cooperatives showed a large increase. Most of these cooperatives are now paid in cash, based on the difference between the bazaar price and some historical price level. It is probably the importance of flour to the workingman's diet that keeps this a variable component of compensation.

It should be emphasized that, along with the general trend toward a cash economy, the evolution of cooperatives stems from a paradox inherent in their conception. The idea that a firm or government agency should purchase stocks of staple commodities to help smooth price and supply instabilities which confront its workers appeals to workers and to paternalistic managers. Yet few firms are willing or able to tie up large quantities of capital in such a form. Thus, during a severe disturbance in the market (as occurred for flour in 1967–68), the firm's supplies are soon exhausted and provision of the cooperative in kind cannot be continued, unless the firm wishes to pay the going high prices. In short, when the cooperative principle could do the most to maintain workers' living standards, the firm finds itself in no better market position than does the individual worker—and the cooperatives are generally suspended.

The net result of all these changes has been to make the compensation packages for blue-collar and white-collar workers more similar. Clerical employees continue to have higher likelihood of receiving free housing and annual bonuses, but the gaps have narrowed. The major differences seem to be that clerks have moved further down the path of transition from cooperatives toward family allowances, and they receive a lunch allowance more frequently than a free meal.

To estimate the total value of compensation, it is necessary to place some value on the fringe benefits provided in various enterprises. For some components of compensation, this is not too difficult: the annual per man cost of providing the goods or services may approximate their price in the bazaar, as in the case of lunches or meals. Here also there is a check, in that some companies pay cash. The researcher may also be inclined to reject a blue-collar meal valuation which far exceeds the same company's cash allowance to its white-collar staff. For the seventeen companies that provide lunches or allowances to blue-collar staff, the average value is about six and one-half afs per day.

Other items are not so easily handled. The value of free housing is subject to a number of problems: different values in different towns, problems of quality evaluation, overcrowding, availability, and the like. Most managerial estimates have been pared down. Valuation of medical care presents similar problems, but managers' estimates of costs per man-year were much less heterogeneous.[12]

When a money value had been given to each of the compensation components for the various occupations in each company, a series of detailed estimates was produced. Occupational, regional, and sectoral averages were then developed, weighted by employment in the various companies. Seven occupations had sufficient observations to warrant calculation of national averages; these figures are shown in Table 5.

Table 5. Average Annual Compensation by Occupation, Region, and Sector (in Afghanis)

Occupation	No. of plants	Overall average	Kabul and vicinity	North	South and west	Govt.	Ownership Private FDPIL	Older
Mechanics	18	30,800	34,400	29,900	(25,100)	(28,100)	29,600	32,500
Electricians	3	(30,900)	—	—	—	—	—	—
Carpenters, masons	3	(29,700)	—	—	—	—	—	—
Operatives	15	20,100	16,300	21,000	21,200	(19,200)	16,800	20,500
Weavers, power loom	8	21,300	16,400	22,300	—	—	18,700	21,600
Unskilled, year-round	14	10,000	9,600	10,000	10,900	9,200	11,000	10,400
Clerks, starting rate	15	26,000	20,700	26,800	—	15,680[a]	16,600	30,700

[a] This is the starting rate in government service, grade 13.

Figures in parentheses indicate averages based on few, or more variable, observations; hence, they are less reliable.

Dashes indicate insufficient information.

12   For further discussion, see Scoville, "Remuneration in Afghan Industry," pp. 385–87.

Occupational Differentials. Skill differentials in Afghanistan appear to be quite wide, considerably broader than the usual 2/1 ratio found by the ILO for most countries in Africa and Asia.[13] To be more specific, contrast some of the Afghan differentials with those found in two major cities in adjoining nations:

	Unskilled	Weavers	Mechanics	Carpenters
Afghanistan (1970)	100	213	308	297
Teheran (1969)	100	177	129	—
Lahore (1969)	100	144	202	250

Managers' persistent reports of a shortage of skilled workers appear to be borne out by these differentials. Moreover, as shown in Table 6, these differentials have widened over the last three years. There is some evidence here of misdirected effort in the educational system, from the side of either students or educators. While skilled wages have risen relative to unskilled, those for clerical and administrative workers have not. Indeed, fragmentary evidence in the ILO source suggests that clerical wages are well above those for skilled workers in most comparable countries, while Table 5 implies this may not be the case in Afghanistan, particularly for the lower clerical grades. The power of the forces of status and prestige is measured by continued outpouring of unemployed graduates, while managers bemoan the lack of skilled men. Although the resulting earnings relationships look more rational than in other countries with the same problem, it appears certain that the skilled and white-collar sectors of the labor market are still far from equilibrium.

Regional Differentials. Geographical differences in earnings in Afghanistan possess one major and one minor anomaly. To take the minor first, an observer is struck by the constancy of the day labor rate across the cities and towns visited. This rate is roughly 30 afs per day everywhere (unchanged from 1967) and shows seasonal variations which are more important than any regional differences. Why are there not more perceptible differences in an underdeveloped country larger than France? In the absence of data, a most likely hypothesis would supplant the "problem of commitment" by a firm commitment to the benefits of a cash economy, origin unknown at present. This appears to be supported and ac-

---

13   See "Results of the October Inquiry," *Bulletin of Labour Statistics,* 1970, no. 2, pp. 104–7, 113–17. The Iranian and Pakistani data refer to hourly rates and hourly earnings, respectively.

companied by cases of substantial labor mobility. Eighty percent of the 700 seasonal production workers in the sugar factory at Baghlan (a small provincial center) come from areas 150 miles away to work twelve hours a day for 15 afs, three meals, and a cot.

The major anomaly of regional differentials is found in their divergence from the usual pattern by size of place. Compensation of semi-skilled, skilled, and white-collar workers is higher in the smaller towns than in the larger cities, Kabul and Kandahar.[14] To say that this is due to influx of workers to these cities is to beg the question. Both the wage differentials and the migration reflect the considerable civilized advantages available, particularly in Kabul. In the case of white-collar workers, this preference for Kabul's amenities is fostered by the city's concentration of educational activities in which these workers get their training.

Sector or Ownership Differentials. In 1967 considerable emphasis was placed on the role of the government wage scales in determining levels of compensation throughout the industrial sector. For government-owned enterprises the government scales were obligatory, but use of these scales was pervasive in the private sector. Clerical workers in all plants but one and an estimated 50 percent of all private company permanent blue-collar workers (except those on piece rates) were paid by this scale, perhaps with a percentage differential. The implementation of government rates seems to have resulted not from official pressure, but from the adoption and application of an arbitrary rule as a substitute for managerial decision-making. This reaction seems appropriate to a situation where managerial talent is sparse indeed.

Using the same procedures, it is now estimated that 78 percent of all clerical workers in industry have their pay based on the appropriate government scale, but only 70 percent of those in privately owned firms. Approximately 18 percent of the clerical workers in plants under FDPIL are paid by government scale. Blue-collar workers in the four government-owned plants are paid by the seventeen-grade scale, plus a regional differential in one case. Roughly one-quarter of the non–piece rate workers in plants under FDPIL are so paid. As this sector grows, government influence on blue-collar wages should diminish. It is difficult to spot a trend among the older, more government-influenced enterprises; one

14 Mechanics were the exception to this rule in 1967 and remain so now, perhaps due to dissimilarities in kind of work performed. The figures for Kabul include a large number of production mechanics in a metal works; those in the provinces are primarily maintenance men.

could perhaps say that the influence of the government scale has declined, simply on the basis of the widespread uncertainty among managers about the exact origins of their wage scales.

As seen in Table 5, government-owned enterprises and the older private companies exhibit the same relationship as prevailed in 1967, where private enterprise paid more—sometimes, as with clerks, considerably more. This last comparison is flawed by a problem that also makes difficult the interpretation of the figures shown for new plants under FDPIL—the large regional differential against Kabul. Most of the new enterprises are in Kabul,[15] while the older private and government plants are more scattered. Thus rates in the new firms might appear low, while actually being relatively high.[16] Unfortunately, insufficient data were produced to permit a test of the interesting question whether expanded private enterprise under FDPIL would be more efficient than older firms, and hence pay better wages.

Changes in Compensation, 1967–70. Table 6 shows estimated annual compensation in 1967 and 1970 for those few occupations which had a significant number of observations in both years. The four blue-collar occupations show increases directly related to skill level, while the starting clerical rate has not kept up with changes in skilled compensation. By way of contrast, the unskilled day labor rate has remained fairly constant at roughly 30 afs per day.

All the percentage changes shown in Table 6 somewhat overstate the increase in disposable compensation. Depending on the occupation, from 500 to 1,000 afs increase in compensation is due strictly to increases in the cost-based valuations of free meals. Thus unskilled year-round compensation net of free meals has changed little, if at all, making its behavior parallel that of the day labor rate.[17]

---

15   This is easily understood and likely to persist. The Miner team estimates that capital costs are 30% greater in the provinces, due to lack of water, electricity, and roads.

16   As in the case of clerks, where FDPIL concerns pay more than the government.

17   A rough check on the percentage changes in Table 6 is possible in two cases. Six enterprises reported directly comparable figures for mechanics in both years; the change in their weighted average compensation was 22%. Seven firms gave comparable data for starting clerical rates; estimated change over three years was 6%. We might thus be led to suspect that some part of the increases shown is due to the inclusion of new firms in the sample, except that these subsamples of six and seven plants contained high-wage plants in 1967. For both mechanics and clerks these subsamples paid 20% more than the national average in 1967. Thus they may have been under less pressure to raise compensation than low-wage firms, and increases may have been less than the average.

Table 6. Changes in Annual Compensation, 1967–70 (in Afghanis)

Occupation	1967	1970	Change
Mechanics	23,000	30,800	+34%
Electricians and carpenters	24,000	30,600	28
Power loom weavers	18,000	21,300	18
Clerks, starting rate	23,000	26,000	13
Unskilled, year-round	9,000	10,000	11

Lack of an appropriate consumer price index prevents us from accurately assessing any changes in real compensation. The price index calculated by the Ministry of Planning gives a weight of 93 percent of the urban budget to consumption of food, although the comparable proportion found in the Household Expenditure Survey at Lashkar Gah was 60.7.[18] As Schiro points out, "No other nation in the world, including nations as poor or poorer than Afghanistan, shows such a high proportion of expenditures going to food."[19] Thus this index is hardly useful for assessing the course of real income levels.

G. Owens of the Kabul University agriculture faculty has developed an indicator which, although it still far overweights food (87%), has the virtue of being based on the AID agriculture division's "Weekly Price Report for Kabul." This is likely to incorporate a more accurate reporting system than that upon which the Ministry of Planning index is based. Using Owens's weights, one finds a price increase of about 2 percent from July, 1967, to the end of that year, then a decline of about 5 percent from January, 1968, to June–July, 1970. By this measure, prices would have declined approximately 3 percent between the two compensation surveys. All the figures shown in Table 6 would therefore reflect increases in real incomes. Unfortunately, as with the Ministry index, the exclusion of rents from the index makes any firm conclusion impossible; these appear to have been under considerable upward pressure, particularly in the Kabul area.

Despite the inconclusive results of our inquiry into changes in the price level, the general impression remains quite clear: wages have behaved in almost perfect accordance with Lewis's model. Common labor rates and unskilled compensation in industry have moved little, if at all. This result may be partly due to the fact that government scales have not been changed during the three-year

18   *Survey of Progress,* 1969, chapter on Lashkar Gah Household Expenditure Survey, Table 7a.
19   Bruno A. Schiro, "The Statistical System of Afghanistan," (USAID/A, Kabul, Summer, 1970), p. 13.

period. Nevertheless, industry's declining reliance on those government scales makes wage changes more of a market phenomenon than an administrative accident.

Other Conditions of Employment. Hours of work and holiday provisions did not change between 1967 and 1970. Almost all plants work eight hours per day, six days per week (except in Ramazan, the month of fasting). Provision is made for the sixteen national and religious holidays, but other leave provisions are more disparate and informal. The typical plant would allow about fifty days per year in some combination of sick leave, recreational leave, and emergency leave. The looseness and informality of these provisions appears to reflect tacit acceptance of the Afghan worker's penchant for absenteeism.

Among the larger and older factories, retirement schemes have become fairly common. Many are of the nature of a "provident fund" financed by employee salary deductions, with occasional employer contributions or interest payments. Several large companies pay a termination bonus of half a month's pay per year of service. None of the new plants under FDPIL reported a formal scheme of this nature.

An Assessment of Afghan Labor Markets. Institutional factors, such as the government wage scales, are clearly quite important in the operation of labor markets. Yet the possibility of adjusting a large number of fringe benefits, the frequent use of percentage differentials above the government rates, and the expanding importance of the private sector under FDPIL suggest that there is considerable flexibility to respond to economic conditions as well. We have seen that the size and movement of wage differentials corresponds closely with managers' and observers' characterizations of labor market conditions. Regional differentials are consistent with variations in the quality of life between the provincial towns and large cities. Evidence from Baghlan Sugar (and other cases not cited) suggests that men are willing to travel significant distances even for jobs that are only seasonal, accounting in part for the striking uniformity of day labor wages across the country. By standards of how labor markets are supposed to work, those of Afghanistan give the appearance of something resembling competitive rationality.

Further evidence of the connection between wages and worker behavior can also be presented, quite dramatically, in Table 7, which reflects an attempt to collect information on labor turnover.

Such data are critical to an assessment of the allegedly existing problem of commitment in less developed areas.

Two major obstacles stood in the way of an attempt to collect such information. In the first place, top management doesn't collect these figures in Afghanistan; hence the only people who would have much of an idea would be the foremen who handle blue-collar hiring. Second, the whole issue of turnover is clouded by the widespread existence of individual labor contracts. These are often of two years' duration for production workers, and frequently of five years' duration for skilled mechanics.

The most frequent cause of labor turnover mentioned by managers was conscription for military service. Several companies, particularly around Kabul, had occasional problems with workers returning periodically to agricultural duties (the so-called mulberry season). Yet the most important factor in managers' minds clearly appears to be the level of compensation. The president of one government plant ascribed last year's quit rate of 15 percent to the narrow grade differentials in the government blue-collar scale, plus the government's policy of never advancing a man more than one grade per year. A manager at a large textile plant complained that he lost skilled operatives to competitors "for the sake of a thousand afs or so," after investing a good sum in their training.[20]

This important link between compensation and turnover is supported by Table 7. Five relatively small textile plants in the Kabul area provided fairly reliable data on this subject. Their small size allows us to circumvent the problem of lack of information by managers, while labor contracts where they existed were for only one year. The relationship between compensation levels and quit rates is quite striking.

Thus available evidence indicates that Afghan labor markets behave much as economic theory leads us to expect, despite levels of illiteracy and poverty that should interfere. Undoubtedly, some part of the explanation is to be found in the social history of the people who comprise the urban population. Yet a good deal of it must stem from the needs for cash which typify the Afghan city-dweller's life, and those of many of his countrymen. He needs cash for imported manufactured items, for fines and taxes, to pay off officials and police; these must be fairly common features in the developing world. Beyond this, the young man faces a hurdle

20   A manager in Kabul has an "agent" (a relative, no doubt) in that plant's town, to whom he pays 50 afs for each skilled worker he steals.

Table 7. Turnover Rates and Estimated Annual Compensation of Weavers: Textile Factories in the Kabul Area

Company		Power loom weavers' compensation (in afghanis)	Annual turnover estimates
A		14,075	40%
B		15,000	20–25
C		16,250	20
D	before wage hike[a]	14,700	"as high as 10% monthly"
	after wage hike	20,700	0
E		18,000	0

[a] According to manager, wages were increased explicitly to combat turnover problems.

which must further commit him to the cash nexus: the need to accumulate sums that often seem staggering to pay the price for his bride. Further research would be desirable, for the answer to the "problem of commitment" in Afghanistan may be as simple as that.

COMPARISONS WITH INCOME IN OTHER ACTIVITIES

In a country so predominantly agricultural, it would be desirable to compare compensation in industry with incomes from farming. The handful of studies available in 1967 led me to conclude that "the average remuneration of a low-skilled worker in industry is at least double the income per adult male in agriculture."[21] Since that time several additional studies of farm incomes have come to light; they strongly underscore the "at least double" of the 1967 situation.

The following data were collected in a 1965 survey of thirty-six farms in the Helmand Valley. These are mostly occupied by new settlers, which gives us a rough comparability with new job openings in industry. The average farm size was 7.4 hectares (18.3 acres), of which 6.6 were farmed.[22] The average number of household members was 9.5.[23] This typical unit produced a net income of 28,104 afs per year. The major problem is to determine the manpower unit to compare with the compensation of a well-defined "worker" in industry. For labor inputs on the farm, the report deals in man-equivalents, where women count as .5 and children range

21 Scoville, "Remuneration in Afghan Industry," p. 396.
22 Shamalan Unit, Helmand-Arghandab Valley Development Project, *Feasibility Report,* September, 1968. Appendix A; Agricultural Economics, p. 27.
23 *Ibid.,* p. 25.

from .3 to .4. Thus the average household equaled 5.2 man-equivalents.

On this basis, net income per man-equivalent would be 5,405 afs per year, slightly more than half the year-round unskilled industrial rate. Such a comparison, however, is not entirely appropriate. One should, in fact, calculate the man-equivalents available to the family unit if it were to locate in the various industrial areas. Depending on the pervasiveness of schooling in various towns and cities, the man-equivalents from children might become negligible. Again, depending on size and extent of land-holdings in industrial areas, the man-equivalents available from female labor might stay at .5 (perhaps around Gulbahar, where small holdings are quite common) or decline sharply (probably in Kabul).[24] Perhaps the simplest solution is to do the same as in 1967 and use adult males as the basis for comparison. Reasonable assumptions would imply that a household of 9.5 persons embodying 5.2 man-equivalents contains approximately 3 adult males. On this basis, net income per adult male comes to 9,300 afs per year, strikingly close to the annual earnings of day labor and unskilled industrial workers.[25]

This finding should probably not be too surprising—and may be irrelevant, as the farms involved are part of a new development project, are irrigated, and are considerably larger than typical holdings. One survey found that 42 percent of rural landowning households had less than one acre, about 85 percent less than ten, and 90 percent less than fifteen.[26] Asiel also quotes from the Third Five-Year Plan, which gives estimated incomes for small holder families of six persons falling in the range from 1,100 to 5,000 afs yearly.[27] This may be more usual than the incomes for the Shamalan region.

As a result of a survey conducted in 1970 by Gordon Whiting (University of Wisconsin), some new data have recently appeared on the incomes of Afghan farmers.[28] These data would be ill suited for any attempt to describe the average condition of farmers: the sample was purposefully drawn from regions with high agricultural

24   Alternatively, we might add the probable income of dependents of an industrial worker to his compensation, adjust for family size and composition, and make comparisons on that basis. Such figures are not yet available.

25   As a note of caution, it is unclear what effect recent changes in the prices of agricultural products might have had on farmers' incomes.

26   Quoted in Murad A. Asiel, "Economic Development and the Problems of Employment in Afghanistan" (USAID-mimeo, 1970), p. 16.

27   *Ibid.,* p. 20.

28   Personal communication to the author, March 5, 1971. Whiting surveyed 718 farm units, by far the largest sample of any study.

development potential, to test (among other things) entrepreneurial attributes of farm decision-makers. Thus the manner of selecting the sample combines with the usual skew in income distributions to make average incomes doubly deceptive. Yet for this very reason Whiting's data would set a firm lower limit to the industry-agriculture differential. The average income per adult male in his study can be estimated as slightly above 6,000 afs, derived from his farm unit income figures shown in Table 8.

One additional study of agricultural incomes focused on vineyards in the Koh-i-Daman Valley. For the ninety-five smaller, more typical vineyards covered by this survey, averaging 3.1 jeribs, the

Table 8. Estimated Measures of Farm Income in Afghanistan

			Income per:		
Study	Unit income (afghanis)	Persons in unit	Adult male	Man-equivalent	Capita
Stevens and Tarzi[a] (Panjawi-Maiwand, 1965)	4,825	3 adults + (?) children	2,400[b]	1,400[b]	750[b]
Wyoming team[a] (1967)					
Baghlan (10 acres)	14,165	n.a.	—	—	—
Logar Valley (5 acres)	10,920	n.a.	—	—	—
Koh-i-Daman					
(3½ acres)	36,162	n.a.	—	—	—
Shamalan (1965)	28,104	9.5	9,300	5,405	2,958
Dawlaty et al. (Koh-i-Daman, 1968)	4,928	9.39	1,650[c]	1,000[c]	525[c]
Whiting (1970)					
All farmers	19,600	10	6,222[d]	3,590[d]	1,960[d]
Owner-operators	20,040	n.a.	—	—	—
Sharecroppers	12,110	n.a.	—	—	—
Landlords	35,610	n.a.	—	—	—

[a] For discussion of these studies, see Scoville, "Remuneration in Afghan Industry," pp 395–96.

[b] I have assumed that the (partially guessed) Shamalan family structure of 9.5 persons: 5.2 man-equivalents: 3 adult males can be scaled down proportionately to the (probable) 2 adult males in the Stevens-Tarzi unit.

[c] Here the Shamalan actual and assumed figures for male-equivalents and adult males, respectively, have been applied to the Dawlaty et al. data.

[d] As in note b, I have scaled the Shamalan family structure for 9.5 persons up to 10, implying 5.46 man-equivalents and 3.15 adult males. Whiting's respondents estimated man-equivalents at slightly over 2 per household. As he states, "This seems unreasonably small. If it is accurate there must be strong sanctions against utilizing the labor of females, the very young, and the very old. It may be that farmers did not understand that they were being asked for family labor available for use rather than family labor actually in use. Also an element of pride in not regarding female members of the household as available may have entered in."

mean annual income was 4,927.64 afs.[29] This income was produced by a typical household of 9.39 persons, 5.44 of whom were of working age (13–60).[30] These figures, along with those from the Third Five-Year Plan, point to very low average farm income and suggest no compelling reason for narrowing the industry-agriculture income differential suggested in 1967.

Indeed, the situation seems to suggest that income differences between the modern and subsistence agriculture sectors may be even wider than figures available three years ago would lead one to suspect. The available studies are summarized in Table 8, with some attempted evaluations of income in relation to various population and manpower indices. The Stevens and Tarzi, Dawlaty et al., and Whiting averages have been produced on the assumption that the age-sex structure of the family unit is similar to that reported in the Shamalan study.[31] No figures can be concocted for the Wyoming team studies—all we can say (referring to Asiel) is that these are rather large landholdings.

These figures point to a gap between agriculture and industry far wider than suggested by Lewis. Whiting's averages, despite being inflated by skew and the privileged nature of the group sampled, show the differential to be at least 60 percent. Looking at his income figure for sharecroppers (28% of his sample) and applying some windage for areas of less agricultural potential, it is clear that the true differential is much larger than that. Two cases from Table 8 suggest that unskilled wages in industry may run four to five times the level of farm income per adult male. The historic hand of the government wage scales undoubtedly had a good deal to do with this differential. Its portent for the future population of the industrial areas, should the Green Revolution come to Afghanistan and displace rural labor, is ominous indeed.[32]

Turning to other traditional pursuits we encounter a virtual absence of data. According to a former Soviet manpower and labor advisor, the typical small *nan* (bread) shops have the following general technical specifications. They employ six or seven men and

29   K. Dawlaty, R. K. Harlan, and G. P. Owens, "The Economics of Grape Production and Marketing in the Koh Daman Valley of Afghanistan," Kabul University, Faculty of Agriculture, Technical Bulletin #7, November, 1967, p. 11.

30   *Ibid.*, p. 5.

31   No compelling justification can be given for this procedure. Most emphatically, neither the procedure nor its results should be attributed to the authors whose data I have borrowed.

32   For an overview of this problem, see W. A. Lewis, "Summary," *International Labour Review,* May, 1970, pp. 550–51.

produce between 2,000 and 4,000 *nan* per day, each weighing 200 grams. In the summer of 1970 the price of flour was about 60 afs per seer, which translates into a raw material cost per *nan* of approximately afs 1.65. Thus, when the retail price of bread is 2 afs,[33] enterprise income is 35 puls per *nan*. Using the lower limit of the expert's output estimates (2,000 per day), net income per worker is about 100 afs per day. If we knew how much goes for capital and other costs (taxes, rent, wood), and how the remainder is distributed among the baker and his hired help, we could say something definite. Yet it is clear that income here must be relatively high, since a group of seven industrial workers would have to be skilled mechanics or craftsmen to earn together 700 afs per day. A collectivity of seven operatives might earn 400 afs together; of unskilled or day labor, 200.

The quest for comparative income data turned up one other item, even less informative than data on *nan* shops. It is alleged that sixty woman-days are needed to produce one square meter of average carpet, which means five meters per year. If we strike a rough average of the two most recent figures for the average price of carpets (1,205 afs/meter in 1967–8, 715 afs/meter in the following year),[34] it would appear that the annual *retail* value of her production is in the vicinity of 5,000 afs. How much of this actually goes to supplement the family income (and thus serve as an impediment to the family's industrial or regional mobility) is an open question.

The available data thus suggest that there is an ample supply of unskilled labor, but that the real wage in the modern sector is far above Lewis's "subsistence plus." The level of this wage has been influenced in part by the importance of government wage scales in fixing compensation in industry. We may expect, with new private plants relying less on government scales, that the level of real wages will be eroded by forces in the labor market, particularly if the price level should rise substantially.[35] As far as skilled labor is

33 As the price of bread is now above 2 afs, all the figures given are underestimates. Calculations as follows: 1 seer = 7.066 kg. = 35.3 *nan* of 200 grams. At the time the calculations were made, the price of wheat in Kabul was fluctuating between 58 and 59 afs per seer. Fifty-eight afs divided by 35.3 *nan* yields the raw material estimate in the text.

34 *Survey of Progress*, 1969, p. S-13.

35 When this essay was being prepared in late 1970, the prospects for price increases were high: large portions of the dry-land wheat crop were lost to drought in 1970. This drought was severe enough in some areas to bake the earth so hard that plowing was impossible, portending another poor crop for 1971. As this book goes to press, grain shortages and localized cases of famine had become a reality in spring, 1972.

concerned, a persistent shortage seems to exist, exerting upward pressure on wages. The shortage may be due in part to better alternatives in some traditional areas, as the data on *nan* shops suggest.

INDUSTRIAL RELATIONS

Part of my discussions with managers centered upon various aspects of the nascent industrial relations system of Afghanistan. They were supplemented by discussions with government officials and observers of the Afghan scene. Some of the following is more impressionistic than the data presented earlier.

Hiring. In contrast to India and some African countries, where distinctive schemes for recruitment of labor were developed at the outset of industrial activity, no peculiar hiring system has appeared in Afghanistan. Among the large firms availability of jobs is communicated through word of mouth in the bazaar and via radio, with all hiring performed at the factory gate. Most companies report applications which far exceed the number of jobs available. A few smaller enterprises showed evidence or admitted hiring from a particular ethnic or family group, with the avowed purpose of reducing friction, but most companies denied such practices. Several companies report policies (and occasionally action) against the practice of foremen taking kickbacks from workers to protect their jobs, but neither the extent of the practice nor of the counteraction is known for certain.

An interesting aspect of the hiring issue is involved in the employment of women, exceedingly rare in Afghan industry. In 1967, some .7 percent of employment surveyed was female; three years later the proportion had risen to 1.1 percent. Only five plants (of twenty-five) employ any women at all in production departments, and one plant employs half the total. Due to the social need to segregate women,[36] a whole department or area of the plant must be given over to them as a group. Thus the managerial decision about hiring women is not whether to hire one or two, but whether to hire twenty or thirty to staff some appropriate cluster of jobs. Current examples of such jobs are sorting raw wool, wrapping bars of soap, making yarn or thread, and nit-picking.

---

36   In the presence of men outside the family, the Afghan woman's traditional dress involves the *chawdry,* which literally covers her from head to toe with only a mesh-covered opening at the eyes. Needless to say, this garment is incompatible with most industrial work.

When employed, women generally receive the same wages as would men in those jobs. Occasionally some special allowance is made; one plant, which provides bus and truck transport for its male workers, gives its women 2½ afs in cash daily so that they may come by more civilized public conveyances.

Work Rules and Labor Contracts. Recalling the kind of work rules which emerged in Britain and the United States in the early stages of industrial development and which frequently regulated the worker's moral, religious, and social life, a search was undertaken for such a list of rules in Afghan plants. No such formal listing was found, evidently due in part to the overwhelming extent of illiteracy among production workers. There is a volume of regulations applying to government plants which spells out wage scales, overtime, holidays and leave, retirement and medical provisions, but this is obviously of limited importance to the daily life of the worker.

The closest thing to a summary of the rules with which the worker is expected to be familiar can be found in the provisions of the individual labor contracts mentioned earlier. A rough translation of one of these agreements is provided below, courtesy of Mohammed Naim (Miner Associates).

FIVE-YEAR AGREEMENT

The Jangalak Factories, called the employer, and Mr._____, son of_____, residence_____, holder of ID card #_____, called employee, have made the following agreement.

1. Employee agrees to respect all the rules and regulations of the establishment and keep secret the confidences of the factory.

2. Employee agrees to keep up with all rules and regulations of the factory and has accepted the attendance regulation. Without logical reasons, sickness or recreational leave, he can't get rid of his duty.

3. Employee agrees from the effective date of the agreement to work for five consecutive years at the factory, in the field of_____, grade_____, salary_____.

4. If employee prior to a certain point in the contract and without agreement of the Head Office or logical reasons (i.e., military service or permanent sickness) leaves the job, he is not entitled to 5% provident fund.

5. Employee agrees to obey all authorized people's instructions in connection with the factory administration.

6. Employee agrees to cooperate with his friends in the factory

and should behave nicely; otherwise, if he makes disturbance to the management of the factory, not only will he be fired, but he also is not entitled to 5% provident fund.

7. Employee agrees that, in case the management regards the attendance of the worker as not being in conformity with the provisions of the contract, the boss or management is authorized to warn him or deduct from his salary as per instructions of the Head Office authority.

8. Employee, during his service or after, except for salary, cooperative, medical insurance privileges and [legal benefits?] is not entitled to ask for other rights, according to the rules and procedures of the factory.

9. If the Jangalak Factory decides to cancel the contract of an employee, the management of the factory has decided to pay one month's salary in cash to those who made service for less than two years. If his service is more than two years, then he is entitled to two month's salary plus provident fund.

The above-mentioned contract made between employer and employee is valid for five consecutive years.

_____Employer Signature   _____Employee Signature

The contract is still quite vague about rules of the workplace, although the repetition of phrases on attendance and contract duration would indicate that these rules are frequently broken and are important to management. The obligations of the worker's factory are quite sharply limited, while the worker's duty to obey unspecified rules, regulations, and authorities is greatly stressed. Clause 8, as with similar ones in other contracts, is to be construed as a no-strike pledge. The threatened loss of "provident fund"—financed by 5 percent salary deductions (plus 4 percent annual interest, in this case)—is held as sanction against all sorts of misbehavior.

Grievance Handling. Formal procedures for handling employee grievances appear to be nonexistent in Afghan industry. Managers of even the largest enterprises insist that they know all their employees by name (highly unlikely), and that the workers are neither afraid nor unable to present their problems directly to the president of the company (equally unlikely). From frequent interruptions of interview sessions, it is certain that some employees do follow this grievance route, but what proportion of total problems this represents and how satisfactorily they are settled remains unclear.

Some evidence of lack of effective communication comes out of the spate of strikes in 1968. Even while professing the omniscient paternalistic philosophy summarized above, managers will say that disturbances over the quality of food served by their companies, over rancid ghee or dirty rice, over work assignment, pay-grade classification, and elimination of overtime, or about overcrowding in company housing were important parts of the unrest. Such complaints, largely nonwage and nonpolitical in nature (although perhaps the vehicle for political activity), appear to have surprised some managers. They also indicate that the traditional labor-management relationship does not work as well as the managers like to think.

Unrest and Strikes. Trade unions and political parties lie in a state of legal limbo in Afghanistan. Their right to exist is constitutionally protected;[37] on the other hand, the law by which they are to be established does not exist. Trade unions might therefore be denoted as nonlegal, to indicate this curious status.

Despite this absence of formal organizations, many of the large enterprises in Afghanistan were troubled by labor unrest, particularly during the first half of 1968.[38] In many cases the facts of the matter are unclear: informed observers differ on where unrest occurred, just what happened, and the relative importance of politics and agitators versus internal company or economic issues. I cannot pretend to add anything to this confusion. Instead, my discussions with managers focused on their perceptions of the issues involved, the manner in which strikes were ended, and the possible appearance of formative labor organizations. Most managers who had gone through strikes in 1968 and were still in their jobs were quite open in discussing what happened. Asked how the strike at his plant came to an end, one manager laughed and replied, "Police force, of course."

Most managers thought that their strikes were basically political acts, instigated by one or another of the four Communist groups with which Afghanistan is blessed and coordinated by "the outside hand."[39] Some evidence for this was offered by one manager, who claimed that this was particularly obvious in the case of his strike:

37   The following passage from Article 32 of the 1964 Constitution covers labor organizations: "Afghan citizens have the right to establish, in accordance with the provisions of the law, associations for the realization of material or spiritual purposes."
38   For a summary of worker and student unrest in April–June, 1968, see Louis Dupree, "Afghanistan, 1968, Part IV: Strikes and Demonstrations," *Universities Field Staff Reports,* South Asia series, vol. 12, no. 7.
39   Radio reports of concurrent events in France probably played some role.

the mimeographed list of demands which was being passed out asked for the introduction of cooperatives and other fringe benefits which had already been in existence at the time of my 1967 survey. Even so, wage increases and the kinds of work-related complaints noted earlier were frequently involved in the dispute, perhaps only as fuel for a fundamentally political event. Yet, where the complaints had some foundation, they had to be dealt with regardless of the motivation and origins of the unrest itself.

The reaction of various managements and their ways of handling strikes were quite varied, but they had one common thread: even if they wanted to negotiate, they had little way of knowing where to turn for an opposite number. Sometimes they resorted to discussions with mass meetings of the workers, descriptions of which sound like chaos of the highest order; at least one of these meetings turned into a rather nasty riot. Other companies refused to deal under pressure with demands that they regarded as unreasonable; they finally relied on the police to break the strike. In one case the president of the company asked the workers to select a committee to formalize their demands and meet with him. This strike was also ended by the police, even though the committee apparently still meets with the president from time to time. Another company has dealt occasionally with ad hoc groups of workers.

In only one case was anything resembling bargaining reported. This company experienced a three-month strike in 1969. During the strike the workers chose a committee (allegedly by formal election) which negotiated with the board of directors. These negotiations ended with a four-point agreement involving the institution of food allowances, payment of bonuses (evidently involving major concessions from both sides' starting positions), payment of salary during the strike, and a pledge that no one be fired. Despite what sounds like a major and orderly success, the workers' committee has since evaporated.

Even where such bargaining did not take place, managements appear to have made some adjustments. In at least two cases managers promised wage increases before they finally broke the strikes; in one case comparison with the 1967 survey data indicates that this promise was kept. The other case is unclear, both with regard to the size of increase promised and to any subsequent action. In another enterprise complaints about the procedures for grading workers on the pay scale led to the creation of a body in the Ministry of Mines and Industries responsible for testing workers' skills and placing them in the proper pay grade. The first round of this apparently resulted in a considerable amount of upward movement and consequent wage increases for many workers. The expansion of medical coverage for blue-collar workers may also be attributed to the demands raised by workers in 1968. On the other hand, a number of companies fired anyone they thought was connected with their strike.

Despite apparent economic gains in some cases and elimination of some grievances, the impact of the strikes on industrial relations, particularly with respect to the development of labor organizations, has been virtually nil. On the workers' side, where committees arose (however chosen), they have almost invariably disappeared. The one workers' committee that apparently continues to function seems to be simply a relic of the strike, with no provisions for elections or other procedures to renew its membership and its mandate. On the side of management, there is perhaps a greater awareness of the need for some authoritative group with whom to deal, if one is going to have a strike imposed upon him. However, this awareness is counter-balanced by a conviction that any committees developed now would sooner or later become the tools of one political faction or another. Meanwhile, the government (which got caught in the middle of the unrest) is contemplating the legalization of strikes and trade unions simply to extricate itself from the situation.

As may be evident from the history above, the type of permissive legislation now under consideration[40] is inadequate to the current state of industrial relations in Afghanistan. To simply legalize strikes and organization, as the current proposal would do in several brief sentences, would still leave a vacuum where the parties have little idea how, when, or upon which issues to act. Since the creation of national or industrial unions would be bound up with the issue of political parties (upon which the government is proceeding most cautiously), the law should envision the formation of works committees, spell out the procedures for their selection, and define the mechanics of their relationships with managements.

OVERVIEW

Judging from a number of items of evidence, Afghan labor markets appear to work more efficiently than might be expected. The move-

[40] The draft, parts of which were verbally translated for me by an official of the Ministry of Mines and Industries, is currently under scrutiny by the Ministry of Justice. From there it will go to the Cabinet. There is little likelihood that its course will be swift; cf. example of law on political parties, passed by Parliament in 1964 and still to be promulgated.

ments of skilled wages in contrast to those of unskilled and clerical workers, the size of skill differentials, the comparatively low level of compensation associated with the amenities of Kabul, and fragmentary data on turnover rates all point to this conclusion. Thus, if we are able to take the competitive model as a working approximation of the Afghan situation, we can evaluate the applicability of Lewis's theory.

The *movements* of unskilled industrial wages (and the day labor rate as well) conform to his predictions—these wages have changed little, if at all. But it is their *level* which most strikingly catches our attention. It is hard to envision "subsistence plus" as describing wage levels at least double (and perhaps much more than double) the income available in agriculture. For the Afghan case, then, the following modifications must be made to the basic Lewis model.

1. Government wage scales have exercised considerable (though decreasing) influence on industrial wages, both through direct ownership and by imitation in private firms short on managerial talent. Why government wages have exceeded "subsistence plus" might be attributed to humanitarian paternalism; that they have been able to remain at such a level may be due to the fact that Afghan manufactures are seldom exported.

2. Workers in the government-owned plants or the politically sensitive large private enterprises possess a modest degree of bargaining power stemming from their ability to embarrass the government. A few examples of this emerged in the events of 1968.

3. The internal wage structure of enterprises may be constrained by workers' or managers' conceptions of "fair differentials," or, more plausibly, by the fact that on-the-job training of unskilled workers is one means of obtaining skilled men. Thus unskilled wages need to exceed "subsistence plus" in order to cut unskilled workers' turnover rates. Although we have no direct evidence on this point, the high levels of skilled and craft wages, determined by forces outside the individual plant, may well serve to pull up unskilled rates.

In connection with the last point, consider the comparative breadth of skill differentials.[41] It was noted above that they appear to be quite broad in comparison with those of other less developed countries. Two factors may serve to account for this: reported shortages of skilled workers (consistent with recent wage trends),

41   This subject, to the best of my knowledge, is one on which Lewis's model is silent.

and the levels of income which may be obtainable in some forms of traditional enterprise. To the extent that entry into traditional trades (such as *nan* bakeries, for which crude data were given, tea shops, *kabob* grilling, etc.) is not restricted by caste systems, extensive capital or knowledge requirements, or legal restraints, high incomes in these endeavors should increase the wages of industrial jobs requiring some skill or supervisory talent.

On the institutional side, despite the wave of strikes in 1968, the Afghan system of industrial relations remains in its primitive state. Evidence for the emergence of plant-level workers' organizations is largely confined to the time of the strikes themselves; no ongoing bodies in the plant or outside have appeared. The managerial philosophy remains highly paternalistic, modified by a recognition of the occasional need to know who speaks for the workers, tinged by the certainty that such spokesmen would become tools of radical political forces. No governmental institutions have been developed to bridge the gap between the two sides in times of industrial upheaval; currently proposed legislation would be inadequate for the encouragement of orderly evolution in the field of industrial relations.

Peter Kilby

Trade Unionism in Nigeria, 1938-66

THIS CHAPTER examines the character of industrial relations in pre–civil war Nigeria and the nature of its influence on the country's political economy. Part I describes the institutional setting and the structural features of the trade union movement, and it reviews certain aggregate measures of the system's performance. Part II presents an analysis of bargaining therein. Part III is descriptive and historical; by scrutinizing what are thought to be the critical features of Nigerian industrial relations, it attempts to bare the underlying dynamics of the transplanted British system. Part IV, based on the preceding analysis, sets forth a general interpretation of why the Anglo-Saxon model has failed to function as it was intended, both in Nigeria and—with some qualification—in the underdeveloped world at large.

I

In 1966 Nigeria's economically active population was approximately 20.6 million, of whom some 75 percent were engaged in peasant agriculture.[1] The bulk of the urban labor force is self- or family-employed, so wage-paid employment in Nigeria amounts

Earlier versions of this paper appeared in the *Journal of Developing Areas,* July, 1967, and as Ch. 9 in my *Industrialization in an Open Economy: Nigeria 1945–1966* (Cambridge, 1969).

1 Based upon a corrected census estimate of 44 million population. See I. I. U. Eke, "Population of Nigeria: 1952–1965," *Nigerian Journal of Economic and Social Studies,* July, 1966.

to only about 1.2 million persons.[2] Of these, 510,692, or about 2.5 percent of the country's work force, belonged to a trade union in July, 1966. With few exceptions unionization is limited to the civil service, public corporations, and the "European" firms—those areas where wages and conditions of service are most favorable. The small-scale sector where wages are low has remained largely unorganized; firms in this sector are usually small Nigerian and Levantine concerns which operate in highly competitive markets. Another important feature of the labor market is that the government and public corporations, whose wage-setting decisions are most subject to noneconomic considerations, employ over half of all unionized labor.[3] Consequently, the government's behavior as an employer, quite independent of its policy objectives in the labor field, exerts a powerful influence on industrial relations throughout the economy.

THE INSTITUTIONAL SETTING

The year 1938 is commonly designated as the beginning of organized industrial relations in Nigeria.[4] In that year the British colonial government enacted the Trade Union Ordinance which endowed labor unions with legal status and laid down a minimum code of conduct for union administration. To assist voluntary negotiation between trade unions and management, conciliation and arbitration machinery was established in 1941. Upon the advice of the Labor Advisory Board (the Wages Board after 1957), the Wage-Fixing and Registration Ordinance of 1943 empowered the governor-general to set minimum wages in those industries where collective bargaining did not exist and where wages were unreasonably low. In 1942 a Department of Labor was established, and in 1946 a special trade union division was created in the department. Staffed with professional trade unionists seconded from the British

2 Interpolated from the 1964 *Employment and Earning Enquiry* statistics, 1966 Provident Fund enrollment, and my own estimate of wage employment in enterprises of less than ten workers.

3 In 1964 reported employment in establishments of ten or more was as follows: government, 22,442; public corporations, 57,000; private and commercial, 284,092.

4 Prior to 1938 three unions were in existence: the Association of Nigerian Civil Servants, the Nigerian Union of Teachers, and the Railways Workers Union. The first two of these groups were more concerned with maintaining professional standards of their members than agitating for higher wages and improved conditions of employment. The Railways Workers Union was active in pressing its claims and is discussed subsequently.

TUC, this unit assisted in the formation of new unions, advised existing unions on their administrative problems, and conducted various programs of trade union education. Extensive overseas scholarship programs for trade union officers were operated by the Ministry of Labour and the Railway Department during the 1940's and early 1950's.

Taken together, these legislative and administrative measures represent a reproduction of the metropolitan institutional framework corresponding to a mature system of industrial relations and wage determination which had evolved over a long period. The system has as its objective the settlement of conditions and terms of employment by a process of negotiating and collective bargaining. On one hand, the Anglo-Saxon model differs from the unorganized free market, where workers individually settle on terms with the employer, by virtue of labor's greater bargaining strength achieved by combination into a single bargaining unit. On the other hand, the British prototype is distinct from external political or administrative regulation of conditions and terms of service in that the issues are resolved on a private and voluntary basis by those directly involved—those who presumably possess the most intimate knowledge of the problems to be settled and who will be most affected by the settlement. There are two major requirements for the system's effective operation: that both parties possess the capability and the willingness to negotiate, "to give and take," and that in the final resort, if all else fails, there exists the freedom to strike and to lock out.

In addition to those enactments designed to promote voluntary collective bargaining between organized labor and management, a wide range of protective and minimum welfare legislation was passed during the 1920's and 1930's. These included prohibition of forced labor, minimum conditions of recruitment and long-term contract, protection of wages, minimum age, paid maternity and sick leave, control of apprenticeship, and workmen's compensation for accident and death. During the 1950's this legislation was revised and extended. To these enactments was added the Factory Ordinance in 1955, laying down minimum safety standards for all establishments employing ten or more workers. In 1961 a compulsory retirement benefit scheme (the Provident Fund) was enacted; by December, 1966, some 572,000 employees had been enrolled with total contributions of £22.2 million.[5]

5 For a detailed discussion of Nigerian labor legislation, see "The Influence of International Labour Conventions on Nigerian Labour Legislation," *International Labour Review*, 1960.

It has consistently been the government's policy that free negotiation within the established institutional framework should be the
central regulating principle of industrial relations. A complete
statement of the government's philosophy was given in early 1955
by the prime minister:

> Government re-affirms its confidence in the effectiveness of volun-
> tary negotiations and collective bargaining for the determination of
> wages. The long term interest of Government, employer and trade
> unions alike would seem to rest on the process of consultation and
> discussion which is the foundation of democracy in industry. Gov-
> ernment intervention in the general field of wages should be limited
> to the establishment of statutory wage-fixing machinery for any
> industry or occupation where wages are unreasonably low by refer-
> ence to the general level of wages. Any other policy would seem
> likely to lead to political influences and considerations entering into
> the determination of wages with effects that might be ruinous eco-
> nomically, and which would have serious adverse consequences for
> the development of sound trade unions.[6]

At about the same time the federal minister of labour, then chief
Okotie Eboh, was addressing a conference in Geneva. In this in-
stance adherence to the British model—which also underlies the
ILO labor conventions—was made explicit:

> Can the various types of collective bargaining familiar to older in-
> dustrial societies thrive in the different conditions of underdevel-
> oped countries today? This is an important question which in the
> view of my government permits of only one answer. We have fol-
> lowed in Nigeria the voluntary principles which are so important
> an element in industrial relations in the United Kingdom. . . .
> There is little doubt that Government intervention in the field of
> wages can have very adverse effects, in developing countries at
> least, on trade union development and therefore on labour-man-
> agement relations, unless it is carefully restricted to those fields
> where collective bargaining is either non-existent or ineffective.
> Equally it is my view that compulsory arbitration must inevitably
> have adverse effects on the seriousness with which both parties en-
> ter into the earlier stages of negotiation. Compulsory methods
> might occasionally produce a better economic or political result,
> but labor-management must, I think, find greater possibilities of
> mutual harmony where results have been voluntarily arrived at by

6 Reprinted frequently in Ministry of Labour *Annual Reports* and the *Handbook of Commerce and Industry*.

free discussion between the two parties. We in Nigeria, at any rate, are pinning our faith on voluntary methods.[7]

The government's continued adherence to the Anglo-Saxon model was expressed both before the Morgan Commission in 1963 and after the general strike in April, 1965.[8]

In practice the government has, with one important exception, lived up to its declared policies. No attempts have been made to influence the outcome of private negotiations. Statutory wage-fixing has been infrequent and limited primarily to a few Nigerian-operated industries in Lagos. The one failure of the government to honor the voluntary principle has been in wage determination in the public sector; wage and salary changes have occurred not as a result of collective bargaining but on the recommendation of specially constituted tribunals.

It only remains to note that both employers and organized labor have long accepted the principle that voluntary negotiations and collective bargaining are the best means of determining wages and conditions of employment—with the caveat for the labor movement that free bargaining should be supplemented by minimum wage legislation.[9]

GROWTH AND STRUCTURE OF THE TRADE UNION MOVEMENT

From fourteen registered trade unions with a membership of 4,600 in 1940, the movement had grown to 663 unions with a membership of 510,692 by June, 1966. It would appear that something like 70 percent of employees in establishments of ten or more are members of a union. While enterprise or house unions are the predominant form of trade union organization, such organization may become the equivalent of a national craft or industrial union

7   Ministry of Labour, *Quarterly Review*, June, 1955.

8   Government statement before the Morgan Commission, *Report of the Commission on the Review of Wages, Salary and Conditions of Service of the Junior Employees of the Governments of the Federation and in Private Establishments,* 1963–64, p. 3. The 1965 statement was made by the Federal Minister of Labour in the House of Representatives, April 7, 1965. Reproduced in Nigeria Employers Consultative Association, *NECA News,* May, 1965.

9   Virtually every labor union federation since 1943 has supported voluntary collective bargaining. For a historical review of central trade union organizations and their policies, see Ministry of Labour, *Quarterly Review,* March, 1960, and for recent evidence see *Report of the Morgan Commission,* p. 33.

where the employer is the federal government or a public corporation.

Table 1. The Structure of Nigerian Trade Unions

Membership	Number of unions			Distribution of membership (%)		
	1948	1957	1965	1948	1957	1965
−50	26	69	91	0.8	0.8	0.7
51–250	42	92	231	6.3	5.8	5.8
251–1,000	24	37	139	12.1	8.5	13.6
1,001–5,000	7	29	47	13.6	31.3	17.6
5,000+	6	8	21	67.2	53.6	62.3
Unknown	22	45	22			
	127	270	551	100.0	100.0	100.0

Source: Federal Ministry of Labour, *Annual Reports.*

Distribution of membership by size of union has remained fairly stable. Unions of under 1,000 account for 80 percent of all unions, and of these three-quarters have a membership of less than 250. The majority of unions with membership above 5,000 are in the public sector, e.g., teachers, railways, electricity, civil service.

Even after making due allowance for the inclusion of certain nonlabor organizations among the smaller-sized unions,[10] it remains true that Nigerian unions are very small, particularly in the private sector. As a very rough indication, the average union size in the United Kingdom is twenty times that of Nigeria.[11] In the absence of a significant number of skilled craftsmen in the early stages of industrial development, it is not surprising that development of unions takes place initially on the basis of the place of employment, in contrast to the economically stronger craft-protective unionism of nineteenth-century England and America. What is more surprising is that despite all the efforts of the Ministry of Labour and the various central labor organizations, "house" unions, once firmly established, have not been able to cooperate and consolidate in order to achieve stronger bargaining units in the form of industry-wide organizations.

At least four conditioning factors can be identified in the industrywide union's lack of emergence. The first is the physical

10 Among these are employer organizations, traditional craft societies, and trade associations.

11 In 1964 there were 591 unions in the United Kingdom with an overall membership of 10,065,000 (*NECA News,* May, 1966).

consideration: the size of the country, distances between centers of employment, and problems of communications make the organization and administration of nation- or even regionwide unions a difficult task. The second and third factors contributing to an atomized trade union structure are the tribal rivalry inherent in any larger grouping and the reluctance of paid union secretaries to see themselves consolidated out of a job. It is a rare instance of union dissension or disintegration where either tribalism or personal competition between paid officials is not observable.

A final factor which may have inhibited the development of industrywide unions was the disposition of employers before independence. Lack of any organization among employers or, indeed, even informal cooperation prior to the government-requested establishment of the Nigerian Employers Consultative Association (NECA) in 1957, together with its cause—the desire for maximum individual autonomy on the part of the foreign firms—may have constituted an indirect deterrent to intra-industry cooperation among trade unions. In addition a significant number of unionized firms were, often as a result of past experience with professional secretaries, reluctant to deal with union officials unless employed by the company. It is difficult to judge how large a role management has played in discouraging amalgamation. In most instances the first three causes appear to have been sufficient to produce the result. However, since 1962 NECA, in an all-out effort to forestall political wage-fixing, has formed its members into "trade groups" for intra-industry consultation on such bargaining issues as job classification, terms of service, and appropriate negotiating procedures.

Despite the establishment of these trade groups in 1962 and the strenuous efforts of NECA and the Ministry of Labour to promote industrywide collective bargaining during 1965 and 1966 pursuant to the recommendations of the Morgan Commission, no significant inroads with respect to "house unionism" have been achieved. Following the wave of labor solidarity after the 1964 general strike, union membership jumped from 352,790 in March, 1964, to 517,911 in March, 1965, along with an encouraging increase in average union size; by June, 1966, membership had fallen to 510,692, and the number of unions had risen from 551 to 633.[12] Any hopes for a secular trend toward industry unions would seem to be for naught.

12   Federal Ministry of Labour, *Quarterly Review,* June, 1966, par. 60.

The System's Performance

One conventional index to the success of an industrial relations system is the extent of industrial unrest as measured by the number of strikes and total man-days lost. By this criterion Nigeria's labor-management relations have been very good; Nigeria's proportionate loss of working time to industrial stoppages (about .07 percent) has averaged less than that in the United Kingdom or the United States[13]—a fact the government has been quick to point out. This is partly due to deficiencies in the official statistics. An unknown but probably significant number of disputes are not registered with the Ministry of Labour. There is evidence to suggest that the reported number of stoppages for 1960–61 is only one-quarter of the true figure. Concerning the general strike of June, 1964, the actual time lost was probably 30 percent greater than the 722,000 man-days reported by the Ministry of Labor. Moreover, sitdown strikes and go-slows are apparently not treated as stoppages. All in all, it is quite possible that comprehensive and accurate reporting would reveal Nigeria's performance with regard to strikes was no better than that of England, America, or many other countries.[14]

A second observation on the relatively small number of strikes is made by T. M. Yesufu: the high degree of labor utilization lies less with industrial harmony than with the unions' incapacity to call successful strikes.[15] The basis for this argument is that both workers and their unions lack the financial resources to abstain from employment. A review of the history of strikes in Nigeria suggests that any such constraint has operated only in the case of the smaller private establishments. For the larger, more conspicuous European firms and government establishments, where management tends to be more tolerant and where public opinion and political factors often favor the workers, the record indicates that unions have not hesitated to call out their members. Indeed, the high propensity to call strikes is reflected in the exceedingly short duration of the average stoppage. An inspection of the individual strike narratives in the appendices of the Ministry of Labour's

13   Federal Ministry of Commerce and Industry, *Industrial Labour* (Lagos, 1963), p. 25.

14   For further discussion, see Peter Kilby, *Industrialization in an Open Economy: Nigeria 1945–1966* (Cambridge, 1969), pp. 273ff.

15   T. M. Yesufu, *An Introduction to Industrial Relations in Nigeria* (London, 1962), p. 56.

Annual Reports and *Quarterly Reviews* reveals that about three-quarters of these stoppages range from three hours to two days. These same dispute summaries disclose that a large share of strikes —on the order of 40 percent—result from the precipitous action of union leaders in calling a walkout before making a serious effort to communicate with management. Once the officer from the Ministry of Labour arrives and management is fully informed about the claim or grievance, such "disputes" are usually quickly settled. Another 25 percent of the reported stoppages—typically in smaller establishments and hard-pressed Development Corporation enterprises—involve violations of labor standards, such as delayed payment of wages or failure to pay for overtime. Here again the corrective procedure is not to strike and thereby call in the Ministry of Labour, but simply to report the matter directly to that agency. Only about 35 percent of reported stoppages involve disputes to which the strike is an appropriate final response—conditions of service, wages increases, contesting an arbitrary firing, removal of a disliked foreman, etc.

In short, even allowing for unreported disputes, it would seem that industrial relations in unionized establishments in Nigeria are comparatively harmonious and dispute-free. However, it would not be correct to ascribe the relative lack of strikes to the successful functioning of the Anglo-Saxon model. Rather, the absence of industrial discord is attributable to comprehensive legislated labor standards, the skillful intervention of the Ministry of Labour, and the superiority of wages and conditions of service in unionized establishments relative to previous or alternative working situations.

II

WAGE DETERMINATION

The major test of any system of industrial relations is how effectively it deals with the central issues of the labor-management relationship, particularly wage determination. Despite the carefully constructed institutional framework and the avowed commitment of all parties concerned, voluntary collective bargaining has failed to function as a significant mechanism for fixing wages. The 1964 Morgan Commission, which concluded that "collective bargaining in Nigeria has been very defective,"[16] disclosed that collective agreements existed for the mining industry, several insurance companies,

16   *Report of the Morgan Commission*, p. 31.

and five other large employers—representing some 10 percent of wage-paid labor in the modern sector. Following the recommendations of the Morgan Report and as a result of intensive efforts of NECA and the Ministry of Labour, some forty new company agreements had been signed by December, 1966.[17] The majority of these agreements appear to be management creations, formally codifying existing terms of employment and having involved little if any bargaining or negotiating from labor's side. The outbreak of the civil war in 1967 precludes us from observing whether this latest attempt to make the Anglo-Saxon model operational might have been more successful than its forerunners.

In place of voluntary collective bargaining, wage rates in the unionized sector of the labor market have been determined by independent commissions in which neither workers nor employers have been represented. Prior to 1954 these commissions were set up in response to pressure from government employees suffering from an erosion of their real wage; since 1964 the "pull" of electoral politics has reinforced the "push" of rising prices in bringing about wage tribunals and wage awards.[18] Unions have played an important role in transmitting these pressures to the government, and they have made clear to the contending political parties the electoral benefits of pre-election wage awards. Government pay raises have been transmitted to the unionized segment of the private sector, both by a tradition that European employers should pay no less than the government and by a wave of strikes that such expectations, if not immediately fulfilled, give rise to.

So far we have been discussing only unionized labor. The unorganized segment of the labor market is generally semi-modern, labor-intensive, and atomistically competitive. Employers in this sector offer wages closely approximating the marginal supply price of labor. There are a number of difficulties in selecting a repre-

17 Reported individually in the Ministry of Labour's *Quarterly Review* and *NECA News.*

18 The unions' political power to precipitate wage tribunals is *not* based upon politically influential labor leaders, direct links with political parties, or inherited political power from the earlier anti-colonial struggle. Rather, the power to precipitate tribunals and subsequent favorable awards stems from the trade union movement's ability to mobilize public opinion in its support, as discussed at length in the concluding paragraphs of this section. For a full discussion of the political factor in government wage fixing, see Yesufu, *An Introduction to Industrial Relations in Nigeria,* pp. 141–48; W. M. Warren, "Urban Real Wages and the Nigerian Trade Union Movement, 1939–1960," *Economic Development and Cultural Change,* October, 1966, and July, 1969; and Robin Cohen, "Further Comment on the Kilby/Weeks Debate," *Journal of Developing Areas,* January, 1971.

sentative minimum wage rate, the two most important of which are the conventional problem of "compensating differences" and payment-in-training. The latter explains the widespread employment of low-paid apprentices and learners in industries not characterized by significant capital entry barriers (e.g., tailoring, tinkering, carpentry, motor repair); current sacrifice of part or all of the wage constitutes an investment in a secure future earning capacity operating one's own enterprise. In those industries where there are appreciable capital requirements (e.g., singlets, baking, building construction) the incentive to serve as an apprentice or learner is far less, and their presence is seldom observed. Employers in these industries have a correspondingly greater capacity to engage paid labor because competition is less intense.

Table 2.   Minimum Unskilled Wage Rates

A. Southern Nigeria (Lagos excluded), April, 1964, hourly rate

Government	7d.	European firms	
Nigerian-owned		Cigarettes	10d.
Bakery	6d.	Steel rerolling	7d.
Shoe manufacture	5d.	Plasticware	10d.
Singlet	5d.	Paint	8d.
Tire retreading	7d.	Cement	9d.
Levantine-owned		Tire manufacture	10d.
Soap manufacture	7d.		
Wrought iron	7d.		

B. Lagos only, daily rate

	Government	European firms
1938	1s.	1s. 2d.
1945	2s.	1s. 9d.
1950	2s. 8d.	3s. 5d.
1957	4s. 8d.	4s. 9d.
1960	5s.10d.	6s. 1d.
1964	5s.10d.	6s.10d.
1965	7s. 8d.	7s. 8d.

SOURCES: Data in A collected by the writer in establishment interviews, 1964. Data in B, Ministry of Labour, *Quarterly Reviews*, and information supplied by the United Africa Company and the Nigerian Tobacco Company. See also the *NECA Wage Survey*, January, 1965, p. 14.

As Table 2A shows, rates of pay range upward in a continuous spread from the unorganized rate, to the government rate, to the rate paid by the "premium" private employers. The spread is further increased when the fringe benefits given by employers at the higher end of the range and the presence of subminimum wage "learners" and apprentices employed by firms at the lower end of the range are taken into account. The explanations for this spread include ability to pay, differential labor quality requirements, the employer's public image, and union activity.

The pattern of unskilled wage rates as between government and foreign firms shown in Table 2B depicts but one phase in a continuing process of narrowing and widening differentials. The government rate remains stationary between its widely separated jumps, the jumps being a function of some combination of politics and inflation. The high-paying European firms' wage rates jump so as to be on a par with government, but they also move upward (for causes discussed in note 22) with rising prices during the intervals. In early 1964, five years after the Mbanefo award, the European firms' wage rates had risen by a considerable margin above the government rate; just after the wage award in 1964 the gap between the two rates was closed.[19]

In order to understand the forces governing the observed configuration of wage rates and their change over time, it is helpful to identify two key rates, the federal government minimum (w_g) and the minimum wage in the competitive unorganized labor market (w_u). The former is the wage fixed by the tribunals and is a disequilibrium rate in that there is an excess of labor supply relative to employer demand at the levels at which it has been set. In contrast, w_u is a market-clearing wage which equates the residual labor supply with employer demand in the unorganized sector.

A simple model has been developed elsewhere which explores both the short-run and long-run effects of different levels of w_g on w_u, labor migration to the towns and urban unemployment.[20] The central point is that, other things being equal, the further w_g is above average earnings in agriculture, the greater the urban in-migration and downward pressure on w_u. What little time-series data on w_u there are for Nigeria appear to bear out these predictions: as w_g has risen, real wages in the unorganized sector have fallen and unemployment has increased.[21]

Having examined the observed wage spread and the impact of w_g on the workings of the unorganized labor market, let us turn our attention to the more conventional and less complicated issue of the influence of labor unions upon the wage level of their mem-

---

19 For discussion of the impact of government rates on skill differentials, see Kilby, *Industrialization in an Open Economy*, p. 280.
20 *Ibid.*, pp. 277ff.
21 *Ibid.*, p. 279.

bers. Dividing the yearly federal minimum area wage rates by urban consumer price indices, we arrive at an approximate measure of the movement of real wages in the organized sector. These indices are given in Table 3, along with available figures on movements in Nigeria's national per capita income over the same period.

Table 3.   Urban Wages and National Per Capita Income (Indices)

| | Urban real wages | | | | |
	Lagos	Ibadan	Enugu	Kaduna	Per capita GDP
1953	100	100	100	100	100
1956	117	139	121	128	106
1959	105	141	113	123	110
1962	118	139	111	127	118
1965	146	185	164	159	126ᵃ

ᵃ Estimated

SOURCES: Federal Office of Statistics, *Annual Abstract of Statistics: 1964*, and *Economic Indicators*, January, 1967, for urban cost-of-living indices and Gross Domestic Product figures.

Real wages in the organized sector have increased at more than twice the rate of per capita GDP. What has been the influence of collective bargaining in bringing about this outcome? Trade unions have played an important role in mobilizing, magnifying, and channeling the discontent of government employees suffering a gradual erosion of their real wage; these union activities have resulted in more frequent wage tribunals and in larger awards than would otherwise have been the case. The critical point, however, is that such union activities have been primarily directed to bringing political pressure on the government and bear little or no relation to private joint negotiation or collective bargaining, the end for which the trade union movement has been so extensively nurtured.[22]

22   In the organized segment of the private sector, however, collective bargaining has contributed to the maintenance of the real wage, the variable margin above the government rate described earlier. Despite the fact that collective bargaining and written agreements were very rare before 1964, a few firms that were already paying premium wages conceded wage increases equivalent to the rise in the cost of living as a necessary measure to keep their unions alive and in good health (a union which does not win wage increases soon loses membership support). The outstanding example of this pattern is the Nigerian Tobacco Company. A few other very large firms, also concerned with their public image, have tended to follow suit, even though collective bargaining and a viable union were frequently absent. The United Africa Company and its union have negotiated collective agreements regularly since 1959, a unique instance of labor-manage-

In contrast with the preceding analysis, John Weeks and Elliot Berg have argued that trade unions in Nigeria have not exerted upward pressure on wages.[23] They contend that in Nigeria, as in most other underdeveloped countries, unions are organizationally too weak and faction-ridden to deliver blocks of votes or call effective demonstrations. The observed rise in real wages is attributable to the humanitarian feelings and social philosophy of the policy-makers and would have occurred even in the absence of unions.

This interpretation can be disproved with various sets of evidence. The historical investigations of Yesufu, Warren, and Cohen reveal that the ruling political parties were actively concerned with gaining the support of organized labor at the time of each wage award.[24] Cohen has further shown that Nigeria's policy-makers have been far more concerned with holding wages down in the interests of development or colonial budgetary self-sufficiency than with raising the wage of unionized employees above average earnings in the rest of the economy; that they did so attests to the political power of trade unions.

In assessing the political influence of trade unions on wages it is important to recognize the indirect channels as well as the more direct linkages to the decision-making process. While direct power was exercised successfully in the general strikes of 1945 and 1964, the more characteristic and enduring trade union power—a moderate power which is perfectly compatible with organizational weakness—is access to and influence upon public opinion. Trade union leaders, with a recognized constituency and a legally protected position, articulate the grievances of wage earners and their relative deprivation vis-à-vis the ever rising salaries and emoluments of the government elite. This articulation takes place in various media, particularly the press. In their criticisms of the government, union leaders are frequently supported in the editorial and syndicated columns. All of the leading trade union figures, the majority of whom represent government employees, owe their positions primarily to their abilities as propagandists rather than as strike organizers.

---

ment relations approximating the specifications of the Anglo-Saxon model. As a result of what happens in these companies, a certain sympathetic pressure comes to bear on other European firms to follow the wage leaders.

23 J. F. Weeks, "A Comment on Wage Determination in Nigeria," *Journal of Developing Areas,* October, 1968; E. J. Berg, "Urban Real Wages and the Nigerian Trade Union Movement, 1939–1960: A Comment," *Economic Development and Cultural Change,* July, 1969.

24 Works cited in note 18.

When the demands for a wage hike and the climate of opinion reach a certain point, the prime minister and his ministers in council order that a tribunal be established. And it is trade unionists who provide the bulk of the testimony which goes to make up the tribunal members' notion of a fair wage award.

The critical aspect of trade union influence upon public opinion is that it could not exist if the wage earners were unorganized. That this power is derived from government policy to sustain trade unions in pursuit of collective bargaining becomes evident when one considers the failure of other interest groups who, though their relative privation is much greater, are yet incapable of protecting or advancing their economic well-being in the absence of delegated spokesmen to articulate their cause. Perhaps the outstanding case is that of the several million peasant farmers producing heavily taxed export commodities. However, a perfect test as to what would have been in the absence of artifically sponsored unions is provided by the unorganized and amorphous labor force employed in private Nigerian firms in small industry, trade, and services. Wage rates are 25–40 percent lower than in the organized sector; conditions of service, by comparison, are extremely harsh. Given that government labor policies are not enforced in this sector, unions have not developed to any meaningful degree, and would-be articulators of worker interests are summarily dismissed as trouble-makers.[25] Without mobilization of public opinion, humanitarian feelings and social philosophy never become operative.

III

The measurable economic results of a particular system of industrial relations, while of vital significance, do not provide a complete picture of the system's performance. In particular, such an assessment fails to disclose important qualitative human interactions of the system and its harmony or lack thereof with the country's overall socio-political structure. The following analysis of central trade union organization, individual house unions, trade union leadership, union members, and employer behavior is aimed at achieving this more complete assessment of the system's performance.

25 Case histories of industrial relations in nine private Nigerian firms may be found in my "Establishment Interviews in Nigeria and Ghana, I.L.O. Industrial Relations Survey" (Geneva, 1965), pp. 1–158, typescript.

HISTORY OF CENTRAL TRADE UNION ORGANIZATION

The same conditions which spurred the rapid growth in trade unions after 1940—the colonial government's cultivation of the British trade union model and the wartime erosion of real wages—fostered the emergence of a central coordinating organization in November, 1942. From the beginning the Trade Union Congress of Nigeria pursued the activities of conventional business unionism, as well as those of a more radical character. By means of monthly consultative meetings with the Department of Labor, the Congress enjoyed productive and harmonious relations with the government. It assisted its member unions in the settlement of disputes, and it launched an ambitious program of trade union education in co-operation with the Department of Labor. At the same time, the Congress supported the establishment of a Labour party; it called for the nationalization of all privately owned utilities and exploitative industries (timber and tin mining); and it established contacts with the (later Communist) World Federation of Trade Unions (WFTU). "Prior to the general strike of 1945, however, the leadership of the congress was very moderate, a fact which ultimately led to its repudiation by the workers."[26]

Between government cost-of-living awards in 1942 and 1945 the consumer price index rose from 151 to 176. Whereas the allowances of European civil servants were revised upward, no such revisions were made for Africans. This combination of wage erosion and racial discrimination led the African Civil Servants Technical Workers Union to give the government an ultimatum that unless the union's demand, set forth eleven months earlier, for a substantial increase in wages of all African government employees was met in one month, the ACSTWU would call a general strike.

The proposed strike was supported by the TUCN until a few days before the deadline, when it was persuaded, by the acting governor's response that such a strike was illegal under the wartime emergency regulations, to revoke the strike order. Nevertheless, seventeen unions, consisting of about 30,000 workers, went on strike for periods up to thirty-seven days.

It was not the number of strikers that made the work stoppage significant, but the fact that most of them were performing services

26   J. S. Coleman, *Nigeria: Background to Nationalism* (Berkeley, 1958), p. 257.

indispensable to economic and administrative life of the country; they were railway workers, postal and telegraph employees, and technical workers in the government departments. Although in many places the workers went back to their jobs after a few days, the strike was not terminated until the government had given assurances that there would be no victimization and that an impartial commission of inquiry would look into their grievances.[27]

Between 1945 and 1963 central trade union organization made no positive contribution to the development of a viable industrial relations system; on the contrary, it impeded development by diverting energy from the fundamental task of building sound unions and, by virtue of repeated fissures at the national level, set in motion yet another divisive force to weaken the already fragile house unions.

In 1946 the Congress was torn by the radicals' recriminations against the way in which the moderates had handled the general strike. In 1947 the ACSTWU was challenged by a rival federation which claimed to represent the government technical workers unions; personal rivalry for leadership in the TUC continued. In 1948, with the emergence of Yoruba nationalism and the founding of the Egbe Omo Oduduwa, an open split occurred when a majority of the Congress representatives voted to disaffiliate from the country's major political party, the Ibo-led NCNC. This caused the leftist political activists, headed by M. A. O. Imoudu and Nduka Eze, to set up a rival Committee of Trade Unionists, which became known the following year as the Nigerian National Federation of Labour. The NNFL's aims were "to impart political knowledge to the workers, to press for the socialization of important industries with a view to realizing a socialist government," and "to work for the triumphant emergence of a World Parliament of the working class."[28]

Spurred on by the wave of emotional solidarity that followed the Enugu shootings in 1949 and assisted by the good offices of the Department of Labor, the two organizations agreed in March, 1950, to a reconciliation and the formation of a new body, the Nigerian Labor Congress. However, when it became known that the militant Nduka Eze was to be the general secretary and that the Congress would participate in politics, the TUC and the successor federation to the ACSTWU (now outside the TUC) refused

27   *Ibid.*, p. 257.
28   Ministry of Labour, *Quarterly Review,* March, 1960, p. 40.

to transfer their assets to the NLC. With funds from Eze's own UAC house union and others from Communist organizations abroad, the NLC established a daily newspaper, *Labour Champion,* won four seats in the Lagos election, and then in December called a disastrously unsuccessful general strike of mercantile workers which wrecked both the NLC and the UAC union. "By the end of 1950 the majority of registered trade unions including most of the largest were outside any of the central trade union organizations."[29]

Save for the revolutionary aspect of Nduka Eze's "positive action," the 1948–50 pattern was repeated with depressing regularity until September, 1963. New all-embracing central labor organizations were established in 1953, 1959, and 1962; each time in less than a year these organizations split into warring factions with one or more competing congresses soon emerging. The issues— whether or not to participate directly in politics and whether to affiliate with the pro-West ICFTU or the Communist WFTU— remained constant, as did the personalities. (The radicals were pro-WFTU and advocated direct political participation; the moderates were pro-ICFTU and advocated no direct connection with any political party.) Lack of interest in the health of constituent unions, self-seeking rivalry for leadership, and a desire for a personal share in the ICFTU or WFTU money kept the cycle in motion.[30]

By 1963 there were five central labor organizations—the moderate group having split into three factions and the radicals into two. In addition, two political parties were launched by trade union leaders in that year.

The general strike of 1963–64 represents the only successful industrial action of the central labor organizations other than the 1945 strike.[31] After the unsuccessful austerity campaign of 1961 to reduce the salaries and allowances of ministers, parliamentarians, and senior civil servants, public resentment against those in positions of power and privilege was on the rise. As October 1, 1963, approached (the day Nigeria was to be proclaimed a republic), a

---

29 *Ibid.*
30 Yesufu has described the situation in even stronger terms: "As things are the T.U.C. in Nigeria has become divided into two factions, each of which is in fact a puppet of one or more foreign organizations, and run almost completely with money from foreign sources: the Ghana T.U.C. and the W.F.T.U. support one section while the I.C.F.T.U. supports the other." Yesufu, *An Introduction to Industrial Relations in Nigeria,* p. 155.
31 This history of the general strike is based on the following issues of *West Africa:* October 5, November 16, 1963; June 6, 13, 20, July 4, August 15, 22, 29, October 3, 17, 1964; and May 15, 1965. See also Nigeria Employers Consultative Association, *NECA News,* published monthly.

rumor spread among junior government employees that a bonus of one month's pay would be given to all employees to celebrate. When the prime minister summarily rejected these rumors, talk of boycotting the celebrations spread quickly; from this the idea of a strike to embarrass the government developed.

It was at this point that the trade union leaders entered and took command of the protest movement. Forming themselves into a Joint Action Committee, the leaders of the five central labor organizations and major national unions widened the original claim into a demand for a commission to review the entire wage and salary structure. Threatened thus, the government modified its position and agreed early in the last week of the month to pay an advance of one month's pay. But this did not satisfy the JAC; led by the railway, dock, and municipal workers unions, a general strike for a full wage review was called on midnight of September 27. Although the work stoppage was only effective in the communications sector, the government was sufficiently concerned with its international image on such an auspicious occasion to concede to the JAC's demand on the night of September 30, a few hours before the republic was to be proclaimed.

The original JAC demand for a wage and salary revision was for a review of the entire wage and salary structure, anticipating downward adjustments for the highest-paid as well as upward adjustments for the lowest-paid wage earners. However, the government succeeded in confining the inquiry's terms of reference to junior employees.

An independent six-man commission headed by Chief Justice Adeyinka Morgan of the Western Nigeria High Court began its hearings in November. On April 30, 1964, the commission submitted its report and recommendations to the federal government. The government did not publish the report as it had earlier announced that it would, nor did it issue a white paper setting forth the official position. After a month of inept stalling on the part of the government (approximately twenty of the thirty-six ministers were abroad), a second general strike was called on May 31. On June 3 a white paper was published granting approximately half the increase recommended in the Morgan report. These proposals were rejected by the JAC; the strike continued. On June 6 the prime minister interrupted his holiday in the northern region to return to Lagos to call a cabinet meeting. On June 8 negotiations between the JAC and the government broke down completely, and the government issued an ultimatum that unless the workers returned to their jobs in forty-eight hours they would be dismissed and would lose their accrued privileges when they applied for reappointment. The following day thirty of the major firms, in response to pressure from the government, issued seventy-two-hour ultimatums. On the same day the Northern Federation of Labour and the Northern Civil Services Union ordered their members back to work after the northern premier had agreed to no victimization, strike pay, and negotiation on the basis of the Morgan recommendations rather than the white paper.[32]

On June 10 the federal government's ultimatum ended with only a few government employees back at work in Lagos. The ultimatum of the foreign firms was more successful, with about half the workers returning on June 12. (Nigerian and Levantine employers were for the most part unaffected by the strike.) On June 13 the contending parties came to an agreement and the strike was called off. The agreement provided that the government withdraw the dismissal notices and give full pay for the period of the strike, and that wage negotiations would be pursued by a tripartite body consisting of the JAC, the government of Nigeria, and the private employers' association. Although resurgent internal rivalry weakened the JAC's bargaining strength,[33] the pressure of nearing December elections induced the contending regional governments to improve their offers beyond the terms which the JAC accepted on June 27.

The terms that were made public on July 1, known as the Okotie-Eboh settlement—after the name of the finance minister—raised minimum wages by 29 percent in Lagos, 27 percent in the west, 47 percent in the east, and 22 percent in the north. In addition, these increases were to be retroactive to January 1, permanent collective bargaining and minimum wage–fixing machinery were to be established, the daily wage system (which does not provide for job security) was to be abolished for employees of more than five years, and government action was pledged in the fields of workers' housing, municipal transport fares, and rent and price controls. The vote-buying element of these concessions was highlighted when the northern premier announced a further wage hike in September "in appreciation of the good leadership and maturity

32 The Northern Federation of Labour was bitterly attacked in the south for "selling out." Evidence supporting the contention that NFL's general secretary was influenced by considerations of personal gain is examined in *West Africa,* October 3, 1964.

33 It was afterward alleged by one of the JAC co-chairmen, H. P. Adebola, that during this time Michael Imoudu paid a nocturnal visit to the prime minister requesting the post of federal labor adviser. (*NECA News,* March, 1965).

shown by the labour leaders in bringing to an end the last nation-wide strike. We hope they will appreciate this gesture and recipro-cate accordingly."[34]

The effective life of the JAC was ended in January, 1965, after an unsuccessful political strike demanding nullification of the December 29 federal elections. The strike had been called by the radical faction without the consent of the moderates. Immediately after the strike the moderates resigned and set up a new body, the Supreme Council of Nigerian Trade Unions. The trade union move-ment thus reverted to its pre-1963 condition of internal wrangling and impotence. Not only did organized labor lose its influence over wage and industrial relations policy; because the feuding parties could not agree on common representatives, progress in implement-ing the gains of the 1964 strike, particularly the establishment of permanent industrywide collective bargaining machinery, was also seriously impeded.

THE PRIMARY UNION

The health of the individual union and the nature of its relationship with the employer is of more fundamental importance to the long-term viability of a system based on voluntary collective bargaining than is central trade union organization. Even in the largest firms with the longest histories of attempted bargaining relationships, the record is poor. Moreover, there seems to have been no evolution toward an improved, stable relationship.

The unions' existence in these larger firms—particularly the railways, Enugu colliery, Nigerian Tobacco Company, and United Africa Company, for which some data exist—has not typically been opposed by management. The companies have recognized the need for worker representation, especially in the area of grievances. By contrast, the unions' response has been to reject the favorable environment and pursue policies of short-run opportun-ism. When the union is strong and public opinion has been whipped up against the company, strikes, violence, and rejection of awards have been the pattern. But these actions are often self-defeating, because the strike ends with serious weakening or actual disap-pearance of the union.[35]

34 Nigeria Employers Consultative Association, *NECA News,* September, 1964.

35 For case histories of these four firms, see Kilby, *Industrialization in an Open Economy,* pp. 290–93.

Many of the characteristics of industrial relations in the four larger firms would apply to a "representative" trade union situation in Nigeria. The major differences would be that in the typical case the labor force would be considerably smaller and management would be a good deal less charitably disposed toward dealing with a union.[36] In this typical case there would be a dormant house union, with no written agreement and no regular contact with management. (There might or might not be a joint consultative committee, but this would be completely independent of the union.) A major claim or grievance arises; mobilized by individuals from the artisan and craftsman ranks, members begin paying their union dues, and the services of a professional trade union secretary are recruited. After a few preliminaries (perhaps including a few statements to the local press) the professional secretary confronts the management and threatens strike action if the claim is not conceded. If in the end (perhaps after a short strike) the claim is not granted, the services of the secretary are dispensed with; likewise, if successful, the absence of any energizing discontent is soon reflected in a falling off of dues and the exit of the professional secretary for want of remuneration—unless, of course, he can manage to generate a new dispute.

TRADE UNION LEADERSHIP

The prevalence of the foregoing pattern has meant that the "strong man" type unionist has tended to survive. One common trait in this type of personality would appear to be his mode of discourse with management; passages like the following can be found in a high proportion of the Ministry of Labour's *Annual Reports* over the last twenty years:

> The projection of personal antagonism between union officials and members of management into the sphere of industrial relations was, as in the past, an unfortunate cause of trade disputes in the country. The inability on the part of some trade union leaders to distinguish between personalities and principles invariably found expression in union-backed demands for the removal of senior management of-

36 The basis for the following characterization of a representative trade union–management pattern are the narratives contained under the headings "Industrial Relations" and "Trade Unions" in the Ministry of Labour's *Annual Reports* and *Quarterly Review,* and my own collection of case histories taken by interview in the autumn of 1964 ("Establishment Interviews in Nigeria and Ghana, I.L.O. Industrial Relations Survey").

ficials on grounds such as "intimidation, oppression and subversive activities against the union."[37]

The alternative to the professional unionist is a company employee. However, company employees usually lack the personality and talent and are fearful lest they lose their job or damage their promotion prospects. The Ministry of Labour has stated the conundrum well:

> The management of a few establishments will not treat with officials who are not members or ex-members of their staff. On the side of the Union . . . it is argued that the professional Secretary owes his existence largely to the fact that in the past attempts by employers to curb Union activity have taken the form of discharging the leaders or promoting them out of the Union sphere. It is also argued that he provides the necessary degree of literacy and, in the absence of other adequate methods of communication, is free to make personal contact with remote branches to obtain support and explain issues. From the management side it is argued that a salaried official recruited from the clerical rather than the industrial class has little knowledge of and less interest in the working of the concern in which the men he represents are employed; that he must, to retain his job, demonstrate his power, create grievances and refuse compromise; and that meetings between management and workers become the occasion not for a calm and logical examination of problems, but for a display of intransigence if not outright rudery towards the management designed, above all, to impress the membership that the Secretary is the right "strong man" for the job.[38]

Other faults widespread among individual company union leaders are failure to comply with legal minima for the administration of union affairs, the mismanagement and embezzlement of union funds, and "a prevalent tendency to repudiate collective agreements and arbitration awards."[39] In the larger unions, particularly in the public sector, leadership tends to fissure into rival factions: northern versus southern, Ibo versus non-Ibo, a mirror of the central trade union organization rifts, or simply unrelinquishing emeritus officers versus newly elected officers.

37 Ministry of Labour, *Annual Report*, 1957–58, par. 100.
38 Ministry of Labour, *Annual Report*, 1956–57, par. 73.
39 Yesufu, *An Introduction to Industrial Relations in Nigeria*, pp. 88–91. In March, 1966, the Local Government Employees union (6,400 members) was removed from the register after failing to submit the legally required financial statement for the preceding eleven years.

A reasonably dedicated trade union leadership, with a certain administrative competence and with an ability to negotiate, bargain, and compromise within an accepted set of ground rules, is an obvious sine qua non for the operation of a system of industrial relations designed after the Anglo-Saxon prototype. Individuals possessing these qualifications have been in the trade union movement: former Premier Obafemi Awolowo, Ayo Ogunsheye, one director and more than ten managers in the United Africa Company, the managing director of the Nigerian Railway Corporation, a number of permanent secretaries, most of the senior officials in the Ministry of Labour, and so on. The relevant fact is that all these men left the labor movement after a fairly short stay. It was for this reason that the Ministry of Labour and the Railway Corporation discontinued their trade union scholarship schemes in 1953 and 1955—returning unionists invariably used their new educational qualification to secure a better appointment outside the trade union movement.[40] Capable and/or educationally qualified individuals have always had opportunities for career advancement outside the movement, and they have taken these opportunities. It is no mere coincidence that all the major figures who have remained in the Nigerian labor movement—Borha, Imoudu, Nzeribe, Goodluck, Bassey, Kanu, Adebola—have failed to complete their secondary education. In short, the cause of organized labor has not commanded any appreciable loyalty, even from its own leaders.

TRADE UNION MEMBERSHIP

A glimpse at the rank and file union membership helps to illuminate the attitudes of their leaders: "The interest of members in their trade unions remains largely intermittent, rising most whenever there are prospects of immediate material gain; otherwise real interest has been lacking. Monthly dues have been allowed to fall in arrears; attendance at union meetings has fallen off, and the machinery of union government has often been virtually surrendered into the hands of a few union officials."[41]

Even during 1964, the year of organized labor's greatest exer-

40   For example, of the six trade union officials who received U.K. scholarships in 1950, three joined the civil service, two obtained jobs in industry, and one stayed in the U.K. to study law (Department of Labour, *Annual Report, 1952–53*, par. 111).
41   Ministry of Labour, *Annual Report,* 1958–59, par. 77.

tions, the Ministry of Labour reported, "Attendance at ordinary union meetings continued to be poor and the state of general apathy continued."[42] The explanation (or at least a substantial part of it) for the worker's general disinterest in his union is admirably stated by Yesufu:

> The worker's tribal organization, or "improvement" union in the town provides benefits in desperate cases, financially assists those who want to get married, pays the burial expenses of a deceased parent, makes a present on the occasion of the birth of a new babe, honours the worker elevated to a chieftaincy, and repatriates the destitute. Some tribal organizations award scholarships to the young educated worker or to the children of others. It is this that explains the seeming paradox that whereas the worker will not regularly subscribe to the funds of a trade union (apparently because he is too poor) he does pay regular subscriptions to the funds of his tribal "union"; and the contributions are usually higher than those required by the trade union.
>
> Thus the trade union is caught in a vicious circle: it is deprived of funds because the services which it ought to render are provided by non-industrial organizations supported by the workers, and it cannot provide rival services because it has not funds. The sociological factors are equally impressive. In the tribal "union" for example, the worker can speak and be spoken to in a language he understands well, against a background of customs and traditions which he comprehends. Those with whom he has to deal give him that due personal respect to which the African attaches so much importance. In one word, the worker feels that in the gathering of his tribal organization, he truly "belongs." In the trade union meeting, on the other hand, matters are often discussed against an industrial and economic background which the worker hardly understands; the secretary of the trade union may be of a different tribe; and if, in addition, he belongs to a rival political party, all the seeds of failure have been sown.[43]

THE EMPLOYERS

Up to this point little has been explicitly said about management attitudes toward industrial relations. In the early years there was some reluctance for small employers to recognize their unions.

42 *Quarterly Review,* June, 1964.
43 *Daily Times* (Lagos), April 14, 1958; cited by R. L. Sklar, *Nigerian Political Parties* (Princeton, 1963), p. 496.

And, as already noted, many firms whose initial experience with a militant professional unionist had been unhappy ones (as for instance the United Africa Company and Nigerian Breweries) were unwilling, until about 1960, to recognize and deal with a union unless its secretary was an employee of the company. While the small firms prior to 1962 seldom encouraged collective bargaining as such, most large firms—who find the process of negotiation and collective bargaining the easiest and most efficient way to deal with the complexities of their labor relations—were more than willing to negotiate and bargain; it is also true that the firms have usually offered these same capable leaders jobs on the management side. On the other hand, management reaction to the "strong man" trade union official has been almost universally hostile, and any opportunity to undermine the official, including fostering dissension and rivalry within the union, has usually been exploited.

Since its inception in 1957 the Nigeria Employers Consultative Association (NECA) had advocated collective bargaining in place of the prevalent unilateral fixing of wages by employers.[44] Beyond its attachment to collective bargaining for its own desirability, the NECA executive continually pointed out to its members that only through the implementation of collective bargaining could the private sector free itself from being tied to the government wage awards. Virtually compulsory large wage increases, backdated as much as nine months, are a very cumbersome and costly arrangement (although it saves on wage costs during the intervals) for commercial enterprises, which are unable to raise their prices retroactively. In 1962 the membership of NECA launched a major effort to establish industrywide collective bargaining; to this end various trade groups were set up for the purpose of agreeing on common bargaining procedures, job classification, etc. However, by the end of 1966, despite the federal government's parallel action to make national joint industrial councils virtually compulsory, only one industrywide agreement had been negotiated (in the shipping

44 NECA's position before the Morgan Commission in December, 1963, was as follows: "Pending the successful complete development of a voluntary system of collective bargaining, the Association is satisfied that the State has sufficient legal powers and the necessary machinery to protect industries which have yet to be brought into the orbit of the voluntary system. The Association believes that problems can be overcome within the framework of the present system, and that with mutual cooperation between Government, employers and workers these problems can be overcome within the framework of the present system, and that a new system is unnecessary" (*NECA News,* January, 1964).

services trade), and two pre-existing agreements (in the construction and tin-mining industries) were renewed. The explanation for this failure was the inability to bring together representatives on the labor side.

In the absence of an effective channel of communication with their workers through the unions, all the larger firms have established some form of joint consultation. In practice, many of the issues theoretically reserved for negotiation with the union are discussed in joint consultation—thus inadvertently further weakening the prospects of unions fulfilling their intended roles.[45]

The actions of the government (particularly the British colonial government) as an employer have been a significant cause of the miscarriage of the Anglo-Saxon model in Nigeria. In failing to fix the wages of its own employees by negotiation with employee representatives, the government has de facto precluded the operation of the voluntary system for half of organized labor.[46] And indirectly, by the quantitative and normative power of its example, the actions of government have done much to undermine the potential for collective bargaining in the private sector.

At least three ways in which the government has adversely influenced collective bargaining in the private sector may be identified. First, the fact of public awards and their obligatory nature for private employers has had the effect of overriding and nullifying all existing collective agreements. Second, retroactive awards have tended to break the nexus between wage determination and economic principles, thus setting up false expectations about the kind of wage claim that might be legitimately advanced against management in the bargaining context. Third, by paying their employees for the period in which they were on strike, the government has removed for the workers the gravity of taking such action, which can only have the consequence of encouraging labor demands, the short-cutting of negotiating procedures, and frequent recourse to the strike.

45   In a survey of twenty-one firms in 1963, it was found that, in six companies where the unions were defunct or in fragments, joint consultative committees had taken over the unions' functions outright, and that, in fourteen of the remaining fifteen companies, matters theoretically reserved for union negotiation were also discussed in the joint consultative committees (Nigeria Employers Consultative Association, *Survey on Joint Consultation* [Lagos, August, 1963], mimeograph).

46   The causes for the failure of collective bargaining in the public sector—union leadership rivalry, status-conscious employer representatives, disagreements over the scope of bargaining, changing government structures—are discussed in Kilby, *Industrialization in an Open Economy*, pp. 298–99.

IV

A review of the literature on trade unionism in other under-developed countries reveals that Nigeria's experience is by no means unique; in fact, it conforms to a very common pattern. The constituent elements of this pattern include a preponderance of many small weak unions, apathetic non–dues paying membership, vociferous but inept outside union leadership dealing with foreign employers, maladministration and theft of union funds, a primary focus on wage claims, inability to sustain strikes, and realized gains won by politically interested government intervention.

The absence of the necessary conditions for a viable system of voluntary collective bargaining has been noted by all investigators. The prescriptions offered are, virtually without exception, to strengthen voluntary labor-management negotiations by promoting joint consultation, works committees, conciliation procedures, and the like; by outlawing certain types of anti-union employer practices; and by training union leaders and developing membership interest and participation.[47] The possibility of abandoning the model of voluntary collective bargaining as inappropriate and unworkable is never seriously considered. Yesufu's position is typical:

> The great necessity in Nigerian industry today, therefore, is not to sweep away the principles of industrial democracy, but for both sides of industry to realize the magnitude of what is at stake, and to heed the exhortation that they must learn to develop the necessary patterns of living together. Essentially, this is a matter of employers reorientating their whole attitude towards labour and the trade unions, and for the latter to develop strong, more inclusive, and responsible organizations. It is believed that these can be achieved partly through sustained education on all sides, and partly through experience. We have nevertheless suggested some amendments to existing legislation or administrative machinery; but these have been few, and intended, not to replace existing policy, but to make it more effective. If previous attempts to improve industrial relations in Nigeria through the educative process have not shown all the results that might have been expected, it is not because such

47 Saad El Din Fawzi, *The Labour Movement in the Sudan, 1946–1955* (London, 1957), Ch. 12; Yesufu, *An Introduction to Industrial Relations in Nigeria,* Ch. 9; Walter Galenson, ed., *Labor and Economic Development* (New York, 1959), Introduction, and *Labor in Developing Economies* (Berkeley, 1962), Introduction; Arnold Zack, *Labor Training in Developing Countries: A Study in Responsible Democracy* (New York, 1964).

efforts have been misdirected; it merely emphasizes the magnitude of the work to be done.[48]

AN INTERPRETATION

Is traditional economic unionism, based on voluntary collective bargaining, a potentially viable socio-economic institution for present-day underdeveloped countries? To answer this question one must first identify the needs to which the development of unions was the natural response, and, second, assess the relationship between the functions fulfilled by unions and their capacity to engage in collective bargaining.

Against a background of pervasive insecurity, the first union function to emerge historically was the provision of "friendly benefits" out of union funds—mutual insurance for sickness, unemployment, old age, and death.[49] A second purpose of labor combination has been to win economic concessions from the employer (covering remuneration, hours, conditions of work and fringe benefits); such economic concessions included the prevention of wage cuts or other forms of "exploitation." Finally, and related to the foregoing, in the psychological-social realm unions have endeavored to restrict management's prerogatives in all matters affecting labor (promotion, discipline, working rules, redundancy, etc.), thereby limiting as far as possible the subordination of the worker which is inherent in the employer-employee relationship.

How compelling have been these three needs, which have traditionally given rise to trade unions, in underdeveloped countries since World War II?

As we have earlier implied, rather than being an exploited group, organized labor is already a highly privileged minority. Implementation, albeit potential, of ILO conventions, in conjunction with traditional arrangements based on the extended family, have obviated the need for trade union friendly benefits at an equal rate. Likewise on the wages side, the laborer's earnings considerably exceed his opportunity income outside the organized employ-

---

48   Yesufu, *An Introduction to Labor Relations in Nigeria,* p. 176.
49   Henry Pelling, *A History of British Trade Unionism* (London, 1963); A. Flanders and H. Clegg, eds., *The System of Industrial Relations in Great Britain* (Oxford, 1954); Neil W. Chamberlain, *Collective Bargaining,* 2nd ed. (New York, 1965); Mark Perlman, "Labour Movement Theories: Past, Present, and Future," *Industrial and Labor Relations Review,* April, 1960.

ment market—in short, he is enjoying a higher standard of living than he has ever known before.

The problems and tensions arising out of the adaptation to the industrial way of life in the less developed areas have proved to be far less significant than nineteenth-century history or twentieth-century sociological theorizing would indicate. Indeed, it is difficult to find instances of industrial unrest in backward economies. There is much labor unrest, but it has little to do with the absolute wage or conditions of work; rather, it is, as in Nigeria, an expression of relative deprivation by the "haves" vis-à-vis the even smaller minority of the "have-mores." As for the "rigors" of factory discipline: these have proved far more congenial than the back-breaking work in primitive agriculture. The relative unimportance of adaptation problems has also been noted.[50]

The absence of an environment and a set of felt needs similar to those which produced the Anglo-Saxon model has far-reaching implications for its institutional transfer. The sustained loyalty and discipline required of union members, which was built up in the earlier era only after long years of struggling for recognition, cannot be generated when the antecedent goals pursued by the trade union lose their primacy. And without such loyalty and discipline, unions cannot achieve the maturity and stability needed to successfully negotiate and uphold voluntary agreements on a regular basis.[51]

In short, the development sequence—the learning process—required to make collective bargaining viable as a technique for determining wages is denied to present-day underdeveloped countries.[52] Beyond its effects for the current situation, the absence of the conditions necessary for this learning process has important implications for the future development of trade union movements in underdeveloped economies. In a very provocative essay setting forth a general theory of trade union evolution in differing environments, Adolf Sturmthal has argued that in labor surplus economies unions will necessarily have little economic bargaining

50 Galenson, *Labor and Economic Development*, p. 3. C. Kerr, J. Dunlop, F. Harbison and C. Meyers, *Industrialism and Industrial Man* (London, 1962), pp. 6, 7, 195.

51 While the original functions of trade unions in advanced countries may have atrophied, the skills and traditions "learned" in the earlier period have carried forward to provide the basis for the mature Anglo-Saxon model.

52 The attempted institutional transfer of parliamentary democracy to Africa has failed for analogous reasons.

strength and can be expected to turn to some variety of political unionism.[53] As structural transformation proceeds and excess labor reserves in agriculture disappear, the labor movement will adopt collective bargaining as the most efficient instrument for advancing its interests. However, if the analysis offered here is correct, because trade unions in contemporary underdeveloped countries are precluded from the learning process whereby the necessary skills and traditions are acquired, it would seem unlikely, contrary to Sturmthal's prediction, that voluntary collective bargaining will, in fact, emerge at the labor-scarce stage.

Under existing circumstances in underdeveloped countries, the trade union ceases to serve any "essential" need and thus elicits no sustained loyalty from either its leaders or its membership. Instead, labor organization becomes a political instrumentality for channeling the protest of relatively privileged wage earners against the distribution of the national wealth between themselves and those at the apex of the distributional pyramid. An evaluation of the political desirability of this outcome (weighing the costs of disruption against the benefits of pluralism) is outside the realm of the economist, but it is important to recognize that the unions' political power is an unintended result of purely economic policies. Couldn't labor's political representation be better achieved through political parties?

The economic consequences of the politicized Anglo-Saxon model stem from organized labor's political power to raise wages in the government and foreign private sector higher than they would be in the absence of such power. First, the higher wage level has raised the cost of production in these sectors and, by causing a diversion of potential investment resources to consumption, may have slowed the rate of economic growth. Given the government's budgetary constraint, a higher wage has meant less public employment. Of far greater significance, a rising urban wage has widened the income gap between the agricultural and the urban sector and has thereby aggravated the rural exodus and urban unemployment, with all of their political ramifications. Finally, and not least of all, in relation to the pre-existing nonunionized situation the politicized Anglo-Saxon model has resulted in worsened, rather than improved, industrial relations.

53 Adolf Sturmthal, "Economic Development and the Labour Movement," in *Industrial Relations and Economic Development,* ed. Arthur Ross (London, 1966).

Jan Pen

Trade Union Attitudes toward Central Wage Policy: Remarks on the Dutch Experience

A CHANGE OF MOOD

ONE OF THE most obvious conditions for a centralized incomes policy is the cooperation of trade unions in the control of wages. Indeed, the main reason why the attempts at an incomes policy in various countries never got off the ground is that governments did not succeed in securing union support for central interference in wage determination. Without wage control, the control of incomes other than wages proves difficult if not impossible; therefore union attitudes are a strategic factor in any kind of incomes policy. In the Netherlands this factor has shown a remarkable development over time. One might ask whether price controls could not have been a substitute for a wage policy. Yet even if price controls could be temporarily enforced, there is no guarantee that this would suppress the wage push. And if wages increased more than productivity, prices would necessarily rise; this would destroy the price controls. Even if governments try to attack the wage-price spiral at both fronts, success is usually meager.

The Netherlands had a system of centrally controlled wages between 1945 and 1970. Although it remained formally in operation for twenty-five years, it worked well only until 1959. Then the system started to crumble; its legal basis was finally withdrawn in 1970. The first period, "the fifties," in which wage policy worked rather satisfactorily, can be roughly distinguished from the second period, "the sixties," in which government control became more and more untenable. Unions, employers' associations, and political parties became increasingly critical of the dominant role of government. The most radical change occurred in the attitude of the greatest of the three Dutch federations of trade unions, the NVV (Nederlands Verbond van Vakverenigingen).[1] This federation is strongly centralized. It has socialist leanings but is not formally associated with the Labor party, although many personal ties and political sympathies exist. From an ardent supporter of a centrally administered wage policy, the NVV became a bitter critic of any government interference in specific collective wage agreements. There was a change from "overleg," the typical Dutch combination of cooperation and consultation, toward hard bargaining. The present position of the NVV is that bargaining should be left to the parties at the industry level and that their agreements should be respected. One of the most puzzling paradoxes in the history of the Dutch experiment is that in the fifties the NVV backed a wage policy, based on the draconic Buitengewoon Besluit Arbeidsverhoudingen 1945[2] (hereafter the BBA), a set of emergency measures which gave a government organ (the Board of State Mediators, hereafter the Board) almost complete formal control over wages; while the same NVV decried the new and rather mild Wage Law of 1970 as a "strangulation law." The latter acknowledges the freedom of collective bargaining but reserves, in Article 8, a marginal possibility for the government to interfere in collective contracts. When the law was accepted by Parliament in 1970, the NVV at once withdrew from all consultative machinery on wage policy at the national level. In August of that year, NVV leaders even refused a polite invitation from the minister of social affairs to discuss methods for getting out of this "blind alley." This radical change of mind must have had its reasons, and the aim of this article is to shed some light on them.

The NVV is not the only Dutch federation of trade unions; two others are the NKV (Nederlands Katholiek Vakverbond)[3] and the CNV (Christelijk Nationaal Vakverbond).[4] Among them they

1   The Netherlands Federation of Trade Unions.
2   Extraordinary Decree on Labor Relations.
3   The Netherlands Catholic Federation of Trade Unions.
4   The Protestant National Federation of Trade Unions. Dutch unions, like many other social institutions, are organized along religious lines. The peculiar folklore of the Dutch social scene is described in John P. Windmuller's highly informative *Labor Relations in the Netherlands* (1969), which also contains valuable chapters on the system of centralized wage policy. The reader who is unacquainted with the Dutch experiment is referred to this book; it is the best there is in this particular field.

organize about a third of all Dutch employees; of this fraction, NVV membership is about 14 percent, CNV membership is 6 percent, and NKV membership is about 12 percent. About 8 percent of the employees belong to unions which are not associated with a federation. NKV and CNV also cooperated in the strict wage policy of the fifties, but their support has always been more qualified than that of NVV. Catholic social organizations, workers, and employers alike adhere to "the principle of subsidiarity," which says that "higher" organs (like the state) should not unnecessarily interfere with the affairs of "lower" organs (like schools, hospitals, municipalities, and trade unions). Protestant doctrine is very similar; it speaks of "sovereignty in one's own circle," a somewhat pompous expression which is often used to stave off centralistic measures. In principle, NKV and CNV favor decentralization; this naturally makes for a critical outlook on central wage policy. The views of NKV and CNV show a development over the years, in the sense that the support for the official policy of guided wages decreased, though there was no such sharp change in policy views as in the case of the NVV. The religious federations agree with the NVV in rejecting the paragraph in the 1970 wage law which provides for government intervention in particular collective wage agreements, but they do so in somewhat more moderate language; they did not follow the NVV when it stepped out of the consultative machinery in 1970.

Paradoxically, the main opponents of wage control in the fifties were not among the unions but among the employers, or at least the employers' associations. They fought the system on the grounds that it gave too much power to the government, that it made the wage structure too rigid, and that it prevented expansionary firms and industries from attracting sufficient additional labor. The argument that central wage control might dampen inflation and protect profit margins was not altogether overlooked by the employers, but strangely enough it was overruled by more ideological arguments; the word "freedom" in particular frequently occurred in employers' policy statements. Ideology and class interest hardly seemed to run parallel. In the sixties, when strong wage inflation became characteristic of the Dutch economy, the employers' attitude changed somewhat. They became belated supporters of a centralized policy which no longer worked. I am not concerned here with the considerations of the employers, but the change in their viewpoint must be mentioned insofar as it explains the change in the ideas of the unions.

The Dutch political parties had viewpoints of their own. The greatest political organization is the Katholieke Volkspartij[5] (about 30 percent of the votes), which is traditionally skeptical of centralized power, in conformity with the "principle of subsidiarity." The various Protestant parties—roughly 20 percent of the votes—share this view. The Volkspartij voor Vrijheid en Democratie,[6] resembling the British Conservative party and commanding about 10 percent of the votes, defends views which show a remarkable similarity to those of the employers' organizations. This adds up to a parliamentary majority against overly centralistic measures, and indeed the Second Chamber (House of Representatives) as early as 1953 moved that wage determination should, as soon as circumstances would permit, be left to the parties concerned. The Labor party, initially having about 30 percent of the votes but gradually reduced to somewhat more than 20 percent by the end of the sixties, regarded wage determination as a responsibility of government, albeit in cooperation with the unions and the employers' associations. In fact, the main architects of the Dutch system of wage control were cabinet ministers belonging to the Labor party, which until 1958 formed various coalition governments with the Catholic People's party and some Protestant parties. However, in the course of the sixties the Labor party's stand became uncertain and confused; under the influence of the NVV, the opinion arose that wage bargaining should be unfettered, but the traditional preference for guided wages remained with influential party members.

After 1958 the Labor party was replaced in the coalition by the Party for Freedom and Democracy. This political shift, which gave the government coalition a more conservative leaning, had a strategic impact on the conduct of wage policy, as will be shown in the next section.

The following quotation may serve to illustrate the main theme of this article. It is taken from an article in *De Vakbeweging*,[7] the biweekly publication for NVV officials. The author, A. H. Kloos, then editor of *De Vakbeweging,* is now president of the NVV. He wrote: "The standpoint of the NVV on wage policy is well-known. We prefer a strongly coordinated—if one wants the expression, guided—wage policy, operating with general wage rounds." And:

5 Catholic People's party.
6 People's Party for Freedom and Democracy. The use of the word "people" aims at combatting the fairly general suspicion that this is a party for the well-to-do.
7 A. H. Kloos, "The Labor Movement," *De Vakbeweging,* April 14, 1959.

"The unions' power—also in industries which do not belong to the strong ones, at least not to those where productivity rises fast— makes us shrink from the experiment of a freer wage determination, even when this would take place on the basis of economic reports."[8] The author of these lines is the same man who, ten years later, led the frontal attack on Article 8 of the Wage Law, which introduces the possibility that the minister of social affairs might declare null and void a particular collective wage agreement within a fortnight after it is concluded. This possibility made the law, according to Kloos, an unbearable piece of "dirigisme." The change of mood is clear.

CHANGES IN POLICY: THE FIFTIES AND THE SIXTIES

Before trying to explain the change in union attitudes, a short review of the changes in policy seems in order. Although the BBA remained in force from 1945 to 1970, several shifts in accent took place.[9] The main legal provisions of the BBA were the following. In the first place, all collective wage agreements were to be submitted to a state organ, the Board of State Mediators (College van Rijksbemiddelaars). Without the signature of the Board, they had no legal effect. With the Board's signature, they became binding, in the sense that individual wage contracts departing from the collective contract were null and void, and employers paying wages other than those approved by the Board came under the threat of criminal prosecution. The Board could also establish wage arrangements in those industries where no collective contract came into being.

The Board operated more or less independently, though the minister of social affairs had the legal power to give directives; in the fifties these instructions were of a very general character and were mostly concerned with wage rounds for the labor force as a whole. Wage fixing in specific industries was left to the Board, and the minister managed to escape parliamentary debate on this aspect

8   For instance, forecasts of productivity increases and balance of payments developments by the Central Planning Bureau. The productivity increase is sometimes called the "room" for wage increases, though it is also asserted by some participants in the Dutch process of wage determination that the "room" is actually greater than the productivity increase because labor may increase its share of the national income at the expense of other groups.

9   In this article I omit the first five years from consideration. This was the period of reconstruction of war damage. Consumer goods were rationed, prices were controlled, and wages were kept as low as possible. In this period, nobody questioned the necessity of austerity.

of policy. In handling particular collective wage agreements, the Board cooperated closely with the (private) Foundation of Labor, a bipartite organization in which the federations of trade unions and the employers' associations are represented. The Foundation officially advised the Board concerning specific agreements, and the Board unofficially advised the Foundation on what to advise. In practice, cooperation of the Board and the Foundation was such that the Board could maintain that it merely legalized the Foundation's decisions, while the Foundation could shift the responsibility for unpopular decisions to the Board. The rather subtle interplay between the two bodies created a welcome opportunity for saving everybody's face and made the system less draconic than it looked on paper.

In 1959 the Labor-Catholic coalition was replaced by a government in which the conservative Volkspartij voor Vrijheid en Democratie participated. The accent was on more freedom for bargaining at the industry level. Yet the legal provisions of the BBA were left intact. The uniform wage rounds were abolished, and wage increases were tied to productivity increases in the industry or the firm. This was the outcome of a long debate over wage differentiation. Although the word "freedom" was frequently used, the Board's signature remained formally required for all collective agreements.

In practice, the calculation of productivity increases proved to be a difficult and rather arbitrary affair. This led to friction between unions and employers, and, in some sectors, to higher wage increases than the government deemed acceptable. The new underminister of social affairs, B. Roolvink, a former CNV-secretary, occupied himself intensely with wage determination. He issued several general directives to explain the productivity criteria, but he also interfered with the daily routine of the Board—in fact, he started giving instructions concerning particular wage agreements. The latter was something new. The practice irritated the parties, who expected freedom and got more government interference, and it also irritated the Board.

In the meantime, some individual employers openly flouted the basic philosophy of the BBA and started paying wages in excess of the official agreements. Of course black wages had never been absent, but now they were paid conspicuously and defiantly. The authorities took no action against these overt illegal practices. This showed to all concerned that the system was no longer acceptable at the grassroots. Thus general disenchantment stimulated the search for new solutions. In 1962 an advisory council of employers, unions, and experts (the Social Economic Council) advised the government on a change in the legal system. They proposed to amend the BBA in such a way that the Board of State Mediators would automatically approve all wage agreements that were accepted by the Foundation of Labor. In other words, the formal decision on wage policy would be taken by a private institution. The minister of social affairs would keep the prerogative of declaring particular wage agreements null and void, but only in emergency cases. The government followed this advice, and in 1963 the BBA was altered accordingly.

The new set-up proved to be a failure. The Foundation did not succeed in keeping wage inflation down; on the contrary, in the first year of its reign (1964) the wage level exploded by 15 percent. The next year the percentage was still over 10 percent; these were record figures in the history of Dutch wages. The government concluded that the Foundation was not a very efficient wage controller, and in 1966 it returned the power of decision to the Board. The situation was legally the same as before 1963.

The next year, 1967, the Foundation (including the unions) advised the government to liberate wage policy, in the sense that no previous approval of collective agreements would be required; in principle, wage determination should be left to employers and unions. In this situation the minister of social affairs could declare an agreement null and void, but only if this agreement would lead to a serious disturbance of economic equilibrium. The Foundation suggested that twice a year it would offer recommendations to all parties concerned about the optimum average wage increases, but these recommendations would have no binding character, and departures from these guidelines would involve no sanctions.

The government accepted this system and came forward with a bill to replace the BBA (1968). It went even further than the Foundation's recommendations: collective agreements would contain minima only; if the parties did not specify otherwise, the payment of higher wages than laid down in the agreement would be legal. The payment of deviating wages would never be a criminal offense; at most it would constitute an actionable tort. The minister of social affairs was given the power to extend the duration of collective agreements for one year ("wage freeze"); this idea did not appear in the Foundation's advice, but it was nonetheless accepted by Parliament. The bill contained an article which made possible the revival of the system of previous approval, but only as an emergency measure. However, the latter article was voted down by the Second Chamber of Parliament.

After a heated debate in Parliament, where the Labor party and some other parties on the left attacked Article 8, providing that the minister of social affairs could declare particular collective agreements null and void, the majority accepted the Wage Law. The NVV had tried to influence the debate by declaring that it would not cooperate at the national level if the law was accepted; non-cooperation would mean that the new system could not work. This statement caused a great deal of confusion, but it did not prevent Parliament from accepting the law (1970). At once the NVV left the various committees that characterize the Dutch organizational system, and wage determination became a matter of collective agreements at the industry or firm level. Consultation and cooperation at the national level came to a standstill, which marked the formal end of the Dutch experiment.

Possible Explanations

A rationalistic approach, viewing the unions as maximizers of some preferably measurable variable (real wages, wage bill, share of labor in the national income), might reason as follows.[10] In the fifties the unions backed a certain system of wage determination, so this must have been a satisfactory system in terms of real wages, wage bill, share of labor, etc. In the sixties they became more and more hostile to the then practiced system, so the latter must have been less productive in these terms. This "bread and butter" approach has the advantage in that its propositions can be more or less tested. This will be tried in the next section, particularly with respect to the distribution of the national income.

A second approach to union attitudes is inspired by the idea that wages are ultimately determined by supply and demand, and that a realistic outlook of the unions must be adapted to the overruling power of these market forces.[11] If a union believes, for whatever reasons, that government control of wages is a good thing, but the situation on the labor market makes this kind of control impossible (e.g., by "black market" wages), then the union is compelled to give up its illusions. In this type of reasoning, which is frequently used in the domestic debate, the Dutch experiment has failed be-

10   This approach is to be found in J. T. Dunlop's *Wage Determination under Trade Unions* (1944).

11   This view is defended by many authors, among them B. C. Roberts, *National Wages Policy in War and Peace* (1958).

cause it tried to keep wage increases below the rate dictated by the strain on the labor market; the unions became aware of this failure, though after some delay, and drew the conclusion that a central wage policy was a chimera not worth defending.

This theory, too, can be tested. In particular, its macro-economic aspect, embodied in the Phillips curve, can be confronted with empirical evidence. This shall be tried in the section on "The Forces of the Market."

A third explanation of the change in the union mood stresses political, psychological, and ideological factors. This may mean different things. Following A. M. Ross,[12] we may look at the union as a body aiming at institutional survival and growth, and at the union leader as a person who tries to reconcile the various pressures exerted on him, including pressures by members, other union officials, management, government agencies, and the public. We may also underline the ideological factor, in the sense that we look for the union view of the "good society," whether it has evolutionary or revolutionary ideas on political development, and so on. An important point is that the Dutch unions consider themselves instrumental in changing society, but these changes should, according to the three federations, be gradual and nonrevolutionary. Moreover, they accept, in principle, the norms of modern macro-economic policy, such as equilibrium of the balance of payments, full employment, and avoidance of strong inflation. While the reconciliation of outside pressures emphasized by Ross views the union's policy as outer-directed, the ideological approach seems to imply a more inner-directed motivation. If we follow this latter approach, we should investigate whether the ideology of the unions, and in particular the NVV, has changed. Finally, one may stress "irrational" factors (such as fear of inflation, mass unemployment, or sudden economic disaster of an unspecified nature) and personal factors (such as friendship between politicians and union leaders, disappointment, irritation, and animosity). In a small country like the Netherlands, where policy-making is in the hands of a relatively small group of people who know each other rather well, it is *a priori* not out of the question that the influence of personal relations and feelings may be important. In that case events must be explained by unique "historical" facts, and we are a long way from the general laws of economics and from simple maximizing behavior.

These three approaches are not mutually exclusive, nor is it easy

---

12   A. M. Ross, *Trade Union Wage Policy* (1948).

to weigh the various influences which played a role in this particular case history. The following sections are unavoidably subjective.

BREAD AND BUTTER

Real incomes of workers increased steadily under the policy of controlled wages. Only in two years (1951 and 1957) was the real wage rate reduced, and this happened as a consequence of a deliberate program to restore equilibrium in the balance of payments. These deflationary programs were devised and executed with the unions' cooperation. Indeed, one of the outstanding features of the Dutch system was that this type of concerted action proved possible.[13] But the trend in real wages has been a steadily rising one. In itself this sheds no light on wage policy; under any type of social system the trend in real wages depends mainly on the trend in production or labor productivity—that is, on the growth rate of the economy.

The Dutch growth rate has been satisfactory. In the fifties this fact was often adduced as supporting the view that wage policy was beneficial. According to official policy statements, moderation in wage increases would stimulate exports (about half of the national income) and investment; lower money wages would lead to higher real wages. This relationship is obviously complex; low money wages might have a negative effect by slowing down entrepreneurial innovation and investments in depth. Growth may be hampered or stimulated by many factors other than wage levels. Moreover, the Dutch growth figures, though good,[14] were not spectacularly better than those of other European countries that had no wage policy to speak of (German Federal Republic, 5.3 percent; Italy, 6.2 percent; France, 4.5 percent; Switzerland, 4.3 percent).[15] And the growth of the Dutch economy did not slow down after the great wage explosions of 1964 and 1965. The increases in real wages are thus not a good criterion for judging the bread-and-butter aspects of controlled wages.

A better criterion is the degree to which labor shares in the growing national income. This type of calculation has always drawn much attention in the Netherlands. Meticulous calculations were

13   An American observer who is rather impressed by this aspect of Dutch policy is J. G. Abert, *Economic Policy and Planning in the Netherlands, 1950–1965* (1969).
14   The average over the 1953–68 period was 5.9 percent.
15   *United Nations Statistical Yearbook,* 1969, 1970.

made, mainly by the Central Planning Bureau, as a guide for government and union action. Discussions in the various committees about desired or possible wage increases were always held with an eye on the distributive shares. There are two ways to define this share: the first takes the total wage bill (wages and salaries from the business and the government sectors, plus employers' contributions to social security and pension funds) and divides this figure by national income at factor cost; this ratio is called Labor's Share. The second method divides wage income *per employee* in the business sector by national income at factor cost *per head of the active population*. The latter is in Dutch jargon confusingly called the Employee Share; a better expression would be Wage Ratio. The second ratio is more significant than the first, because it is not influenced by the transfer of small businessmen and farmers toward paid employment. Both quotients have risen over time; Labor's Share was still 55 percent in 1955; in 1960, the quotient had risen to 57; in 1961, the figure was 61, and the increase went steadily on in the sixties until it reached almost 70 percent in 1969. The share of profits and incomes of professional people remained more or less constant at about 20 percent of the national income; the pure share of capital (dividends, interest, rent of land and buildings) bore the full impact of the increase in labor's share and is now less than 10 percent of the national income. While production becomes more and more capitalistic in the sense that the capital-labor ratio increases, distribution becomes more laboristic. In this respect the sixties were more favorable to labor than the fifties, and the increasing opposition to wage policy is difficult to understand.[16]

A better criterion for measuring distribution is the Employees' Share. In 1950 it was 72 percent; in 1955 this quotient was lower (67 percent). In 1960 the figure was 68 percent. After that the ratio increased, until in 1966 a percentage of 77 was reached. In 1969 the percentage was slightly lower (75). Here too we notice the paradox that the unions started opposing a wage policy which improved labor's relative position, while they had supported a more stringent policy which was less favorable.[17]

These figures relate to primary distribution. If we calculate Labor's Share after deductions have been made for taxes and social security premiums, we see a different picture.[18] The ratio declined steadily from 50 percent in 1950 to less than 40 percent in 1970.

16 *Annual Report* of De Nederlandsche Bank N.V. for 1969.
17 *Central Economic Plan,* 1970.
18 *Annual Report* of De Nederlandsche Bank N.V. for 1969.

But profits and capital incomes also declined if they are calculated after taxes, as a percentage of national income, from more than 20 percent in 1950 to 16 percent in 1970. This reduction is explained by the increasing share of the government (from 20 percent to 25 percent), and in particular by the substantial rise in social security payments. The latter, including old age pensions, represented only 8 percent of national income in 1950; in 1970 the figure was almost 20 percent. It is obvious that workers paid their share in the financing of these expenditures and that, therefore, the increase in disposable real wages was smaller than the increase in labor productivity. But this has no direct implications for the evolution of wage policy. Redistribution via taxation and social insurance is a matter of parliamentary decisions; it would be asking too much if one wanted to offset the consequences of these programs for labor alone. This would mean that other groups, earning about a quarter of the national income, would bear the full brunt of the new policies. Moreover, shifting the burden to profits and capital by higher money wages would certainly fail, because a new process of shifting via higher prices would try to restore the old situation.

The relative decline in labor's disposable share may have had some psychological impact. Some workers felt that their real income did not rise fast enough. This may have contributed to the general discontent. Also, the inflationary process itself leads to frustration, because many people believe that their money incomes fall behind the rise in prices. But the main reason why many workers are not satisfied with their welfare is simply that the Dutch level of real income is still very modest. All the talk about affluence notwithstanding, a family of four in 1970, living in a crowded city, had no particular reason to feel free of financial cares. This does not explain the change in attitude of the trade unions, but it does not facilitate a controlled wage policy, either.

At first the conclusion of this section seems mainly negative. Bread and butter considerations do not explain why the unions changed their minds: in the fifties, they (and in particular the NVV) backed a wage policy which caused only a slight improvement in the worker's relative position; in the sixties, when this relative position improved quickly, they became opposed to the wage controls. This looks like a paradox. However, the paradox disappears if we reason as follows: in the fifties the NVV believed, for ideological reasons, that a strictly controlled wage policy would be beneficial to the nation in general and to the weak groups in particular. This policy proved to be a modest success. In the sixties wage controls were gradually loosened, wage explosions occurred, and the strict system started to fall apart. But no economic disaster followed. Full employment remained intact. Economic growth was not impaired. Labor's relative position improved more spectacularly than in the fifties. Bread and butter were better assured under the rather messy conditions of the sixties than under the well-ordered system of the fifties. The NVV has obviously drawn the conclusion that the ideological viewpoint of the fifties was too austere. This growing preference for the struggle ties in with other shifts in ideology which will be discussed below.

THE FORCES OF THE MARKET[19]

The relationship between unemployment (U) and the rate of increase in wages (w) over the period 1950–70 is illustrated by the Phillips curve shown in the diagram; its equation is $w = 10 - 1.4U$. Correlation is very poor. $(R^2 = .20)$, which implies that there were other factors at work in determining wages than the labor market

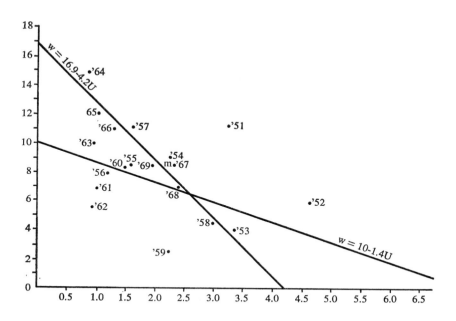

19   The calculations mentioned in this section were made by T. Huppes. His sources were various editions of the Central Economic Plan and the *Annual Report* of the Nederlandsche Bank.

situation. Such other factors included prices (in particular, 1951 and 1952 show a higher wage raise than corresponds with the Phillips curve; this was caused by the desire to keep real wages constant in the face of sharply rising prices), productivity (particularly in the sixties), and government interference. The latter influence appears in 1959, 1961, 1962, and 1963.[20] It is conceivable and even probable (but difficult to prove) that wage policy has shifted the whole Phillips curve downward, in the sense that unfettered market forces would have led to higher wage increases. An indication of the general influence of the controls lies with the dots of the 1964–69 period, when effective policy had virtually ceased to exist. The dots lie on the straight line $w = 16.9 - 4.2U$ ($R^2 = .90$) which shows a much higher correlation and a much stronger market impact than the regression line for the whole period 1951–69. It would be rash to conclude that this latter equation represents the "true" Phillips curve, but the difference between the two lines is not without significance.[21] The late fifties and the early sixties were critical years in which the government promised freedom and wage differentiation to the bargaining parties, but effectuated more control, i.e., detailed instructions to the Board, interference in specific collective agreements. The dots for 1959, 1961, and 1962 lie well below *both* regression lines. This happened in an extremely tight labor market. The graph points to the economic reasons why employers and unions alike rebelled against the government—the stress of the controls was too great. In 1963 the Foundation advised the government to deprive the Board of its wage-fixing power and to leave the control of wages to the Foundation itself. The government followed this advice—it hardly had a choice—though some

20   It is remarkable that a year like 1957, in which a deliberate restrictive program was carried out and real wages were lowered, does not show up in the regression analysis as unusual. The reason is that prices rose in that year; this was partly compensated for by higher money wages.

21   A complete regression equation for the wage increase, used by the Central Planning Bureau, has the following form: $w = 0.43\ p + 0.33\ (h_{-1} - 0.68\ h_{-2}) - 0.93\ (\Delta C - 0.68\ \Delta C_{-1}) - 2.14\ (\Delta C_{-1} - 0.68\ \Delta C_{-2}) + 0.68\ w_{-1} + 0.52$, in which w is the percentage wage increase, p the rise in the price level of consumption goods, h the rise in labor productivity, and ΔC the change in an index of capacity utilization. The latter is correlated negatively with the U of the Phillips equation. Subscripts refer to years. A remarkable feature of this equation is the term which relates wage increases to the wage increase of last year. The labor market is conspicuously absent; its influence is indirect, via ΔC. This, and the strong influence of other terms, suggests that there exists no Phillips curve for the Netherlands. The equation was published in P. Verdoorn, *The Short-Term Model of the Central Planning Bureau and Its Forecasting Performance 1953–1963* (CPB Reprint Series no. 108).

observers had predicted that the Foundation, where employers and unions were by themselves, would not be able to take unpopular steps and therefore was not the proper organ to combat wage inflation. These predictions turned out to be realistic. No sooner had the Foundation taken over than the wage level exploded (1964). The 15 percent increase fits in nicely with the "new" Phillips curve. The Foundation proved to be such a poor wage controller that the government restored the powers of the Board in 1966, but this was not accepted by organized business or labor. In 1967 they advised the government to liberalize wage determination. This was the basis of the Wage Law of 1970. In the meantime, the dots in the diagram remain quite near the Phillips curve.

From this experience the adherents of the theory that market forces determine wages might conclude that the policy of the Dutch government was doomed to failure. By clinging too long to controls and guidelines which were too strict, the system blew itself up. Not only did the wage level explode in 1964; the institutions also went to pieces.

Although there certainly is truth in the statement that the early sixties exemplified excessively high aims being defeated by the market, the simple theory of the iron market forces as formulated above is certainly one-sided. For one might also reason that the experience of the early sixties shows an unusually marked deviation of the Phillips curve. According to the equation $w = 16.9 - 4.2U$, the total wage increase from 1959 to 1963 should have been 58 percent; actually it was only 33 percent. If the controls had been a little less draconic, and if the government had moved a little more tactically, the system might have been saved. The employers and the unions were embittered by the promise of freedom which was not fulfilled and by the type of interference which was more frequent and harsh than before. In this view it is not the labor market but the psychology and the politics of the moment which destroyed the setup.

There is, however, one more argument in favor of the market theory. Under the Dutch system the unions might be depicted as institutions for keeping down wages. This unfriendly description was rather uncommon in the fifties, but under the tense labor market conditions of the early sixties it often happened that employers were overbidding each other, thereby openly flouting the rules of the game. This got a good deal of publicity that put the unions' officials in an awkward position. Compliance with the employers' illegal acts would be contrary to the system to which the unions adhered; unions protesting the higher wages would reveal the Achilles' heel of the unions' position and be contrary to what Ross calls "institutional survival and growth." The way out of the dilemma was the proposal to change the system and charge the Foundation with the responsibility for administering the controls. The union leaders might have predicted the Foundation's ineptitude as a wage fixer, but they did not have much choice.

The change in the unions' position was accompanied by another reference to market forces. In the early sixties the wage difference between Germany and Belgium on the one hand and the Netherlands on the other became so significant that a number of workers, mainly in the border areas, went to work for foreign employers. Particularly in the building trades, some commuting went on. Although the numbers involved were limited, this practice drew a good deal of attention. The argument was heard that the wage policy, which was aiming at promoting exports, was now promoting the export of Dutch labor, wrecking family life, and threatening the moral fiber of the nation (a few of the workers left their families behind and forgot to send money). The publicity did not fail to cause harm to the unions' image; after all, their officials cooperated in the wage policy. Therefore the union spokesmen used the argument that one cannot have controlled wages in the Netherlands when the rest of Europe leaves wage determination to the free forces of the market. This reference to supply and demand forecast arguments heard in the late sixties when the Wage Law was discussed.

THE CONTROL OF OTHER INCOMES

A condition for trade union cooperation in controlling wages has always been the government's willingness to exercise at least a minimum of control of other income categories. This mainly applies to profits, rents, and salaries. NVV officials often explained their later change of mind by stating that the government's treatment of these incomes was overly kid-gloved. Let us consider this argument.

Control of profits was part of the official anti-inflation policy of all Dutch governments, but the intensity with which the policy was carried out differed from time to time. The minister of economic affairs has statutory powers to interfere in all prices if he wishes to do so. Prices of single goods may be fixed, ceilings may be imposed, and binding rules of conduct may be issued. Since 1959 the general rule is that prices should not be increased as a

consequence of higher wages—a principle which aimed at supporting the productivity-oriented wage policy. It has been maintained
when the latter policy was abandoned as a means to suppress the
wage-price spiral. The logic of this measure is unassailable; its practical effect, doubtful. If the order had been fully effective, profit
margins would have been squeezed out of existence by now. Actually, the share of profits in national income has been roughly
constant, so we may conclude that at least some infringement of
the rule took place. Enforcement is, of course, difficult and hap-
hazard. Yet the rule gives the unions a certain satisfaction, and
they know that the minister of economic affairs cannot bend iron
with his bare hands.

However, the unions have had their specific complaints about
price policy. A critical year was 1969, when the new Common
Market tax on value added was introduced and the price level rose
by a far greater percentage (7 percent, a record figure) than even
the full shifting of the tax warranted. Businessmen seized the opportunity to increase their profit margins, which had been under
the pressure of rising labor costs for many years. In a number of
cases these price increases were not only an economic necessity but
also a protest against tax policy and continuous wage inflation. The
struggle of the pressure groups came to the fore at the very moment
that the new Wage Law was under discussion. There can be no
doubt that the attitude of the unions was influenced by these events.

A perpetual thorn in the flesh of the unions is the problem of
rents. The scarcity of housing—one of the sore spots of the Dutch
social situation—pushes up rents; this inflationary movement was
watered down by strict regulations. Rents were increased by bi-
annual rounds until 1967, when the government decided to abolish
the system of frozen rents for most parts of the country and leave
the outcome to supply and demand. Although rents form a very
minor income category (less than 3 percent of the national income), this controversial move created resentment and paved the
way for the claim that wages should be freely determined as well.

Another and more important income category that attracts attention is salaries of higher personnel. Wage controls only apply to
collective wage agreements; these do not reach the higher echelons.
Foremen, supervisors, and specialized technical personnel are above
the limits. Staff personnel, junior management, and all higher employees escape the controls. This is a continuous source of trouble.
Although the statistics do not show a clear increase in vertical differentials—on the contrary, there are pointers in the opposite direc-

tion—the psychological influence of this tremendous hole in the system has always been great.

But perhaps the main cause of irritation lies with the individual and very spectacular cases of flashy speculators—mainly speculators in real estate—who get a good deal of publicity. Well-known Dutchmen such as Zwolsman and Caransa, who buy and sell pieces of Amsterdam and The Hague which many consider public property, seem to escape all pathetic endeavors at an incomes policy, thereby impairing the willingness of others to submit to the rules of the game.²² This point is often brought forward in discussions with union leaders. People find it difficult to accept wage ceilings for the working populations when these dealers go scot-free. The counter-argument that these incomes constitute only a tiny fraction of the national income is not well received; it is said to miss the point of social psychology and social justice.

THE POLITICS OF FRUSTRATION

The control of wages implies the frustration of some of the union's immediate desires. A union may have a broad outlook on the national interest; it may adhere to macro-economic principles of equilibrium; it may have a keen eye for the growth of exports and the requirements of the balance of payments (the NVV in particular cannot be blamed for overlooking these goals). But all the same the moderation in wage claims is felt to be a sacrifice by union officials, and even more by the rank and file. The sacrifices will only be made if the union feels that its policy is appreciated, at least by the authorities.

This condition was fulfilled in the fifties. The government's attitude toward the unions was sympathetic. The Labor party was in office, and the minister of social affairs used to be a former NVV secretary. The very influential chairman of the Board of Mediators, J. A. Berger, was a former NVV official. Trade union chairmen and secretaries had easy access to the government; there was an atmosphere of mutual trust and confidence. Appreciation of the unions' work and of their cooperation in policy matters was general in government circles.

All this changed in 1959. The Labor party was replaced by the (conservative) People's Party for Freedom and Democracy. Immediately "freedom" and "wage differentiation" became the watch-

22   In the sixties many successful deals came to the fore.

words of wage policy, much to the NVV's dismay. Moreover, the secretary of state for social affairs (deputy minister) who handled wage policy in the new cabinet was B. Roolvink, a former CNV (Christian Federation of Unions) secretary, who was viewed by many union leaders as a kind of renegade. Personal relations deteriorated quickly. The bizarre haggling over productivity figures irritated everyone. Roolvink started interfering with the work of the Board, and members of this highly regarded committee publicly declared that they did not appreciate this activity. The only man who might have saved the system, Chairman Berger, died.

The NVV had special reasons to be bothered. One of its most cherished policy goals was equal pay for equal work, the quality being established by job evaluation. The reasons for this preference stemmed partly from an egalitarian ideology and were partly inspired by the wish to keep the various unions in line and avoid trouble at the federation level. The NVV also wanted to compress the wage structure somewhat, in the sense that priority should be given to low wages. All this was frustrated by the government's policy of "freedom" and productivity-oriented wage increases.

The political situation worsened for various reasons. The Labor party in opposition was bound to criticize the government for whatever it did; this implied a negative and sometimes strongly worded opinion on wage policy. These criticisms were generally shared by the NVV's rank and file. The union members were inclined to criticize their leaders for cooperating in a wage policy which was depicted by the opposition as being harmful to the interest of the workers. This was something new; in the fifties, workers were accustomed to hearing how beneficial the wage controls were. At the same time, "black" wages became more and more general, and the unions were blamed by critics from the left for being institutions betraying the worker.

In the mid-sixties there was another change in the government coalition; the Labor party came back into office. For a short time it looked as if the atmosphere of the fifties might be restored, but the cabinet fell after one and a half years; the move in Parliament was made by the Catholic party. The ensuing conflict between the Labor party and the Catholic party was unusually bitter. This, too, had its repercussions on the consultations over wages. NVV feelings were not improved by the fact that Roolvink came back, now as minister of social affairs.

In 1967 a disappointed and cynical Foundation of Labor advised the government on a new wage policy. Employers' federations and unions were in agreement[23] about the principle of the new policy. This principle would be free bargaining at the industry level. The Foundation itself might issue guidelines twice a year, but these would not be mandatory and there would be no sanctions. In highly exceptional cases the minister of social affairs might declare specific collective agreements null and void. At that moment the NVV's opinion was still in line with that of the other members of the Foundation. Minister Roolvink agreed to revise the BBA on the basis of the Foundation's recommendations.

But in 1968 a new conflict arose. The government deemed the wage increases of that year excessive and announced a wage freeze. Collective agreements would be prolonged for a period of six months. This announcement was a unilateral step—the unions and the Foundation were not consulted. This was an enormous blunder in a country that has a long tradition of cooperation and consultation ("overleg") in wage matters. The reaction, inside and outside Parliament, was tremendous. Mass demonstrations were held all over the country. It was in this year that the unions' position changed. In 1967 the three federations had still agreed to accept the ultimate power of the government to intervene. In 1969 confidence in all governments was at such a low level that the NVV, together with the Catholic and the Protestant Federations, rejected this possibility. Yet it was embodied in Article 8 of the bill which Minister Roolvink introduced in 1968.

In the parliamentary debate a number of Catholic party representatives opposed Article 8, together with the Labor party and a number of small factions on the left. However, the majority accepted the law. The debate was not decisively influenced by the NVV's announcement to refuse all "overleg" in wage matters with the government if the bill were to become law.

A SHIFT IN IDEOLOGIES

The changed evaluation of a centrally guided wage policy cannot be fully understood without reference to the differences in ideology between the fifties and the late sixties. After the war Dutch socioeconomic ideology was molded by a strong desire for peaceful cooperation between social groups and a deep distrust of the viability of the European economies. Strict regulations also were considered more or less unavoidable. (The BBA was introduced at the time

23   With the exception of a federation of small businessmen.

when one needed a special pass to travel from Amsterdam to Groningen). Even when (around 1950) economic life returned more or less to "normal," rationing was abolished, and prices were left virtually free, anxiety remained. Would the growth of industry be sufficient to provide full employment? Would exports ever be sufficient to cover import needs? Could a return to the depression of the thirties be forestalled? Would it be possible to avoid ruinous inflation? This feeling of doom and disaster stimulated the national propensity to "overleg" and moderation. The growing welfare of the fifties was often explained as a reward for this peaceful behavior.

Moreover, strong government intervention, including wage controls, was at that time in line with the generally accepted progressive *Weltanschauung*. "Planning" had a progressive ring, and wages should be planned. The government was seen as the natural defender of the weak. The Labor party in particular wanted to reform society via government measures in a formal democracy. The strike was considered slightly obsolete and in any case a last resort; a political strike was clearly anti-democratic. Trade union officials should participate in official policy by means of the elaborate Dutch committee system.

This outlook was hardly challenged from the left. Some critics saw the class struggle as the only road to a better society, and indeed the Eenheids Vak Centrale had a substantial membership (mainly in Amsterdam and Rotterdam), but this federation of unions was obviously tainted with Communism. Communist propaganda was easily countered by anti-propaganda and not taken seriously, at least not in an intellectual sense. The atmosphere of the cold war was hardly conducive to Marxist or neo-Marxist ideologies, and the NVV in particular had nothing to fear from the left.

All this has changed. Industrialization has, notwithstanding the baby boom, led to a tight labor market. The fear of mass unemployment has abated. Inflation continued steadily without leading to visible disaster. The vague economic anxiety of the fifties was replaced by the criticism of the capitalist system which is now in vogue all over the Western world. The younger generation takes social security and a reasonable level of income for granted. Its vociferous part speaks out against bourgeois consumption, the stress on achievement and performance, pollution, the hierarchical structure of society, inequality of economic and political power, the conditions in the underdeveloped world, Vietnam, and the nuclear threat. With a small but influential group these ideas take the form of neo-Marxist ideology. Other groups—rebellious artists, "provos," "kabouters"[24]—get a good deal of public attention, as well as sympathy from liberals, students, and young people generally. All this changed the intellectual climate in which the unions operate.

These critics from the left see the unions as part of the capitalist establishment. Cooperation with employers can only be detrimental to the interests of the workers. A controlled wage policy is a device for increasing surplus value on behalf of the capitalists. The government protects the "structure"—that is, the interests of the strong. According to this theory the unions, by participating in the typically Dutch system, acted as caretakers of the rich. The sudden upsurge of this radicalism in the late sixties was embarrassing to the unions. They were not accustomed to this kind of attack, and their reaction did not excel in clarity. Many union leaders hesitate between the notion that Marx, Marcuse, and Che Guevera have no relevance for the Netherlands, and the view that much is to be learned from these prophets if one takes them with a grain of salt. A good deal of contradictory comment has emanated from union circles. Although their confusion was less than in the Labor party, where a New Left faction caused lively debates and no less lively struggles for power, one cannot say that the convictions of the fifties were unshaken.

A complicating factor was the desire, mainly among students, for "direct democracy" and the accompanying resort to the strike, the sit-in, and the riot. A highlight of the student unrest was the occupation of the administrative building of Amsterdam University in 1968. The action was applauded by the left factions in the Labor party. The NVV was not required to take a formal stand on the matter, though its general position was that the students' aims were acceptable but their means dubious. However, the students' demonstrations and their quest for direct democracy lent these issues a new topicality among workers. This is embarrassing in two ways: it may lead to wildcat strikes, which are a nightmare to any union official, and it may give rise to the claim for direct labor control over the business firm. The latter is not in line with union policy. Moreover, union structure itself has always been characterized by highly indirect democracy. An impartial observer[25] remarks that union leaders "have the same tendency to deal with their members in a spirit of benevolent authoritarianism or highhanded paternalism which they want employers to abandon in dealing with

24   "Provos," an approximate counterpart to American "hippies," are now defunct. "Kabouters" are an anarchist group, eager to go "back to nature," with considerable popular appeal.

25   Windmuller, *Labor Relations in the Netherlands,* p. 223.

their employees." This went unnoticed for a long time, but recently the situation has attracted the attention of the leftist critics within and outside the unions. This contributes to uncertainty among union leaders and makes them eager to show that they, too, are still capable of fighting the establishment.

The practical impact of these ideological shifts is difficult to ascertain, but so much is sure that a wage policy of the Dutch type would be much less feasible now than in the fifties. This is a time of polarization, of sharp distinctions, of loud denunciations. The cosy atmosphere of "overleg," low wages to help economic expansion, and the paternalistic government balancing the interests of the various groups against each other has gone. There is no doubt that this shift in ideological climate contributed to the NVV's changed position. The expression "strangulation law" is in line with the vocabulary of the activists.

CONCLUSIONS

This sketch of the socio-political happenings in a small country may have shown that the fate of wage policy is not decided only in the labor market. It takes a subtle interplay of economic, social, ideological, political, and personal factors to make wage controls feasible. Several conditions must be fulfilled simultaneously. One of them is a rising "employee share" in national income, an objective often explicitly stated by the unions. Indeed, when there is a decline in that share, as happens from time to time, there is an immediate call for its restoration. In fact, the share has risen over the years; yet the unions are not satisfied.

Another condition is a not overly tight labor market. An unemployment rate of less than 1 percent, sustained for a couple of years, gives rise to excessive tension. The graphs presented above point in this direction. Further requirements are discipline of employers, appreciation of union policy by the government, preparedness to restrict other incomes as well, satisfactory personal relationships between union leaders, employer representatives, and wage-fixing authorities, an atmosphere of confidence and trust, and absence of too-powerful influential ideologies on the union's left. Since 1959 several of these conditions have been absent in the Netherlands. The decay and the eventual downfall of the Dutch system of wage controls cannot be ascribed to one single factor, nor can it be explained by purely economic reasoning.

Looking back upon the Dutch experiment, it surprises by its

direction rather than its ultimate demise. Its recent downfall needs less explanation than its existence in the fifties. The latter was, as I see it, mainly conditioned by the then-ruling ideology of the strong and benevolent democratic state, which protects the weak and takes care of macro-economic equilibrium. The main federation of unions, the NVV, adhered to this ideology. In the meantime, it has shifted its position toward one in which direct bargaining at the industry level is stressed, and in which pressure groups take care of themselves.

A persistent strain in post-war Western ideology has been the desirability and social utility of a process loosely called "free collective bargaining." Such positive evaluations of the process and its institutions have often led to pronouncements asserting its generalizability, that free collective bargaining can and should be the model for industrial relations throughout the world. However, there are a number of disagreeable facts which tend to draw this conclusion into question. In the first instance, it has not proved easy to export and implant the ideology and institutions of free collective bargaining—especially American style—around the world. In the second place, several decades of Western experience have suggested that truly free collective bargaining may be gravely inconsistent with broader social objectives, such as full employment. Thus, at both ends of the scale of economic development, common-sense propositions about the social worth and workability of collective bargaining have come into question. General prescriptions derived from transitory phases of social development often meet that fate.

That, in brief, was the starting point for this book. We wished to examine some characteristics of those places and times where organized labor movements have appeared, in an effort to identify some of the forces at work. This is the major task of the first three essays. But we also sought to explore a number of situations, some contemporary, some from the history of industrial relations, where the apparent economic and political pre-conditions for the development of meaningful and independent collective bargaining have not been satisfied, with an eye on the adaptations and alternatives open to the institutions of labor, management, and the state.

The first major factor in the social environment shaping the strategy and structure of the labor movement is found in the political area. Without much doubt, the role and functions of political institutions must be of a specific sort for the appearance of an economically oriented labor movement. If conditions of at least minimal levels of democracy and public education are not met, the labor movement sees workers' rights, the elimination of social discrimination against the working class, and the acquisition of education as its main *raison d'être*. This holds true in nineteenth-century Europe as well as in the twentieth-century colonies of the Western powers.

But if the political pre-conditions are met tolerably well (remembering that we must define these in terms of each culture at a particular time), does this mean that the field is wide open for the emergence of the institutions and processes of free collective bargaining? Our general conclusion on this question takes the following form: a long-term general balance between supply and demand in the labor market appears to be a necessary (but not sufficient) condition for such institutions and processes to develop. The Anglo-Saxon experience generally illustrates the proposition for cases where the political *and* economic conditions have been satisfied. Two aspects of post-war Japanese history also lend support to this view; first, the failure of American-style institutions in the chaotic labor market of the late 1940's, and second, the trend (although retarded by institutional lags) toward collective bargaining that developed as the labor market moved to long-run dynamic balance. Nonetheless, the essays in this volume suggest at least three kinds of cases where different outcomes occur.

In the first place, Sellier has argued that the structure, functioning, and self-conceived "mission" of the state can be such that the labor movement will find that it can do better economically via the political route, even if the labor market balance condition is satisfied. In such an institutional framework of active and fairly evenhanded state intervention, the unions may persist in using political means and pressures instead of collective bargaining. Historically, the "Sellier case" may be rare. Moreover, there may still be some uncertainty whether the observed sequence of events did not flow from a different source—namely, that the political and social preconditions were not in fact satisfied.

We note in passing that the two cases just mentioned—France

and post-war Japan—illustrate the importance of lags in the process of adjustment to changing conditions. Traditions (the general strike) and institutions (enterprise unions) form which change only slowly in response to changes in the political, social, and economic environments. The adjustment lags which result may be quite long, although the Japanese experience suggests that rapid growth in a large industrial sector may accelerate the pace of change.

When the criterion of labor market balance is not met by virtue of chronic excess labor, we do not see the emergence of stable, nationwide systems of collective bargaining. When the trappings of economic trade unionism have been imposed by the colonial power (as in Nigeria), they tend to disappear in the independence struggle and in the face of the realities of the labor market. Yet, even in a generally slack market, small oases of collective bargaining may still be found where the trade involved requires significant skill, where responsibility for expensive capital goods is involved, or where even common industrial jobs require more talents or education than are possessed by the bulk of the population. These factors might explain (as would a hypothesis of ideological naïveté) the apparent economic concessions sought and occasionally won by Afghan strikers, as well as explaining the width of the earnings differential between modern industry and farm labor in developing countries.

Numerically far more important are cases where, in a loose market, the government grants economic power to a union in the form of closed shops, by requiring employers to grant concessions (e.g., profit sharing) to specified workers' organizations, and so on. For value received—usually in the form of political labor support—governments are able to make grants of economic power. Unfortunately, the interrelations between political and economic power imply that favored unions may be periodically cut down to size by their sponsoring government, or replaced when the government itself changes (as attempted in Argentina). None of this implies a great deal of stability in the bargaining processes and institutions. Nevertheless, it is likely to remain a favored means of handling industrial relations problems in many developing countries, and especially of dealing with foreign firms in countries that have recently acquired political independence.

Finally, it is possible for the labor market balance condition to be broken from the other side, through a chronic labor shortage. As Pen so ably shows, this case can do as much to hamstring the workings of free collective bargaining as does its opposite number. The concepts of free decision-making by the two parties, independent of social controls and objectives, without having social responsibility loaded onto the industrial relations and compensation arrangements reached by the parties, appear to be incompatible with long-run overfull employment. In recent years governments throughout the Western world have been groping toward new ways of getting the parties to work within the bounds seen as necessary for the well-being of the whole society.

Is this the final outcome of our work, to suggest that "the rise and fall of (private) collective bargaining" will describe the industrial relations history of today's developing countries? We doubt that the evidence so far supports so broad a conclusion—in many nations the political pre-conditions have hardly been met, at least in terms familiar to the European mind. Moreover, we do not know what political or social techniques of income distribution may be developed by today's less developed countries to avoid Western-style growing pains during the long years before labor market balance will be attained. Perhaps most important, the migration of ideas, the fact that people—even governments—learn, will lead to new and different institutions and processes in response to national conditions. But whatever those new institutions and processes are, they are not likely to resemble the classical paradigm of "free collective bargaining."

CONTRIBUTORS

ALDO A. ARNAUDO is professor of economics and director of the Instituto de Economía y Finanzas, Universidad Nacional de Córdoba. In his studies of monetary theory and policy he has conducted research on the role of inflation in the Argentine economy. He is the author of *Economía monetaria* and *La velocidad de la inflación en la Argentina 1958–66,* as well as various journal articles.

BERT F. HOSELITZ, author of *Sociological Aspects of Economic Growth,* is professor of social science and director of the Research Center in Economic Development and Cultural Change, University of Chicago. He also edited *Theories of Economic Growth, Industrialization and Society* (with Wilbert E. Moore), and the *Encyclopedia of the Social Sciences.*

HISASHI KAWADA, professor emeritus, Keio University, Tokyo, is author of *Amerika Rodo-Undo-Shi* (History of American Labor, vol. 1) and has contributed articles to other collections, including "Continuity and Discontinuity: An Approach to Industrial Relations Systems" (in *The Changing Patterns of Industrial Relations*) and "The Government, Industrial Relations, and Economic Development in Japan" (in *Industrial Relations and Economic Development*).

PETER KILBY draws upon lengthy experience in West Africa for his essay. He has explored themes of economic development in

African Enterprise: The Nigerian Bread Industry, Industrialization in an Open Economy: Nigeria 1945–66, and numerous journal articles. He is associate professor of economics, Wesleyan University.

RYUJI KOMATSU is assistant professor of economics, Keio University. His most recent work on Japanese labor is *The Development of Enterprise-Wide Unionism in Japan.*

PETER LÖSCHE is assistant professor of political science at the Free University of Berlin. His special field of research involves international and comparative labor history, with particular emphasis on Germany and the United States. In this connection he has published *Der Bolshewismus im Urteil der deutschen Sozialdemokratie 1903– 20,* and a variety of journal articles.

JAN PEN is professor of economics, Groningen University, and a former director of general economic policy in the Netherlands Ministry of Economic Affairs. Well known among his works are *The Wage Rate under Collective Bargaining, Modern Economics, Harmony and Conflict in Modern Society, A Primer on International Trade,* and *Income Distribution.*

CARLOS E. SÁNCHEZ is professor of labor economics and social accounting and assistant director of the Instituto de Economía y Finanzas, Universidad Nacional de Córdoba. In his concern with human resources and social accounting, he has published *Un enfoque económico de la educación* and *Unemployment in Argentina.*

JAMES G. SCOVILLE, associate professor of economics and labor and industrial relations, University of Illinois, is author of *The Job Content of the U.S. Economy, Manpower and Occupational Analysis: Concepts and Measurements,* and numerous journal articles on work, training, and the structure of the labor force. His previous work on international labor questions includes "Remuneration in Afghan Industry," (*International Labour Review,* 1969) and "The Occupational Structure of Employment, 1960–1980," in *Sectoral Aspects of Projection for the World Economy.*

FRANÇOIS SELLIER is professor of economics and industrial relations, University of Aix-Marseille, and director of the Laboratoire d'Economie et Sociologie du Travail. He has authored numerous books—*Morale et vie économique, Strategie de la lutte sociale, Dynamique des besoins sociaux*—co-authored others, and contributed frequently to journals and conference volumes.

ADOLF STURMTHAL is professor of labor and industrial relations at the University of Illinois. He is the author of *The Tragedy of European Labor 1918–1939, Unity and Diversity in European Labor,* and many other books, as well as a contributor to various journals and to the *International Encyclopedia of the Social Sciences.* Many of his works have been translated into a variety of foreign languages.

KOJI TAIRA is professor of economics in the department of economics and in the Institute of Labor and Industrial Relations at the University of Illinois. He is the author of *Economic Development and the Labor Market in Japan,* and *Ningensei no keizaigaku (Humane Economics).* He has also translated *Capitalism Today* (ed. Irving Kristol and Daniel Bell) into Japanese.